Private Equity Exits

A Practical Analysis

Consulting Editor **David Walker**

Consulting editor
David Walker

Publisher
Sian O'Neill

Editors
Carolyn Boyle, Emma Gillett

Marketing manager
Alan Mowat

Production
Natalie Clarke, Russell Anderson

Publishing directors
Guy Davis, Tony Harriss, Mark Lamb

Private Equity Exits: A Practical Analysis
is published by
Globe Law and Business
Globe Business Publishing Ltd
New Hibernia House
Winchester Walk
London SE1 9AG
United Kingdom
Tel +44 20 7234 0606
Fax +44 20 7234 0808
Web www.globelawandbusiness.com

Printed and bound by CPI Group (UK) Ltd, Croydon, CR0 4YY

ISBN 978-1-905783-50-2

Table of contents

Preface

Fraser Robson
The Carlyle Group

"We work for our investors," stresses Bill Conway, chief investment officer of The Carlyle Group, and it is from an understanding of this simple truth that every aspect of what makes exits – by which I really mean successful exits – so critically important to private equity. It is investors' expectations as to returns and their time horizon that are the crucial drivers behind fund structuring, decisions on investments (and their oversight), as well as incentive schemes. In a maturing industry, a demonstrable track record of exits has also become a prerequisite for future fund raising, without which private equity firms cannot survive.

A key characteristic of private equity is that investments are held for only a limited period of time. The standard 10-year closed-end fund means that investors and investment teams alike are focused on a period of five years to invest the fund and five years to hold their investments, with rolling exits thereafter through to the fund's conclusion. This typical fund lifecycle has consequences for investment choices and portfolio management, and while the expanding list of potential exit routes provides a range of options, having a strong view on exit when appraising an investment is key, as it is the path to value realisation. Sponsor-to-sponsor transactions, sales to strategic acquirers and initial pubic offerings still form the main bases for discussions regarding exit, but each poses different challenges in terms of understanding how your investment will be assessed by a new purchaser five years from inception, how the trade buyer universe might change and questions around liquidity and control.

Investing for the long term and planning for exit from the outset are not mutually exclusive concepts and this is the priority following the close of any deal. With this in mind, all decisions – spend on marketing, new products and territories, improvements to controls, reporting and monitoring, for example – concentrate on growing value, which will be realised on exit.

As the private equity industry has evolved, the exit process itself has become more standardised and management savvier. Vendor due diligence, for instance, is now commonplace, facilitating compressed timetables, more participants and consequently greater competition. In addition, dedicated management advisory firms have multiplied, and while these organisations exist to secure best terms for their clients, they also provide useful assistance for executive teams by guiding them through increasing complex choices, which are often compounded by differing and potentially conflicting priorities. An understanding of how these factors interrelate is not just crucial to any acquirer; it is vital to conducting a well-run exit process.

Exits are also the leading indicator of fund raising activity for the private equity industry. The value of buy-out exits and new buy-out funds is highly correlated, albeit with a time lag, as distributions are recycled back into commitments to those general partners that have outperformed the market. Successful exits therefore afford investors both the capacity and the confidence to enter into further long-term commitments, as limited partners are less willing to sign up to new funds on the basis of unrealised performance or carrying value, which offers no guarantees as to the returns that a fund will ultimately generate.

It comes as little surprise, therefore, that incentives in the industry are structured around a profit share based on delivering cash on cash returns to limited partners, often subject to rate of return hurdles which comes full circle to investors' return thresholds and their time horizon. This ensures that the interests of deal teams are well aligned with those of their limited partners.

Overall, successful exits that meet investors' return expectations are the ultimate focal point for the myriad workstreams that any private equity deal involves. Deepening one's understanding on topics most closely linked to the exit of private equity investments is therefore critical for any industry practitioner. This book, under the oversight of David Walker as its general editor, features contributions by leading specialists on a range of topics relevant to exiting private equity transactions. Together, the contributors provide an invaluable guide to the legal, regulatory, tax and practical elements in play.

Fraser Robson is an associate director focused on European buy-out opportunities in the industrial, consumer and services sectors. He is based in London.

Since joining Carlyle in 2005, he has been actively involved with Carlyle's investments in Britax and Talaris, where he serves as a member of the board of directors. He was also a member of the transaction team that executed Carlyle's investment in RAC.

Prior to joining Carlyle, he worked at Lazard in London. He received a BA with honours in economics and politics from the University of Durham.

Introduction

David Walker
Clifford Chance LLP

Private equity exits are those corporate transactions that ultimately result in private equity funds being able to return cash to their investors. As such, they form a critical part of the private equity lifecycle; without exits, there are no returns to a fund's investors; without returns, there will be no money invested in the private equity house's next fund; and without money invested in the next private equity fund, there will be no transactions from which to exit. Exits are therefore the lifeblood of private equity: for private equity houses, the top of their list of priorities when making an investment is an understanding of when and how they will realise that in due course. There is no point making an investment unless it results in a (successful) exit.

This is why investors plan their exit strategy at the time they invest, and why private equity investors have developed sophisticated contractual mechanisms to give their investors the best chance of exiting an investment at a time and on terms of their choosing.

The methods of exiting private equity investments have developed over the years, and particularly in the more challenging economic environment of recent times. To the usual trade sales and initial public offerings have been added secondary, tertiary (and more) buy-outs, refinancings, partial sales and liquidations (or indeed a combination of these, known as dual or multi-track processes). In 2010 the aggregate amount of investments divested by private equity houses in the United Kingdom, according to British Venture Capital Association statistics, increased by over 150% on 2009, and this significant growth is reflected across Europe and globally. The trend had appeared to be continuing into 2011 as economies recovered, private equity houses looked to raise new funds to invest in the upturn and cash-rich trade buyers flexed their financial muscle; although given recent market turmoil, the opportunities for exits could start to decline quite quickly. Assuming that the economic environment continues to improve, exits ought to become easier to achieve; but in these uncertain times, private equity houses will continue to put a significant focus on what options might be available to them to realise their portfolio investments, being mindful of not just the economic risks, but also the legal, tax, regulatory and reputational issues at stake. Portfolio company management teams are key to this process and their economic, commercial and personal priorities cannot be underestimated in what is a very complex environment of often conflicting aspirations.

Indeed, it is these potentially conflicting perspectives that make private equity exits so intricate and interesting. A private equity fund needs to return cash to its investors in as tax efficient a manner as possible and free from contingent liabilities. A private equity house acting as fund manager/adviser wants to create a strong track record to raise new funds and to reward its staff, while protecting itself and its portfolio company directors from legal, regulatory and reputational risk. Management teams have their own personal interests to contend with and will of course wish to minimise their own exposures while maximising their gains. Finally, the portfolio company itself will be looking to the future and the ongoing success of the business for shareholders, employees and other current and future stakeholders.

As Fraser Robson from Carlyle makes clear in his preface, private equity exits are key not just in returning funds to investors, but also in raising further funds. For practitioners, it is critical to understand these dynamics when considering potential exit routes and how they might be structured. Globe Law and Business's sister publication to this book – *Private Equity: A Transactional Analysis* – examines the issues around private equity investments; this book focuses on the key issues that need to be considered when exiting from these investments and how potential liabilities for the funds and their advisers can be minimised.

The chapters in this book focus on the different methods of effecting an exit and the key issues that need to be borne in mind by private equity professionals and their advisers in order to create an efficient process, minimise risk and maximise returns. All of the contributors are expert in their fields and can provide insight into the intricate complexities of the exit process.

The book focuses on UK issues, but contains a Luxembourg-specific chapter given the number of private equity investments that are owned by, and therefore exited at the level of, a Luxembourg holding company. In addition to the usual methods of exiting investments referred to above, a chapter has been included on exits of private equity houses themselves, usually from their bank owners, which have been popular in recent times – not least because of the increase in regulatory constraints for banks in owning these types of businesses.

David Walker is a partner at Clifford Chance and global head of private equity. For more than 18 years he has focused on private equity clients and their portfolio companies, assisting them with all types of corporate transactions. He is rated as a leader in his field in numerous legal directories.

Preparing for exit

Philip Sanderson
Travers Smith LLP

1. When do preparations begin?

Exit planning starts before an investment has been made. It is not uncommon for a private equity investor to commission an exit report from a financial adviser as part of the buying due diligence process. One potential exit route could be a sale to 'trade' (ie, to a non-financial buyer – usually a corporate in the same sector and/or with potential economies or commercial benefits in acquiring the target company). If a trade exit is the objective, an exit report will analyse the likely buyer group and each potential buyer's stated ambition for acquisitive growth, its financial constraints and, if the exit report is part of the investor's upfront due diligence, often why a potential buyer did not bid for the target company in the current sale process.

The exit report will help to frame the thoughts of stakeholders and, in particular, force them to ask the question: how do we make this business most attractive to the buyer likely to pay the most? This is fundamentally different from the mindset of a non-private equity investor. A private equity investor will always be preparing for an exit.

2. How is an exit route chosen?

When preparing for exit, a private equity investor will examine multiple exit routes. Other chapters in this book examine each exit route in more detail.

Often, different potential routes are left open. A formal 'dual-track' route may be chosen in which a company is prepared for an initial public offering (IPO) at the same time as potential trade or financial buyers are identified. This is done with a view to maximising the price and terms of exit. A dual-track process requires the most planning and the most management time, and historically has led to few successful IPOs – making them unpopular with the broker community, which is wary of working on researching a potential new issue only to be gazumped by a trade or financial buyer. This may make dual-tracks less common in the immediate future.

An IPO is often ruled out as an option, perhaps because of:

- market sentiment in relation to the sector;
- market appetite generally;
- the suitability of the business for increased public transparency (eg, some business models are successful exactly because they are private); or
- the financial consistency of the business (public markets expect steady growth).

The pull of other exit routes may also be a factor. Ultimately, the choice will follow perceived demand, and in recent years the financial muscle of private equity – where firms have huge amounts of committed but uninvested capital or 'dry powder' – has led to an increase in the number of secondary and tertiary buy-outs. This trend is unlikely to diminish until 'trade' becomes more confident in its collective need to grow by acquisition or until public markets have strengthened considerably.

Identifying an exit route – a case study

One of the more successful exits we have seen recently proceeded broadly as follows:

- Private equity investor X beat Y to an asset in a competitive auction process.
- X immediately focused on why Y wanted to acquire the asset and analysed what would make Y want it even more.
- This led to X carrying out a reorganisation of the asset.
- Within two years of X's acquisition, X sold the reorganised asset to a delighted Y at a significant profit.

3. When to sell?

A private equity investor will sell an investment when it believes that it can maximise its internal rate of return (IRR) on the investment. IRR broadly represents the compound growth rate of an investment from the date of acquisition to the date of exit, and is widely used as a measure for financial performance in the private equity industry. So an investor may, for example, believe that the profits of the investee company will keep rising (and with them, the price achievable on an exit), but will still sell because its IRR may start to decrease over time. A smart private equity investor can pick the time when its IRR is likely to be maximised and ensure that all other stakeholders – in particular, the management team – work to maximise the attractiveness of the business at this point. This will be carried out partly by establishing historic financial performance and partly by presenting a credible vision for future growth.

4. Practical steps when preparing for exit

Every exit is different and the issues raised are manifold. Many of the practicalities of preparing for an exit will differ depending on whether it will be a full or partial exit and whether the portfolio company is to be sold, listed or wound up. However, a number of steps are common to all types of exit situation. These include the appointment of advisers and general housekeeping matters such as ensuring that the statutory books for each group company are complete and up to date.

4.1 Appointing advisers

The purpose of this section is not to detail how each exit adviser is chosen, but it is worth summarising some of the issues that emanate from the letters of agreement recording the terms of their engagement. Typical advisers that are core to a sale process include the legal adviser appointed by the sellers (and commonly a further legal adviser acting for management on their potential ongoing employment and investment), a financial adviser (usually an investment bank or accountancy firm) and any providers of vendor due diligence. Each adviser or provider needs to be legally bound to the engagement from the outset. The engagement letter for the financial adviser is likely to address the following issues.

(a) ***Fees***

It is common for fees to ratchet up depending on the success of the sale, and the parties will need to agree what constitutes 'success' for this purpose. While it is common for no fee to be payable where the sale process fails (making the fee fully contingent on the sale taking place), increasingly advisers seek a retainer or at least a minimal 'abort fee' to cover the basic costs of the engagement. In all cases it is critical that the engagement letter clearly sets out the basis on which fees are payable.

(b) ***Tail fees***

Tail or, more evocatively, 'tail gunner' fees are often negotiated. Such fees are payable if a sale process fails, but the sellers proceed to exit within a specified period, usually 12 months, after the engagement has been terminated. The negotiation of such fees often focuses on issues such as whether it is appropriate for the tail fee to become payable only where the adviser introduced the eventual buyer and whether such a circumstance should warrant a full or reduced success fee.

(c) ***Indemnities***

An adviser will often seek to obtain an indemnity from the company being sold or from the sellers. Such an indemnity will seek, in particular, to cover an adviser against third-party claims relating to its engagement. While some private equity investors accept such a clause, many do not, arguing that advisers must rely on their contractual right to seek damages for a breach. Even if an indemnity is agreed, care must be taken to limit its potential scope – for example, by carving out liabilities arising from the adviser's own negligence or default.

4.2 Pre-exit legal audit

On engagement, a legal adviser should take time to assist in the preparation of the company for the chosen exit. At the outset, this will commonly include a pre-exit legal audit (which will often feed into the processes detailed in sections 4.4 and 4.5, being the preparation of a data room and any vendor or pre-flotation due diligence). This should be a critical part of the process for a legal adviser. A legal adviser should challenge the company's management team to explain the legal framework of its business and seek to anticipate a potential buyer or the market's questions and concerns. This will in turn lead to planning how any identified issues should be presented to potential buyers. For example, on a recent sale of a business in a sensitive, regulated sector, it became clear that a regulatory vendor due diligence exercise was critical to explain the operation of the whole business, and that the presentation of such issues would be critical to the ease of the process once potential buyers commenced their own due diligence.

The audit can also help to identify issues which may need to be resolved either prior to exit or as part of the exit process – for example:

- corporate 'housekeeping' may need attention and resources;
- key contracts may need to be renegotiated (or properly executed);
- employment agreements may need to be improved;
- option schemes may need to be implemented;
- pensions issues may need to be addressed, particularly if there is a defined benefit scheme within the group; and
- IP registrations or agreements may need to be processed or negotiated.

Once the audit is complete, a legal adviser should be able to predict the key legal issues that are likely to feature in discussions with potential buyers.

4.3 Structuring the exit

Once a private equity investor has identified a proposed exit route (or routes, in the case of a dual-track process), it will need to consider how best to structure the exit. For example, will a sale be presented to potential buyers as a straightforward share sale or are there benefits in structuring the disposal as an asset sale? Is it necessary to carry out a pre-sale reorganisation (eg, to separate out different business sectors within the portfolio group) or to return excess cash to the shareholders? On an IPO, the investor will need to consider which company will be listed: will it be the existing holding company of the portfolio group or would it be preferable to incorporate a new holding company?

Usually, tax planning will be a key driver when structuring an exit. The various tax considerations relevant to exit planning are considered in more detail in the chapter on tax.

4.4 Preparing for a sale

Before kicking off a sale process, the investor will carry out a valuation exercise to establish an indication of the price that it can expect to achieve. A range of methods may be used to value a business, including:

- the discounted cash-flow method, which calculates the present value of future operating cash flows;
- the earnings multiple method, which applies a price multiple to an estimate of future earnings; and
- the net asset valuation method, which relies on the valuation of the net assets of the business, but may not take account of the value of intangible assets, such as goodwill. This is more commonly used as a valuation method on asset sales and carve-outs.

Valuation based on multiples of future earnings is the most commonly used method by private equity investors.

The financial adviser will usually be responsible for organising and administering the sale process. Unless a buyer has already been identified, it is common for a sale to be run as an auction and the financial adviser will work with the private equity investor to identify potential buyers.

If the sale is conducted as an auction, the seller will usually prepare an information memorandum. The information memorandum acts as a marketing tool and includes key information about the portfolio company, such as an overview of the business, the management team and financial information. Before it is circulated to potential buyers, the information memorandum will need to be checked to ensure that it is factually correct and includes no false or misleading information. This verification exercise is usually carried out by the management team in conjunction with the seller's lawyers. The information memorandum will also include disclaimer wording, informing potential buyers that the seller accepts no responsibility for the accuracy of the information memorandum and makes no representations or warranties regarding its contents. This is to ensure that the eventual purchaser can rely only on the negotiated warranties set out in the sale and purchase agreement.

In any sale process potential buyers will want to conduct their own comprehensive due diligence exercise on the portfolio group. To facilitate this, the seller will usually set up a data room. A data room is a collection of information about the portfolio group which is made available to potential buyers. The information disclosed to potential buyers in the data room will relate to all aspects of the portfolio company business and will include financial information, constitutional documents, material commercial contracts, employment contracts and other information relating to employees, pensions, IP rights, IT systems, property interests and details of any litigation involving the portfolio group. Highly sensitive information, such as customer and pricing information, is usually kept out of the data room during the initial stages of the sale process and released only to the successful bidder immediately prior to signing the sale and purchase agreement. The data room can be prepared in hard copy, with potential buyers invited to come to a specified location to review documents, or as a virtual online data room. The popularity of online data rooms has grown in recent years, as they have become increasingly sophisticated and the technology now allows sellers carefully to control and monitor access to data. In a competitive auction process, sellers may monitor how frequently potential buyers access an online data room, to assess how much time they have spent on due diligence and therefore how well positioned they are likely to be to proceed quickly to signing the sale and purchase agreement.

The investor may also appoint its own advisers to carry out vendor due diligence, which is intended to speed up potential buyers' own due diligence processes. Vendor due diligence reports generally aim to identify material issues that have potential deal or value implications, and in most cases the successful buyer will ultimately be able to rely on the reports.

Before granting a potential buyer access to the information memorandum and/or the data room, the selling private equity investor will require the potential buyer to sign a confidentiality agreement or non-disclosure agreement. Confidentiality agreements can often be quite heavily negotiated and should include the following provisions to protect the seller's interests:

- a duty not to disclose the information to any person other than the buyer's

officers, employees and professional advisers;
- an undertaking to use the information to evaluate the business and not for any other purpose;
- restrictions on the solicitation of target employees;
- a non-compete undertaking; and
- an undertaking to destroy or return the confidential information if the transaction does not proceed to completion.

At this stage in the sale process, the private equity investor may also carry out its own antitrust analysis based on publicly available information relating to the potential buyers. It may be possible to form a preliminary view on whether a particular buyer is likely to have any substantive antitrust issues which could delay completion of the sale and result in some uncertainty for the sellers where the sale and purchase agreement is made conditional on the relevant antitrust clearances being obtained. This is likely to be one of many factors, including pricing, deliverability and other commercial terms, taken into account when determining who will be the successful bidder in an auction situation.

4.5 Preparing for an IPO

The choice of market for launching an IPO will be important in securing a successful flotation. If the IPO is to take place in the United Kingdom, it will be necessary to decide whether it is appropriate for the company's shares to be admitted to trading on AIM or the main market of the London Stock Exchange. In making this decision a number of factors, including the company's size, objectives and funding needs, will need to be considered. An investment bank will be appointed to manage the IPO process and the portfolio company's legal advisers will advise on the regulatory requirements for listing on the relevant market.

In preparation for the IPO, the portfolio company will need to carry out comprehensive due diligence on its business and financial position, and identify any major risks associated with the business. The flotation due diligence exercise can be extremely time consuming for the senior managers of the portfolio company, but it is essential to ensure that the information included in the prospectus is complete and accurate. A number of other practical steps may also need to be taken in preparation for the IPO, including:

- re-registering the company as a public company;
- amending the company's constitutional documents;
- reorganising the company's share capital; and
- agreeing revised service agreements and incentive arrangements appropriate for the senior management of a publicly quoted company.

A key element of preparing for an IPO will be deciding who will sit on the board of directors of the listed company and developing the company's corporate governance procedures. In particular, it is likely that additional independent non-executive directors will be needed, including possibly a new chairman. Companies seeking a premium listing on the main market of the London Stock Exchange will be subject to the UK Corporate Governance Code, which sets out principles relating to leadership, board effectiveness, accountability, remuneration and relationships with shareholders.

4.6 Winding up the portfolio company

Broadly speaking, there are two obvious scenarios in which a portfolio company may be wound up. The first is where the portfolio company has become insolvent. This is clearly the worst-case scenario for the private equity investor, which in such circumstances will almost certainly lose some or all of its initial investment; but insolvent winding-up is not unheard of, particularly given the recent economic downturn.

The second scenario is where the business and assets of the portfolio company have been disposed of, leaving the portfolio company as a shell. If the portfolio company is to be wound up following the sale of its business, the investor's main concern will be to ensure that all of the proceeds from the sale are distributed by the remaining group up to the investor and the other shareholders. Much of this will be determined by tax considerations – for example, the company may choose to pay cash out as a dividend or it may be more tax efficient to carry out a reduction of capital prior to commencing the winding-up.

5. Role of management and other stakeholders

A strong management team is an essential element of a sale or an IPO, and other stakeholders may also play an important role in the exit process. These will include material suppliers or customers of the portfolio group, the lending banks that financed the original acquisition of the portfolio company by the private equity investor, and employees and second-tier managers of the portfolio group. Preparing for an exit includes preparing each stakeholder for the process, explaining what will be required of it and what it stands to gain (or lose) from the process.

5.1 The management team

In a typical private equity transaction the senior management team will have received shares in the portfolio company and will have entered into an investment agreement with the investor at the time of the initial buy-out. As well as governing the relationship throughout the life of the investment, the investment agreement will usually set out some parameters for an exit – typically, an obligation on the management team to work towards an exit and cooperate fully with any exit process.

On an IPO, it may be necessary to reorganise the management team and bring in external managers who are experienced in sitting on the boards of listed companies. The investor directors appointed to the board by the private equity investor will usually step down immediately before an IPO and be replaced by independent non-executive directors.

In the context of a sale, financial buyers are likely to want to retain the existing management team, although this factor may be less important to trade buyers. The management team will usually be heavily involved in the due diligence process and in negotiating the sale and purchase agreement, particularly any warranties relating to the business which will typically be given by the management team only.

When it comes to an exit, the interests of the management and the private equity investor may not be fully aligned. Where the managers intend to continue in the business after a sale, they may find themselves in the position of being both selling shareholders and potential buyers. As a result, the selling private equity investor may seek to limit potential buyers' access to the existing management team for as long as possible, to ensure that the managers continue to view the transaction as sellers rather than buyers and seek the best possible terms for the sale of their interests.

For managers who are 'rolling over' some or all of their existing investment into the buyer group structure, tax advice will be important and should be sought early in the process.

On a sale, it will be important for the investor to be able to deliver 100% of the issued shares in the portfolio company to the buyer. If for any reason a member (or members) of the management team who is also a shareholder refuses to participate in an exit, several options will likely be available to prevent the dissenting manager(s) from holding the other shareholders to ransom and potentially preventing the sale. These possible options include:

- exercising drag-along provisions, which will typically be included in the articles of association of the portfolio company. Drag-along provisions are often cumbersome to operate and this route is not without its potential hurdles. As a result, it is relatively uncommon for private equity investors to exercise drag-along rights without management cooperation;
- terminating the employment of the relevant dissenting manager. This would usually result in the manager becoming a leaver for the purposes of any compulsory transfer provisions in the portfolio company's articles of association and would enable the investor to require the shares held by or on behalf of the dissenting manager to be transferred to another person; or
- using the Companies Act 2006 squeeze-out procedure, which can be exercised where a buyer acquires 90% of the shares in the portfolio company. This can be a complex and time-consuming process, and therefore is not frequently used.

A buyer will usually be extremely reluctant to conclude an acquisition where a dissenting minority shareholder refuses to participate in the exit and remains as a shareholder of the business.

5.2 Key customers and suppliers

The portfolio company will need to identify the key contracts with its customers and suppliers, to ascertain whether there are any potential issues that will impact on the business and/or the timing of the exit process. This will usually be done as part of a pre-exit legal audit (discussed in section 4.2).

Material contracts should be reviewed to establish whether any are due for renewal or whether they contain change of control provisions that could be triggered on an exit, enabling the counterparty to terminate the contract. If any of the material contracts include change of control provisions, the private equity investor will need to consider engaging with the counterparty at an early stage in the exit process to obtain comfort that any termination rights will not be exercised as a result of the sale or IPO of the portfolio business or used as a means of renegotiating the terms of the contract.

5.3 Lending banks

Other interested parties include any external debt providers that assisted in financing the initial buy-out by the private equity investor. When preparing for an exit, potential buyers and incumbent private equity investors will need to give significant consideration to whether these debt facilities are to be repaid on exit and also whether any external debt finance will be required to help fund the acquisition and/or the portfolio group's working capital and operating requirements following exit.

If the private equity investor is planning to sell the portfolio company to a trade or financial buyer, then more often than not the sale will be on a cash-free, debt-free basis. Consequently, the existing debt facilities will be repaid in full and all security over the portfolio group and its assets, together with any guarantees, will be released on exit. Therefore, it is important that the private equity investor involve the outgoing finance providers (and possibly their legal advisers) at a relatively early stage of the exit timetable to agree the necessary release documentation and mechanics. This is particularly important where the release of security and guarantees granted by overseas companies is required, since the instruction of foreign legal advisers may be necessary and the procedural requirements of certain foreign jurisdictions can often be complicated and time consuming. As part of the release process, outgoing lenders will also need to hand over any title deeds, share certificates and other documents of title in their possession; again, this can cause a delay if they are not requested early enough in the timetable.

In addition, the private equity investor should obtain an up-to-date redemption statement from the outgoing lender in respect of the outstanding debt facilities well in advance of the exit, as this will assist any potential buyers in estimating the final amount to be repaid on completion. The repayment of existing debt facilities may give rise to break costs (where the facilities are repaid other than at the end of an interest period), the payment of accrued but unpaid interest and fees and, in particular, pre-payment fees. The investor should try to ensure that the exit occurs at a time which will minimise the risk of these payments arising, as often the triggering of a substantial fee or break cost can impact on the ultimate purchase price offered by any potential buyers.

In certain circumstances a potential buyer may consider that the quantum and terms of the portfolio company's existing financing arrangements (which it will have reviewed as part of its initial due diligence exercise) are sufficient to support its proposals for the future growth of the business. This is a particular consideration for potential trade buyers, as often they will be able to finance the acquisition from their balance sheet or by drawing on their own banking facilities. In the event that the facilities are to remain in place following exit, the incumbent lenders will again need to be involved at an early stage in the sale process to avoid any delays or unexpected costs arising as a result of the terms of the existing facilities. In particular, consideration will need to be given to whether any pre-exit structural reorganisations or payments (eg, interposing any new holding companies in the existing portfolio group structure, upstream distributions or recapitalisation exercises) will breach the terms of the existing facilities and therefore require the prior written consent of the lenders. In addition, it is likely (particularly under typical leveraged finance facilities) that the exit will trigger a requirement for mandatory pre-payment of the facilities in full as a result of the change in control of the portfolio group. Naturally, the ongoing finance provider will be keen to ensure that the proposed change of control will not materially weaken the underlying credit, which will have been based on the initial investment by and relationship with the private equity investor, as well as the underlying business and management of the portfolio group. Consequently, it will want access to (and possibly reliance on) the due diligence material, reports and financial models provided to the potential buyer well in advance of the proposed date for exit.

Needless to say, the incumbent lenders will often seek to charge a fee for any consents, waivers and/or amendments that are required under or to the financing documentation to facilitate the exit, and any such requirements will need to be factored into the proposed timetable.

Another option available to a private equity investor before it kicks off a sale process is to arrange a 'stapled' finance package. Essentially, this is where the bank that is also advising the portfolio company agrees a financing commitment letter and term sheet prior to the bid stage which offers debt facilities to prospective purchasers. This can be beneficial as it will result in a financing package being available to all potential buyers, thereby removing some of the risk associated with potential buyers that require third-party funding to finance their bid. A stapled financing package can therefore be a useful tool, particularly during periods of illiquidity in the credit markets. As one might expect, the negotiation of the stapled debt documents should be undertaken by the private equity investor well before the start of the bid process to ensure that a suitable package is in place by the time that bids are being solicited.

Where an exit is to proceed by way of a flotation, smart private equity investors may start the planning for an IPO from as early as the initial buy-out by negotiating the initial leveraged finance documents with a listing in mind. It is often the case that the flotation will trigger a requirement for mandatory pre-payment of the facilities out of the proceeds of the flotation (which consequently gives rise to similar concerns as might arise on a trade or financial sale). However, in certain circumstances finance providers and the private equity investor can make the portfolio company a more attractive proposition to potential investors (depending on their views) by permitting certain flotations (ie, 'qualifying IPOs') and agreeing in the existing finance documents that only a proportion of the flotation proceeds are applied in mandatory pre-payment of the facilities by reference to agreed leverage thresholds. This would mean that some of the existing debt can remain in place post-exit, while at the same time the portfolio company will be able to retain a greater proportion of the flotation proceeds (which may improve the state of the post-exit balance sheet). In connection with this, a mechanism will be included in the financing documentation to adjust automatically the pre-exit financial covenants and operational restrictions to reflect the reduction in the portfolio group's leverage. Of course, these provisions are negotiated on the basis that the existing finance providers view the flotation as a realistic possibility and are happy to continue to finance the portfolio company once it is listed. Clearly, in certain circumstances this may not be appropriate.

5.4 Employees and second-tier managers

When preparing for exit, the private equity investor will also need to consider the employees of the portfolio group. The fate of the employees will depend on the type of exit. On a share sale or an IPO, the employees will continue to be employed by their existing employer. However, where the portfolio business is being sold by way of an asset sale, employment-related issues will factor more highly in preparations, as the Transfer of Undertakings (Protection of Employment) Regulations 2006 (TUPE) are likely to apply. Where TUPE applies, employees will usually expect their employment to transfer to the new owner of the business; however, this will need to be considered in each case. TUPE sets out a range of measures designed to protect employees, including information and consultation requirements that will have an impact on timing and will therefore need to be factored into the sale timetable. If any part of the portfolio group's workforce is overseas, there may also be additional consultation requirements under local law which the private equity investor will need to take into account when planning an exit, and local law advice should be obtained at an early stage.

Employees and second-tier managers may also be party to incentive arrangements such as share option schemes. Whether any such arrangements are in place should become apparent through the pre-exit legal audit (see section 4.2). If share options have been issued, the terms of the share option scheme will need to be reviewed to assess the treatment of the share options on exit and this will need to be taken into account when preparing for exit.

At a glance – key steps when preparing for an exit

- Identify an exit route: this will usually be done before the private equity investor acquires the asset.
- Consider when is the right time to exit to maximise the investor's internal rate of return.
- Engage legal, financial and other advisers.
- Conduct a pre-exit legal audit to identify key legal issues to be resolved prior to the exit.
- Consider how the exit can be structured in a tax-efficient way.
- Engage with the management team, existing lenders and other stakeholders at an early stage to ensure that they are fully prepared for the exit process.

Vendor diligence

Rachel Bond
Stephen Drewitt
Macfarlanes LLP

1. Introduction

Due diligence is the process by which a potential purchaser and its advisers investigate the business, assets and liabilities of a target company. From a purchaser's perspective, the due diligence investigation is a very important part of the transaction. Through such investigation, the purchaser will seek to verify its understanding of the risks and opportunities of the proposed acquisition and, in doing so, determine whether it wishes to proceed with the transaction and, if so, at what price and on what terms.

With the assistance of its advisers, a purchaser will typically undertake due diligence in a number of areas.

1.1 Financial due diligence

A purchaser will usually instruct its accountants to undertake a detailed review of the target company's financial position. This will include matters such as:

- historic financial results;
- current trading;
- budgets and forecasts;
- profitability and margins;
- trends in results;
- analysis of assets and liabilities;
- required capital expenditure;
- accounting and financial controls;
- key customers and suppliers;
- the group's management structure;
- staff costs;
- competitors;
- future development opportunities;
- tax; and
- potential synergies.

1.2 Legal due diligence

Similarly, a purchaser's lawyers will usually undertake a legal due diligence review which will cover a range of topics, depending on the target company's business. These typically include:

- the corporate structure and share capital of the target company;

- constitutional documents and existing shareholder arrangements;
- financing arrangements;
- material contracts;
- title to key assets;
- real estate;
- environmental and health and safety issues;
- employment, pensions and employee benefits;
- rights to intellectual property;
- legal compliance, including issues such as compliance with data protection rules and confirmation that the target has all licences and permits required to carry on its business;
- any outstanding or recent litigation or other disputes; and
- insurance arrangements and, if necessary, regulatory issues.

1.3 Commercial and market due diligence

In addition, a purchaser will undertake commercial and market due diligence. Often, a purchaser can undertake this due diligence exercise itself, but it may appoint advisers with specialist knowledge in the sector. The purchaser will also undertake due diligence on the management team.

1.4 Specialist due diligence

Where appropriate, a purchaser may also commission specialist due diligence for the business of the target company. A broad range of matters might fall into this category, including the following:

- Where a target company has a valuable property portfolio, the purchaser might commission valuations or surveys;
- Where the company is engaged in heavy industry or occupies a site where contamination is likely, the purchaser might engage environmental consultants;
- Where the target operates a final salary pension scheme, the purchaser will want to make sure that any deficit and the funding requirements of the scheme are reviewed by its actuary; and
- Where the target has valuable intellectual property, the purchaser might require that its IP rights be reviewed by a patent or trademark agent.

2. Vendor due diligence reports

Preparation by the vendor is key to a successful due diligence exercise. As highlighted in the chapter on auction sales, by planning appropriately the vendor should be able to make the purchaser's due diligence review as smooth as possible, which will greatly assist in the negotiation process and help to ensure that the vendor achieves the best possible outcome in relation to the price and terms of the transaction.

In some transactions, in addition to preparing an information memorandum and providing a data room full of documents and information, a vendor may decide to commission vendor or 'sell side' due diligence reports. The practice of commissioning vendor due diligence reports became relatively common in the late

1990s in a strong sellers' market. At the time, good target companies attracted significant interest, particularly from private equity buyers, and financing for acquisitions was readily available. With reasonable certainty that a sale could be completed, vendors saw significant advantages in providing vendor due diligence with a view to controlling and accelerating the acquisition process. By providing these reports, a vendor could highlight all material issues relating to the target group, including all key selling points, and minimise the disruption caused to the target company by multiple purchasers asking questions and seeking information to carry out their own review.

Financial vendor due diligence reports were particularly common; legal vendor due diligence reports were seen less frequently, but were not uncommon, particularly on large multi-jurisdictional transactions with private equity sellers. In addition, where relevant to a particular target company, vendors would often commission specialist due diligence reports – for example:

- a business with manufacturing operations in a number of jurisdictions might provide Phase I environmental reports;
- a company with material property interests might provide certificates of title; or
- a business which owns valuable intellectual property might commission a trademark report.

In more recent years, and particularly since the start of the credit crunch, vendor due diligence reports have been seen less frequently. The principal reasons for this are:

- the shift of power from sellers to buyers;
- the relative strength of trade buyers compared to private equity buyers (given the difficulties faced by private equity buyers when seeking leverage); and
- the lack of certainty of execution of the transaction at an acceptable price.

Over the past few years, target companies which have been sold in auction processes have been the subject of vendor due diligence reports. However, the number and proportion of target companies sold in auction processes have declined significantly. Generally speaking, only highly successful companies have been sold by auction. Less attractive assets have been traded off-market, typically with purchasers undertaking due diligence.

The vendor and the target company should be aware that if accountants, solicitors or other professional advisers become aware of any criminal offence which has been committed by the target group, they may come under an obligation to make a report to the Serious Organised Crime Agency (SOCA) under the Proceeds of Crime Act 2002. The relevant adviser will need consent from SOCA to continue to advise on the transaction. However, the adviser will be unable to inform the vendor or the target company that it has made a report, as doing so would constitute an offence of 'tipping off'. There is no concept of materiality within the legislation; therefore, advisers may be required to report to SOCA in circumstances where it would not immediately be apparent to their client that this would be necessary. Such circumstances include:

- breaches of health and safety legislation which have resulted in cost savings for the target;
- failure to provide a stakeholder pension scheme when required to do so;
- breaches of environmental legislation, such as failure to carry out required asbestos surveys; and
- certain breaches of companies legislation.

2.1 The vendor's perspective

The production of vendor due diligence reports inevitably requires a seller to incur significant upfront costs. However, it provides a number of advantages:

- It enables a vendor to identify all issues which are likely to be of importance to a purchaser or limit the availability of financing for the acquisition, and to resolve or mitigate as many of them as possible. Carrying out a full due diligence exercise enables a vendor to be proactive in dealing with any problems and avoids the risk of being put in a weak negotiating position by a purchaser which discovers problems of which the vendor was unaware.
- By presenting any negative issues in a clear and upfront manner, a vendor can require a purchaser to take a prompt view of those issues and take them into account in proposing a price. It is much more difficult for a purchaser to seek a price reduction or contractual protection (eg, indemnities or amounts held back in escrow) in the later stages of a transaction for issues of which it is made aware by the vendor at the outset.
- A vendor can make sure that the opportunities available to the target business are highlighted clearly in the vendor due diligence reports and ensure that, where appropriate, its professional advisers comment positively on those opportunities.
- Where confidentiality is important (eg, in relation to customer contracts), vendor due diligence reports can provide a significant amount of important information in an anonymised fashion. For example, the vendor's accountants can comment on the aggregate profitability of the target company's contracts with its top 10 customers without disclosing the detailed terms or the identity of the relevant customers, and the target company's lawyers can comment on provisions such as termination rights on change of control and indemnities. The purchaser will still expect to see material customer contracts before signing the purchase agreement, but the provision of vendor due diligence may make it easier to delay the provision of these contracts until later in the process.
- A vendor can use the vendor due diligence process to frame certain aspects of the negotiations on the terms of sale. For example, the financial due diligence report can be used to support a suggestion that the target company should be sold on a locked box basis, rather than on the basis of completion accounts.
- Similarly, the vendor due diligence process can be used to anticipate negotiations which might otherwise take place on conditions and

completion deliverables. For example, the vendor will be aware of relevant change of control provisions and can outline clearly for a purchaser the extent to which it is prepared to seek waivers/consents to the transaction from third parties as a condition of completion.

- The provision of vendor due diligence should minimise the disruption to the target company's business as a result of the due diligence exercise. It is easier for the management team to provide as much of the relevant information as possible to the vendor's advisers in advance of the sale process than to be faced with lengthy requests for information from advisers to a large number of potential purchasers. The management team will still need to be available (eg, to make presentations to purchasers and answer questions), but the vendor should be able to resist providing material additional documents and information.
- While private equity sellers themselves do not typically give warranties on a sale, members of the management team will often be required to do so, either in the sale documentation and/or in the new equity documents (in circumstances where the purchaser is another private equity house and management are expected to rollover all or part of their interest in the target into the acquisition vehicle). The vendor due diligence exercise will assist the management team's advisers in the negotiation of the warranties and the drafting of disclosures against those warranties. In addition, the management team will be able to argue strongly that the vendor due diligence reports should be disclosed generally against the warranties.

2.2 The purchaser's perspective

From a purchaser's perspective, vendor due diligence reports can be a valuable resource, but should be approached with some caution. The reports are useful, principally because they highlight the key issues relevant to the target company. For example, if a target company is engaged in material litigation, this will be evident from the report and a purchaser can focus on this issue at an early stage. Vendor due diligence reports also enable a purchaser to discover certain information about the target company quickly. For example, if a company has 10 key suppliers, a purchaser can review a legal due diligence report to confirm quickly whether any of the relevant supply contracts contain change of control provisions. Without this report, all 10 supply contracts would have to be reviewed in detail by the purchaser's legal advisers in order to reach the same conclusion. The purpose of the reports is to anticipate the questions that a purchaser is likely to ask about the target company and provide answers to as many of those questions as possible. In the early stages of a transaction, the ability to identify the key issues in relation to a target company quickly without incurring substantial costs can be of assistance to a potential purchaser and its lenders in deciding whether they wish to pursue a particular transaction.

Purchasers are often concerned that vendor due diligence reports will present issues in a way which is favourable to the vendor, making it more difficult for a purchaser to form its own conclusions on the risks and opportunities relevant to the target business. For example, will a financial due diligence report prepared by the target company's accountants challenge the achievability of its business plan to the same extent as a truly independent review? These are legitimate concerns. Purchasers should always review vendor due diligence reports in detail, taking advantage of the work which has been carried out by the vendor's advisers and avoiding unnecessary duplication of effort. However, purchasers should assess the credibility of the work and, where appropriate, review the underlying documents and data with their own advisers to confirm the findings. It will often be possible for purchasers and their advisers to speak directly with the vendor's advisers who prepared the reports, particularly in relation to financial due diligence. Purchasers can take this opportunity to discuss in detail any areas where the analysis is finely balanced or where there is a concern that information might have been presented with a positive spin.

There will almost always be certain areas where a purchaser requires more detail than has been included in the vendor due diligence reports or where it requires an independent review of particular issues. A vendor due diligence report cannot take into account the particular circumstances of each purchaser and its finance providers. For example, a trade purchaser may need to consider restrictive covenants entered into by the target company in more detail than a private equity-backed newco. Furthermore, a vendor due diligence report will not cover issues arising out of the purchaser's plans for the business. It will highlight opportunities to grow the business or perhaps to expand into new but complementary areas; however, it is unlikely that the vendor due diligence reports will contemplate the break-up of the target group or the closure of a particular part of its business. Therefore, a purchaser will need to undertake its own due diligence in certain areas. Finally, while the vendor due diligence reports can provide much of the information in relation to the target company which is relevant to the antitrust analysis (eg, by presenting the sales of the target group in each jurisdiction in the appropriate manner), it clearly cannot consider any overlap with the as-yet-unidentified purchaser. Therefore, further work will be required to reach a conclusion on antitrust issues which might arise in any particular jurisdiction.

2.3 Reliance on the reports

Vendor due diligence is commissioned by the vendor or the target company and made available to potential purchasers on a hold harmless basis. This means that prior to receiving the report, potential purchasers will have to sign a letter with the provider of the report in which the potential purchaser will agree that it cannot rely on the report and has no right of action in respect of it. The potential purchaser will also be required to agree not to disclose the report other than to a limited category of persons, such as professional advisers and senior employees who need to review it for the purpose of the transaction. The same will apply to any lenders to the potential purchaser.

On exchange of contracts, the ultimate purchaser and its lenders will enter into a reliance letter with the provider of the report, under which they will have the right to rely only on the final version of the report. The report should set out clearly the basis on which it has been prepared – in particular, that it has been prepared on instructions from the vendor and does not consider issues specific to the purchaser or its lenders, and that it is limited to the matters expressly within its scope. In addition, the reliance letter will contain a number of limitations which a purchaser may try to negotiate with the providers of the reports. The principal areas to be considered are as follows:

- The cap on liability – in relation to accountants, in 1998 the British Venture Capital Association published a memorandum of understanding on limitation of liability in private equity transactions, which is still used today to provide a reference point for liability for financial due diligence reports. The cap on liability depends on the size of the transaction. For any deal with a value in excess of £55 million (which will almost certainly be the case if a vendor due diligence report is to be commissioned), the relevant cap is £25 million and it is unusual for accountants to agree to a higher cap. There is no equivalent memorandum of understanding in relation to legal due diligence; however, in relation to vendor legal due diligence, a cap on liability will almost invariably be included and will often be the same as that which applies to the financial due diligence.
- Time limits for claims – generally, claims will have to be brought within a certain timeframe of perhaps two or three years.
- Proportionate liability – this is to ensure that where more than one adviser has contributed to a loss, the liability of any adviser without a financial cap on liability, or with a higher cap, will be reduced proportionately in line with the reduction in liability of the adviser who benefits from a cap.

Consideration should be given to which entities on the purchaser's side can rely on the vendor due diligence reports. The acquiring entity, whether a trade purchaser or a newco established by a private equity house, will be the primary beneficiary of the report and the entity most likely to suffer direct loss as a result of having relied on it. Particularly where the purchaser is a newco established by a private equity house, the vendor's advisers may argue that their liability should terminate on any change of control of that newco (ie, that their liability should not survive an exit by the private equity house).

The report will also be addressed to the providers of debt finance to the purchaser. Where there is a syndicate of lenders, it will normally be addressed to the lead debt provider for itself and as agent for the syndicate members (on primary syndication). Only the lead debt provider will be entitled to bring a claim and will do so on the instructions of the majority lenders on behalf of all relevant syndicate members. Lenders that join the syndicate after primary syndication are generally unable to rely on the reports.

It is also possible that group companies of the acquiring company or, where it is a private equity-backed newco, the private equity fund, fund manager or investment adviser will seek the right to rely on the reports. Where this is agreed, the lenders will expect to agree with the other addressees that the lenders have a first ranking claim against the providers of the reports.

2.4 Initial engagement of report providers

Generally, the correct person(s) to engage the providers of any vendor due diligence reports and to pay their fees will be the selling shareholders (ie, the private equity house or perhaps one of its holding companies, if the sale is to take place at that level in the structure). This assumes that the reports are commissioned in connection with a proposed sale rather than, for example, as part of a strategic review by the investee company, one possible outcome of which might be a sale.

However, given the upfront costs of commissioning vendor due diligence reports, it is not unusual for the private equity house to seek to make the target company the engaging party, or at least to have an agreement that the target company will pay the fees associated with the reports if no sale results from the auction process. This has become easier in the United Kingdom since October 1 2008, which marked the abolition of the prohibition on a private company providing financial assistance in connection with the acquisition of its own shares or those of its private holding company. Financial assistance remains relevant for public companies (or subsidiaries of public companies), but it will be relatively rare for a private equity investee company to be a public company. Even where the target company is a private company, if there is a proposal that it should bear the costs of the vendor due diligence reports, careful consideration will still need to be given to the legality of that proposal, taking into account issues such as capital maintenance and corporate benefit for the target company.

3. Portfolio sales

This chapter has focused on sales by a private equity house of a single portfolio company by way of auction. However, in recent years there has been an increasing number of examples of sales of portfolios of companies by one private equity house to another (or by a corporate to a private equity house). The approach towards due diligence on portfolio sales differs substantially from the approach taken on the sale of a single portfolio company, and one of the particular differences arises in relation to vendor due diligence.

Generally, where a private equity house proposes to purchase a large portfolio of assets, it will carry out less detailed due diligence on the underlying businesses than it would on the acquisition of a single company. There will still be a data room, which will contain detailed financial information and information on other material issues relating to the investee companies; but, for example, the number of contracts provided for review will be smaller and limited to key items. It is likely that some of the companies in the portfolio will have material value and those may be subject to fairly detailed due diligence. Others will be of limited value and will be included in the transaction for nominal consideration. The key objective of the due diligence exercise in relation to those companies will be to ascertain whether any liabilities could attach to a purchaser of those companies. For example, do any of them have a defined benefit pension scheme which is underfunded or any material environmental liabilities? It is quite common to see focused vendor due diligence reports being prepared to consider these sorts of specific material issue.

In addition, there is one significant area of due diligence which must be covered in relation to a portfolio sale, which does not arise on sales of individual investee companies. It will usually be the case that, ideally, the acquiring private equity house wishes to take over the position of the exiting private equity house without triggering any rights of other shareholders under the financing documents, shareholders' agreement or articles. For example, the purchaser will not want the shares to be offered to other shareholders under pre-emption rights or rights of first refusal. Equally, it will not want existing shareholders to be able to exercise tag-along rights or the lenders to be able to treat the transaction as a change of control (and hence an event of default under the loan documents). In practice, it will almost invariably be the case that there are some rights in relation to transfers which need to be waived, or some consents which need to be given, in order for the transaction to proceed. The task of reviewing all investment and financing documents, reporting on the relevant rights and restrictions, and proposing solutions will usually fall to the vendor and its advisers in the first instance, and the legal advisers to the vendor will provide a detailed vendor due diligence report on those matters.

4. Conclusion

Due diligence is often considered to be a matter for the purchaser: vendors and target companies passively provide relevant information which the purchaser analyses for its own benefit. However, with the right approach, the due diligence exercise can provide significant opportunities for a vendor to ensure that it achieves the best possible terms of sale at the best possible price. Planning is key and a vendor must remember to view the target company and the information to be provided from the perspective of the potential purchaser. Vendor due diligence can be a valuable part of the process in appropriate circumstances.

Management issues

Emma Danks
Taylor Wessing LLP

1. Introduction

The ability of a management team to understand the emphasis placed by private equity houses on driving towards an exit in the medium term, thereby effectively aligning its interests with the private equity house, will make the management team far more attractive to a private equity investor. However, the management team's perception of and attitude towards an exit can be very different from those of a private equity house and this is important for all parties to understand. For a management team, it represents a new period of ownership and potentially a time of unsettling change. If the managers are also selling shareholders, it may not even represent a full exit if the sale is to another private equity house and management is being required to roll over some of its current investment into the new deal. Understanding management's concerns is equally imperative for any private equity seller on an exit and for a private equity and trade buyer acquiring a company from a private equity house. In particular, on a secondary buy-out there will come a tipping point in the transaction where management will move from being primarily on the sell side to being primarily on the buy side. Conflicting interests may also arise within the management team itself, as the personal situation and goals of each manager may be very different.

This chapter first considers what impact the form of the exit has on management and looks at the duties of management and potential conflicts of interest during the exit process. It then considers the terms of the original deal documents – in particular, the obligation on management to give warranties on an exit and what price management will get for its equity. Finally, the duties of management and potential conflicts of interest are considered. Tax planning also plays an important role in a manager's exit or decision to re-invest. The main factors considered in that regard are discussed in the chapter on tax.

2. What form is the exit taking and what impact does that have on management?

The recent private equity market has primarily experienced trade sales and secondary buy-outs as the key exit routes, with initial public offerings (IPOs) being less common. However, there are some common themes for management, regardless of which exit route is used, as well as variables dependent on the route, market conditions and practices at the time of the exit.

2.1 Secondary buy-out

(a) *Dynamic*

On a secondary buy-out, being the sale of a business by one private equity house to another, management's negotiations with the incoming private equity house will have a different dynamic from that which the managers would have had at the time of the original investment with the first private equity house. The dynamic hinges on the facts that:

- management is both a buyer and a seller; and
- the managers will have undergone the experience of private equity ownership and will know what did and did not work well in the original private equity investment from their perspective.

The secondary buy-out of a successful business will normally be only a partial exit for management, as all (or at least many) of the managers will be expected to continue with the business, and so in this way their interests will not be aligned with those of the outgoing private equity house. If the original investment was unsuccessful and/or the incoming private equity house believes that there are weaknesses in the management team, or if a manager wants to leave the business for personal reasons, the incoming private equity house may want to bring in an entirely new management team (or certain new managers to work alongside the incumbent team). This will inevitably lead to a period of transition and change for all management.

Having already gone through one private equity buy-out, management will be familiar with the parameters and nature of private equity ownership and is likely to use the set of equity documents negotiated on the first buy-out as a starting point for negotiations on the secondary buy-out. Although market practice may have moved on during the lifetime of the investment, unless there have been any radical changes, it will cause real negotiation tension if the incoming private equity house seeks to agree any provisions which are substantially worse for the management team than those agreed in the original investment. However, some private equity houses have their own preferred terms which, even if less favourable than those in existence, can be difficult to move them away from.

(b) *Reinvestment*

The management team may be personally entitled to reap significant financial rewards from the exit of the primary buy-out, and may be reluctant to reinvest a large portion of this back into the secondary buy-out and effectively see this money 'locked up' until the incoming private equity house exits. By contrast, the incoming private equity house will want management to demonstrate its continuing commitment to the deal by reinvesting a substantial amount of its proceeds. The end result of these contrasting positions in any secondary buy-out tends to reflect a delicate balance between the acknowledgement, at least in the context of a successful business, that managers should receive some reward for growing that business, but not enough to disincentivise them from delivering an even greater return for themselves and, importantly, their new owners.

(c) ***Warranties***

On a secondary buy-out, the outgoing private equity house will provide no warranties other than as to ownership of the shares that it is selling and authority to sell those shares. In order to close the 'warranty gap' which would otherwise exist on a sale by a private equity house, the managers will usually be required to give 'look-back' warranties relating to historic issues in the business, as well as the more 'look-forward' warranties relating to, for example, the accuracy of their business plan. Where the original deal was an acquisition by a private equity house from a trade seller, this will be a fundamental difference for the management team from the original deal, where the managers may not have had to give such warranties. The management team's advisers will need to explain carefully the implications of giving these statements and ensure that the team has sufficient time to understand the warranties and undertake a proper disclosure exercise. The negotiation of the warranty package with management will be a key commercial issue for any buyer and will be a particularly emotive issue for management, given the potential risk of personal liability. In addition, and in respect of secondary buy-outs, the negotiation will need to dovetail with the wider discussions on the amount which the incoming private equity house requires management to reinvest and the terms of that reinvestment. The key concerns for management, other than the scope of the warranties, will be the limitations on those warranties. The financial limitations in terms of the 'look-back' warranties will usually be calculated as a percentage of management's sale proceeds (in cash and after tax), and this percentage is very much a function of commercial negotiation; whereas those 'look-forward' warranties given by managers in the equity documents with the incoming private equity house will typically be calculated by reference to a low multiple of their gross salary.

(d) ***Restrictive covenants***

In addition, management will be required to give various restrictive covenants as sellers pursuant to the sale and purchase agreement, such as a non-compete obligation or non-solicitation of other employees or customers/suppliers. It will have already given restrictive covenants in the original deal, in both the equity documents and service agreements; given that the managers will have entered into the equity documents on a commercial footing rather than as employees (as is the case with the service agreements), the restrictive covenants in the equity documents are generally considered to be easier to enforce.

2.2 Trade sale

Many of the considerations referred to above will apply equally to a trade sale. The fundamental difference will be an emotional one, and a trade sale is an area where the existing private equity house and management are most likely to have issues to discuss. During the lifetime of the investment, management will have become accustomed to acting on a day-to-day basis effectively as the owner of the business with an equity stake (albeit a minority one) in the business. A trade sale could take away this day-to-day autonomy, which might have been the reason why management supported a buy-out in the first place. If the trade buyer is a large corporate (or worse, a competitor), the day-to-day experience for management will be radically different. In addition, management is unlikely to have any equity interest in the business or, if the trade buyer does offer any such equity incentives, they are likely to be restricted to the very top tier of management only and may be in the form of share options in the parent company rather than shares themselves. This creates a problem for the top tier of management in incentivising the more junior tiers of management who may have previously participated in the equity either directly or via a 'pooling vehicle' (eg, an employee benefit trust). It is perhaps unsurprising that trade sales do not involve the continued involvement of 'existing' management for any extended period of time.

2.3 IPO

Management's reaction to an IPO can vary. Many management teams will relish the higher profile which it brings for the company. However, after the IPO has taken place, the continuing obligations with which listed companies must comply will impose more onerous duties and obligations on the management team.

As with a sale, the management team will be required to enter into warranties and indemnities (in favour of the underwriter) and take responsibility for the contents of the prospectus. In addition, it will need to enter into a lock-up agreement and orderly market restrictions. The lock-up agreement prevents any sale of management's retained shares (or any other transactions in those shares) for a specific period. The lock-up is an important message for the underwriter to be able to present to the market, as it demonstrates that management will bear the risk of share price fluctuations for a period of time following the IPO. Management may also be required to enter into orderly market obligations in respect of its retained shares; these provisions are designed to promote continuing stability in the market for the company's listed shares for an additional period after expiry of the lock-up period.

Even when the lock-up period expires, any dealings by the management team in shares will be subject to intense market scrutiny and it may be that the stock is illiquid in terms of selling off material interests in any event. These factors will combine to mean that for the management team at least, it is not an 'exit' in the purest sense of the term. It is possible that the institutions may also be required to retain some shares as a confirmation of their confidence in the future of the business.

In terms of their ongoing incentivisation on an IPO, new incentive arrangements will often be put in place in the form of share option schemes and sometimes bonus plans.

3. What rights and obligations were there in the original deal documents?

The shareholders' agreement will usually include a statement as to the parties' intentions as regards an exit, in terms of both timing and process. As well as the private equity house wanting to ensure the managers' buy-in to the process, given that they will be crucial to the success of any exit, it will also want them to give further transaction comfort through warranties (and, if necessary, indemnities).

Given the reluctance of private equity houses to give warranties which go beyond the ownership of the shares that they are selling and authorising to sell, they will usually look to the managers to provide operational warranties, and possibly also any indemnities if required (for a further discussion on the 'warranty gap', see section 2). The original equity documents will tend to include an explicit statement that the outgoing private equity house will give no warranties or indemnities on an exit, other than as to title and capacity, but that management will give such customary warranties and indemnities as are reasonably required by the purchaser and agree to such lock-ups as may be required (but see the paragraph below regarding enforceability). There will typically be an explicit statement that no greater value will be attributed to management's shares as a result of these warranties and indemnities.

In an actual exit scenario, these provisions in a shareholders' agreement, given their unspecific nature, are not necessarily enforceable and merely provide broad parameters for the negotiation of exit terms at the time that the exit eventually takes place. They ensure that all parties are continually driven towards a successful exit during the lifetime of the private equity house's investment in the company; but in reality, a successful exit needs the management team's support and the private equity house will not want to have to force a sale (see section 4 with regard to 'drag-along'). Hence, as a practical matter, there is likely to be more flexibility at the time of an eventual exit than the provisions in a shareholders' agreement might suggest.

4. What price will management get for its equity?

4.1 Tag-along/drag-along

All private equity houses will want to be able to deliver the entire share capital of a portfolio company on an exit, regardless of whether it is a trade sale or a sale to another private equity house. This is essential in order to make the target company as attractive an asset as possible and thereby achieve the highest value for the target company. The existing equity documentation will usually contain drag-along provisions, enabling the private equity house as the majority seller to 'drag' (ie, force a sale by) the managers. Such a sale is usually at the same price (and in the same form of consideration) and on the same terms as the sale by the private equity house. The threshold at which the drag-along provision can be triggered will vary from deal to deal; if the management had strong bargaining power when the equity documents were drafted, it might have been able to agree a threshold which would be required to be reached before the drag-along right can be used by the private equity house to involve at least a proportion of the managers' holding shares. In some instances the drag-along rights may be suspended for a period of time after completion of the original deal (eg, three to five years), or be capable of being triggered only once an agreed exit value had been achieved. The principle behind these qualifications is to ensure that management cannot be forced into a sale before having had the opportunity to deliver growth. Institutional shareholders are generally resistant to such carve-outs.

Difficulties can arise in the exercise of the drag-along right if the drafting of the original equity documents is too prescriptive and if the documents stipulate that all shareholders will receive consideration on the same terms and/or at the same price. This is a particular issue on a secondary buy-out, where certain managers will be 'rolling over' into the new equity (see section 4.6), whereas the outgoing private equity house and certain other managers will be receiving cash for their shares. If the drag-along rights are drafted in such a way that they are triggered only once an offer has been made for the target company, the acquisition of the target company may well be carried out by way of a takeover offer under the Companies Act 2006 (thereby enabling the drag-along right to be triggered by the bidder); similar issues may arise in such circumstances. The Companies Act 2006 requires the offer to be on terms which are the same in relation to the shares (or all shares of the relevant class(es)) to which the offer relates. Thus, the offer document needs to be carefully drafted and the offer constructed in such a way as to ensure that the drag-along right can be triggered.

Equally, the managers will want to ensure that they will not be 'left behind' if the private equity house finds a buyer for its shares. Therefore, the equity documentation will usually contain corresponding tag-along provisions requiring a buyer of some or all of the private equity house's shares (often subject to a minimum) to offer the same price and terms for the shares held by management as are being offered to the selling private equity house. However, tag-along differs from drag-along in that there is no obligation on the managers to accept the offer.

There are additional complexities for the exit if there are managers who had held equity from the original private equity deal and who have left the target company, but still hold shares due to the way in which particular leaver provisions operate. Their interests will not necessarily be aligned with the rest of the shareholder base; thus, it is essential to ensure that they can be dragged if necessary. For similar logistical reasons, where there is a wide management shareholder base, structuring the exit will be made significantly more straightforward where a pooling vehicle has been used for management investment (see section 2.2).

Again, although tag and drag provisions are typical, the use of these mechanics to achieve a sale is unusual, as a successful exit is generally dependent on a cooperative management team.

4.2 Ratchet

In a secondary buy-out scenario, the outgoing private equity house may have further sought to align management's interests with its own by using a ratchet to redistribute the total equity pot of the company at the time of the exit according to whether certain milestones have been met. Ratchets are usually constructed by reference to either a target value of the company on exit or the internal rate of return (IRR) or exit multiple of the outgoing private equity house. Although the former construction will be more familiar to management and will be easier for it to keep visibility of, the latter construction is more commonly used, given that it is the measure of performance which private equity houses tend to use for their investments. Therefore, management must be sure that it understands how the IRR is calculated by the private equity house, including the effect of any partial exits done by the private equity house before the eventual exit of 100% of its investment.

Some private equity houses do not offer ratchet arrangements, arguing that management's share of the equity pot at the outset operates as an effective incentive to deliver future growth. Whether this is right may depend on the initial equity on offer, the nature of the business and the bargaining position of the management team.

The tax considerations around the structuring of ratchet-type mechanisms are complex and are the subject of the chapter on tax.

4.3 Sale bonuses

Although ratchets are a popular method for private equity houses to incentivise management, incentives can be provided (or supplemented) by other means, such as bonus arrangements. To achieve this, managers are given a contractual right to a cash bonus payable by the company on exit, provided that, for example, they have remained employed until the exit and have contributed properly towards the exit process. This method of incentivisation is a tax-inefficient means of incentivising management and pushes down reported earnings; however, it can help where, for example, management equity is 'underwater' at the time of the exit or where managers deemed key to the sale process do not themselves hold equity and hurdle shares have not been deemed appropriate (for further discussion please see the chapter on tax).

4.4 Options

If a manager has options in the company, these options are usually triggered by an exit (regardless of the timing of the exit), allowing the manager to acquire a fixed number of shares in the company or its group at a specified price. The shares which are allocated as a result of the exercise of the option will then be sold to the purchaser for the same price as the existing shares in the company (for further discussion please see the chapter on tax).

4.5 Unallocated shares

Often at the beginning of an investment, the private equity house might agree to the reservation of a percentage of the share capital to be used to incentivise new management during the lifetime of the deal. If any of that pool remains unallocated at exit, the original equity documents should provide for what happens to the unallocated shares pool – for example, whether it is allocated across the management team only (and in what proportion) or to the outgoing private equity house too and for what value. Again, it is inherently tax inefficient to leave the allocation of these shares until immediately before an exit, and management will be very much alive to the need to allocate this pool at an early stage in the investment cycle.

4.6 Reinvestment

In a secondary buy-out scenario, management is likely to be offered the opportunity to reinvest a proportion of its exit proceeds in the new bid vehicle going forward (or will possibly even be required to do so by the incoming private equity house). Management must take specific tax advice in this instance, as it will usually be tax inefficient for managers to receive cash for the sale of their existing shares on the exit and then immediately reinvest some or all of that cash in the new equity, as a capital gains tax charge will be crystallised immediately and become payable on the gain. The normal method is for managers to roll over into the new equity by exchanging some or all of their current equity for new equity (if necessary via a sequence of steps to roll the managers' equity up through the buyer's newco group) (for further discussion please see the chapter on tax).

5. Duties of management and potential conflicts of interest

On an exit (as during the lifetime of the investment), managers should be mindful of their duties as directors under the Companies Act 2006, their service agreement and their common law fiduciary duties.

During the course of exit negotiations, management will inevitably be faced with an array of situations in which potential conflicts of interest and duty will arise. In broad terms, under the Companies Act 2006, a director should avoid putting himself or herself in a position where there is a conflict between his or her own interests and those of the target company. Management is likely to be wearing a number of different 'hats' for the purposes of the exit. On the one hand, management owes duties to the outgoing private equity house and the company; and on the other, management has a personal economic interest in the outcome of the exit (whether by way of secondary buy-out, trade sale or IPO).

In an auction process, the interests of the outgoing private equity house and management may diverge significantly in terms of choice of buyer and price to be paid, and the pressure on management to manage its conflicts can become particularly acute. As referred to previously (see section 2), management may favour a particular financial bidder which supports its business plan and is willing to offer an attractive equity incentive package over a trade buyer which already has a management team in situate. Management will be faced with a delicate balancing act; while securing its own future, it must also satisfy the outgoing private equity house that it has not switched to the buy side, and that its priority continues to be achieving the optimum sale price for existing shareholders as a whole. This being so, the outgoing private equity house may well be keen to retain control of the auction process and, in particular, the flow of information and access to management, in order to create an even playing field among bidders.

While it may be frustrating for management to be sidelined in this manner, it can be helpful in terms of mitigating the risk of conflict. If management has not sought and obtained its employer's consent to proceed with the auction process, this is likely to constitute a breach of a number of terms of the relevant managers' service agreements (eg, the use and disclosure of confidential information, devoting their whole time and attention to their duties as employees and holding no other business interests). In particular, consent to proceed will need to include use of confidential information for the purpose of creating a business plan and disclosure of the business plan and related information to bidders. Given the importance to the eventual disclosure exercise of keeping an audit trail of documents disclosed to bidders (whether through the data room or otherwise), it is also important for an outgoing private equity house to keep control and have visibility of the information flow to bidders rather than leaving this solely to management.

To avoid any allegation of breach of duty, management should seek prior authorisation of the potential conflicts that may arise during the course of the exit process. Although under the Companies Act 2006 conflicts can be authorised at board level (such authorisation being effective only if the required quorum is met by the non-conflicted directors (ie, the outgoing investor and non-executive directors)), it is more prudent for the target company to seek authorisation from its shareholders. It may also be appropriate for the management team to take further mitigating action by establishing a sub-committee of non-conflicted directors to evaluate and, where necessary, negotiate the terms of the proposed transaction.

As directors of the target company, the managers have a continuing duty to act in a way which they consider, in good faith, to be most likely to promote the success of the target company. The effect of this can be twofold in the context of an exit. First, management should be satisfied that any offer which it is supporting is likely to have a long-term positive impact on the business of the company going forward. For example, in the context of a secondary buy-out, the level of debt can be cause for concern. If newco is highly leveraged, the return requirements of the capital structure may put substantial pressure on the business of the company, requiring management to refocus its attention on cost containment and, potentially, the sale of business assets, rather than growth. In some instances this may cause friction between an offer at an acceptable level to the outgoing private equity house and the interests of the target company, notwithstanding the fairness of the price. Second, management will be expected to continue to run the business of the target company in an efficient manner throughout the exit process. The difficulty that this presents should not be underestimated; any exit process will require a serious time commitment, but management should not be unduly distracted from running the target business by pressure from the outgoing private equity house to assist in the marketing process or by negotiations with any incoming shareholder as to the nature of its incentive package.

A manager who is also a director of the target company must not allow his or her relationship and negotiations with any incoming private equity house to interfere with his or her overriding duty to act in the way that he or she considers most likely to promote the success of the company for the benefit of the members as a whole. A breach of duty by management is capable of ratification by the shareholders of the target company (the votes of management being disregarded for the purposes of determining whether the shareholder resolution has been validly passed). If no ratification is forthcoming, a breach of duty entitles the company to bring a claim for damages or, in appropriate circumstances (eg, the unlawful distribution of confidential information), equitable relief against management. Any such breach is also likely to constitute a breach of his or her service agreement with the company, resulting in immediate dismissal.

6. Conclusion

The position of the management team on an exit must be considered from a variety of different perspectives. The managers' role is a hybrid of acting as sellers, buyers, directors and employees, and they have ultimate day-to-day responsibility for the continued successful performance of the underlying business. To add to this complexity, while the managers will have some commonality of interests, their individual aspirations may well vary. Given the current economic environment and the additional operational pressure which many private equity houses are imposing on their portfolio companies, understanding the role and motivation of management teams is more important than ever.

The author would like to thank Martin Winter, Nick Hazell and Eleanor West of Taylor Wessing for their contributions to this chapter.

Auction sales

Tim Wright
SJ Berwin LLP

1. Introduction

1.1 Overview of process

In many ways the auction process is ideally suited to a private equity sale. Private equity sellers are not burdened with some of the commercial constraints that may affect trade sellers (eg, concerns about a sale to a buyer that is a competitor). They can instead focus on achieving the highest possible return for their limited partners and investors, and securing the minimum amount of contingency to the price or the process. By leveraging off the competitive tension between the bidders, a well-run auction process of a good asset (and sometimes a not-so-good asset) can achieve those objectives handsomely.

1.2 Choice of process

Among other things, the competitive tendering process is intended to maximise the price of the asset by encouraging potential buyers to bid against each other. Well-advised prospective sellers will consider what type of sale will maximise the price of the asset that they are seeking to dispose of, and for the general partner of a private equity house an auction has the added attraction of demonstrating to limited partners that the best price was achieved.

A key factor in the decision to seek an exit via an auction process will be identifying potential bidders and assessing the optimal pool of bidders. This will require a detailed assessment of the target company, its group, its rivals and the wider industry and sector. In most situations neither the target nor the private equity seller will possess sufficient research and analysis resources or breadth of industry expertise to undertake this task adequately in-house. A financial adviser is appointed to advise the seller at an early stage in the auction process and to provide the necessary transaction management. The involvement of a reputable investment bank may also be seen to enhance the credibility of the process and is likely to provide access to a wider bidder market.

Factors which may militate against the use of an auction process include the situation where the seller believes that there is insufficient depth of bidders to sustain a competition. Although this can be difficult to gauge at the outset of a process, it is important that this be properly assessed sooner rather than later. Once the process has commenced, the seller's negotiating position will be severely weakened if deadlines need to be extended to encourage further or improved bids. Despite the mostly tightly drafted confidentiality agreement, news of a failed auction process invariably becomes widespread in the investor community and can lead to a medium-term loss of shareholder value until the asset shakes off the tag of 'damaged goods'.

2. Key issues

2.1 Role of management sellers

The involvement of management can be a sensitive area where the private equity seller and management interests are not well aligned and this conflict of interest can impact on the maximisation of value for one or both of these parties. It is crucial to the private equity seller that the key management team be properly engaged at the appropriate stage. A private equity house will buy and sell many assets; a manager may have only one or, at best, a handful of opportunities. The stakes are therefore high, but the expectations and the process need to be managed; divisions between the sellers simply present opportunities for bidders.

2.2 Conflict

Potential for tensions between management investors and the private equity sponsor play a key role in any buy-out or exit negotiations (and indeed throughout the lifetime of the investment). In general, these arise from the disparate economic positions and competing aims of each party. In an exit situation this is particularly the case with regard to the form of proceeds to be received by each party and the difficult subject of the giving of warranties (or other commitments which entail an ongoing relationship with the investment following the exit). These tensions are often exacerbated in an auction scenario – all the more so where the exit is investor-led and driven, and where prospective purchasers expect management to continue to play key roles, in terms of both time and exit proceeds that they commit.

2.3 Warranties and indemnities

In the United Kingdom, the typical position is that no warranties or indemnities will be given by the private equity seller other than a warranty that it owns its own shares and has the capacity to sell them. Any warranty or indemnity cover that the prospective bidders may seek will therefore need to be given by the management team. However, management in turn may often be unwilling or indeed unable to give such protection – "Why am I being asked to stand behind 100% of the risk when I am not taking 100% of the cash?" is often the plaintive cry (and not without some justification). Even if the management sellers are happy to give warranties, they may be reluctant to assume liability on an absolute basis, or indeed have the financial resources (even after the net sale proceeds) to allow them to provide suitable cover. Negotiation of the basis of warranties will therefore be a key issue to be resolved between the private equity seller and management sellers at an early stage of the auction process. If a substantially complete draft of the sale and purchase agreement is to be provided to prospective bidders, management will need to be substantively engaged at an early stage in the sale process and agreement reached upon the basis of the approach to be taken.

From the bidder's perspective, it is proposing to pay a full and fair price. It may therefore feel that it should have proper recourse if it transpires that what it has bought is not quite what it was hoping that it would be.

Although it is certainly not the only solution, warranty and indemnity insurance is increasingly being used in transactions to bridge the gap between the buyer's need to have recourse for breaches of warranty and the seller's ability and willingness to provide such recourse. Generally, the parties will seek a policy that mirrors the warranties in the sale and purchase agreement and the tax deed, if a tax deed is given. The advantages of such a policy are that it allows proper cover to be given from a party with good covenant strength which would not otherwise be available.

Clearly, this approach involves an increased cost, and while availability, terms and premiums do change in line with the insurance market, it is not going to be a cheap option. Whether such cost is to be borne by the buyer or the seller (and if so, which seller) is again a point for clarity earlier rather than later in the process.

What does appear to have permanently changed (for the better) over the last decade is the relative ease with which the insurance can be put in place during a transaction.

2.4 Europe

In other jurisdictions, the 'no warranties other than as to title and capacity' approach that is invariably taken by private equity sellers in the United Kingdom is not so firmly set, although to the extent that a trend can be detected, it is generally towards the 'no warranty' approach. This in itself can cause differences in expectations from bidders that otherwise feel that the seller is just taking a negotiating position; therefore, such false expectations need to be managed early in the process and the approach of the seller made very clear.

2.5 Rollover

If the successful bidder is a private equity house that regards incumbent management as key to the business plan and future success of the investment, management is likely to be required to roll over (ie, reinvest all or part of its exit proceeds in the same mix of shares, preference shares and loan notes as the investor is taking) a significant portion of its existing equity investment into securities in the new investment structure. More detail on this is included elsewhere in this book, but once again, expectations and the process need to be managed.

2.6 Equity terms

Crucial to the rollover decision and negotiation is not merely the prospective bidders' commercial assessment of the target company and management's value to the continuing business, but also the future relationship between continuing management and the bidders as prospective majority investors in the target company. A manager who it is proposed will 'roll over' will want to be very sure that he or she has a future with the new owners and not end up simply providing equity financing from what would otherwise have been cash proceeds. The competitive tension and dynamics of an auction may mean that management sellers who are expecting to retain their roles in the target company will have significantly more bargaining power with prospective bidders than might be the case in a 'straight sale' situation.

In a genuinely competitive auction where management's continued involvement is key to the commercial success of the target company, there is the risk that management may seek to favour the bidder that offers management the most advantageous terms for its continued involvement in the business – a position that is obviously not well aligned with the interests of the private equity seller. In order to avoid or at least mitigate this, the private equity seller must plan and manage the involvement of management (and its separate set of advisers) throughout the process. This needs to be handled alongside and concurrently with the provision of information relating to the target company by management to the prospective bidders, both through the data room and in face-to-face meetings with bidders. In some cases a private equity seller may seek to avoid this situation by insisting on limiting management's involvement and seek the best institutional offer before an engagement with management on equity terms – an approach that is unlikely to help discussions on the proportion of rollover.

In practice, where management and private equity sellers are well advised, the friction is much less than might be imagined; however, the risk of sell-side division remains one that needs to be recognised.

3. Seller preparation

3.1 Opportunity

Sell-side preparation is vital to the success of the auction. In general, an exit via auction (whether it is a full formal auction process or a less formal competitive sale) will present the seller with significant opportunities for control over the sale process and, in particular, the flow of information, which a seller may not otherwise expect to have on an exit. For example, the seller will generally be in a position to produce a first draft sale and purchase agreement for issue to bidders and will expect to defend its key points by leveraging the competitive tension between bidders. The bidders may be wary of providing aggressive mark-ups which may be seen as unreasonable where they believe that this will lead to them being eliminated from the process. Acceptance of the seller's position certainly seems to come easier for a buyer before rather than after exclusivity.

3.2 Process preparation

Depending on the competitive situation (ie, the level of interest in the target company that the seller reasonably expects from the market), well-prepared sellers should be in a position to control tightly the scope and flow of information to bidders. While much of this can be managed by the investment bank or financial advisers, the seller will need, at an early stage, to identify the internal team and resources of the target company which will be required, and to ensure that the internal team is correctly briefed at an appropriate stage in the process.

The other critical part of the process preparation will be identifying the key issues in advance of them being raised by the bidders. If a key contract contains a change of control clause, what approach will be taken? Can a bidder realistically be asked to take a view or is it something where consent or at least comfort needs to be sought from the counterparty? If so, when will this be undertaken? Equally, there may be a potential issue (eg, a tax query) that, with sufficient time and advanced planning, can be resolved prior to signing. All of these decisions and actions are always much better taken when there is time and not in the heat of the transaction.

3.3 Information management

The scope of the target documentation to be provided to bidders will be established at a relatively early stage in the process, having regard not only to the nature of the target business and likely bidders, but also to the level of market interest anticipated. It may also be appropriate to consider producing a seller due diligence report, prepared by the seller's legal and financial advisers. Management of information flow is crucial both in monitoring what information is provided to bidders and in ensuring that the process itself is managed efficiently. This also avoids the danger of criticism – and legal action – from bidders that believe they have been treated unfairly and are disadvantaged in the process.

3.4 Seller due diligence

Virtually all processes now include a vendor due diligence accounting report, sometimes accompanied by commercial and legal due diligence reports. These reports are prepared by advisers to the target company under a scope determined by the sellers. The successful bidder (but only the successful bidder) will be allowed to have reliance upon these reports and so, theoretically, vendor due diligence reports remove duplication of effort and cost. In practice, bidders may have certain scepticism (whether justified or not) as to how genuinely independent, adequately scoped and useful these reports actually are, and many bidders are likely to want to prepare some form of 'top-up' report. Notwithstanding this, vendor due diligence reports do have the advantages of:

- saving time;
- allowing bidders controlled access to some detailed information at an early stage;
- allowing bidders to make competing bids based on comparable information; and
- saving that very valuable resource in any exit process – management's time.

3.5 Evaluation preparation

In preparing the seller's drafts of key transaction documents, the seller and its advisers will be keen to identify the key issues and priorities for the seller, and in particular those which are likely to be crucial to the evaluation of bids. In this respect, private equity sellers are gloriously uncomplicated: they want the maximum cash consideration with the minimum of execution risk and very limited, if any, recourse to the private equity seller following completion.

Once the bids are received, and assuming that they are at the right level, the seller will want to keep the momentum of the transaction going. Therefore, while it is to be expected that there will be some time to evaluate the bids, it is unlikely that there will be an excess of time to evaluate the bids. A properly prepared sell-side team will therefore have briefed the seller on the likely positions to be taken by the bidders and ensured that all on the sell-side team understand the significance (or not) of key areas. They will also probably have had preliminary meetings on some of the issues with all bidders and will have agreed with the seller the key areas of focus for the analysis of the competing bids.

3.6 Timetable

The auction process will usually include the following elements, albeit that the timing and order of the steps may vary depending on the transaction:

- retention of advisers;
- confidentiality undertakings from the bidders;
- preparation of the information memorandum and due diligence;
- preparation of the data room;
- first-round 'indicative' bids;
- bidders' due diligence and investigations (prior to second-round bid);
- second-round bid (from a limited number of bidders, accompanied by their responses to the seller's draft documents); and
- negotiations with one or more bidders, leading to the conclusion of a sale.

4. Bid process

4.1 Confidentiality

As in all sales, confidentiality is important; but in an auction sale, because of the greater number of parties involved, the risk of a leak of the existence of the sale discussions and confidential information of the target business is much greater. The lawyers for the seller will seek to negotiate a confidentiality agreement with each bidder before the first contact is made or any confidential information is provided, seeking to bind not only the bidders and their affiliates, but also their professional advisers and anyone else whom they may need to involve in the evaluation process.

The confidentiality agreement will impose an obligation to keep the contemplated sale confidential and to use the information disclosed only for the purposes of evaluating the target company. It will also ensure that all of the information disclosed is kept confidential by each bidder and that no approaches are made to the target company's customers, suppliers, management or employees, whether with a view to poaching them or simply to obtaining more information. The confidentiality agreement will also typically prevent the bidders from being permitted to communicate with each other.

4.2 Information memorandum

The information memorandum is one of the key documents in the auction process. Typically, it will be drafted by the investment bank or other financial adviser, with input from management. It is essentially a selling document and seeks to provide bidders with a reasonable amount of information about the target company in order to elicit meaningful first-round bids.

The information memorandum will contain at least the following:

- a description of the target business and its history;
- the principal assets of the business;
- current and historical financial information and future projections;
- information relating to employees and consultants;
- depending on sensitivity, information relating to major customers and contracts; and
- a statement that no reliance can be placed on it.

The seller and its advisers will carry out due diligence before the information memorandum is distributed to bidders, to ensure that it contains no misleading statements. Aside from the considerable reputational risk involved, they will wish to avoid any risk of a breach of Section 397 of the Financial Services and Markets Act 2000 and, in the worse case, an action for fraudulent misrepresentation, more details of which are set out in section 5 below.

4.3 Preparation of the data room

The preparation of the data room is an important part of an auction process and involves input from management and the seller's advisers. It is usual now for the seller to instruct a data room provider to establish a virtual data room via the Internet, through which each bidder and certain of its advisers can securely, under supervision and in a controlled environment, obtain access to the confidential information relating to the target business.

The data room will need to be a well-indexed comprehensive set of documents, since the contents will be an item for discussion when the warranties and disclosures are debated with the preferred bidder. The time taken to compile it should not be underestimated. Although sometimes this is perceived as a simple mechanical task, in practice the process needs close supervision from a member of the seller team of sufficient seniority. The potential for error is huge – for example:

- not uploading the back pages of a double-sided original document;
- failing to ensure that the standard 'click-through' terms of use of the virtual data room match the key protections put in place in the confidentiality letter signed with the bidders; and
- making sensitive information available too early.

Following discussions with the lawyers, decisions will be taken on how to deal with issues such as:

- documents that are legally privileged in ongoing litigation (and where the privilege would be lost if disclosed);
- commercially sensitive agreements; and
- commercial contracts that have confidentiality clauses preventing their disclosure.

While in some cases it will be sufficient to provide summaries or to blank out the sensitive parts of key contracts, alternatives include having an independent report prepared by legal counsel summarising the target company's contractual arrangements with suitable anonymity or holding back key agreements until later.

The documents provided to bidders in the data room may also include seller due diligence reports and other independent third-party reports to minimise the delay that would be involved if each bidder were to carry out its own full financial and other investigations from scratch.

4.4 Process letter

The information memorandum will be distributed to the bidders together with a process letter (typically drafted by the investment bank or other financial adviser) inviting the recipients to submit indicative first-round bids by no later than a specified date. The purpose of the process letter is not to elicit bids capable of resulting in a legally binding contract, but to ensure that all offers are made on a basis which enables the seller to make meaningful comparisons between them. It also serves to identify at an early stage whether there are regulatory problems, merger clearances or other conditions which reduce the likelihood of concluding a transaction quickly with particular bidders. From the point of view of the seller, it will want to structure the process letter to require the bidders in their offer letters to crystallise as many points for future negotiation as possible at this early stage of the auction, to enable the seller to obtain a realistic view of which bidders are worth moving forward with.

The process letter will usually not set out the criteria for evaluating bids, so as to protect the seller in the evaluation process, and often state that the highest price will not necessarily succeed, so as to retain maximum flexibility for the seller. It will also typically reserve the right of the seller to amend or discontinue the auction process at any time. The seller may in any case be running a dual-track process with, for example, an initial public offering as the alternative. However, even if it is not, it is very possible that it may receive a pre-emptive offer from a bidder before or shortly after the second round has been completed.

4.5 Indicative bids

The seller and the advisers will consider the indicative bids and decide which bidders to invite to participate in the second round of bidding, recognising that the first round of bids will invariably have been based on little information other than that contained in the information memorandum and what is publicly available. Depending on the transaction and its particular auction process, the data room may not necessarily be made available to the bidders prior to the deadline for receiving first-round bids.

4.6 Bidders' due diligence and investigations

Following assessment of the first round bids, certain bidders will be invited to participate in the next round. Access to the data room, meetings with the management and site visits will usually be granted to such bidders remaining in the process, and the draft sale documents will usually also be provided at this stage. The art is trying to ensure that there is a sufficient number and type of serious bidders to maintain competitive tension while not proceeding with so many that they cannot be serviced.

The seller will also seek to use this opportunity to transfer transaction risk to the ultimate buyer (eg, by seeking to limit any potential warranty claims by disclosing in full the contents of the data room (or vendor due diligence report), and by reference to any knowledge that the buyer has on entering into the transaction.

4.7 Transaction documents

The draft sale documents, typically made available to the bidders via the data room, will at the very least comprise a draft acquisition agreement (including the business warranties to be provided by management). In addition, ideally from the seller's perspective, a draft disclosure letter against the warranties in the acquisition agreement will be included. This has two advantages:

- The second-round bids will be subject to the disclosures made; and
- The disclosure process acts as an initial health check, allowing issues to be identified in sufficient time to deal with them ahead of exclusivity.

The transaction documents may also include a draft management term sheet for private equity bidders to mark up. Whether this happens at this stage will depend on the private equity seller's appetite for the potential diversion of management's attention from the sale process to its future equity terms, and bidders' financial resources from the bid terms to the future management.

4.8 Site visits and management presentations

Management and site visits will be managed by the seller. The management presentations will usually be carefully prepared and scripted, so that all issues are handled consistently between the different bidders and disclosure of any sensitive issues is handled in accordance with a pre-set plan, as discussed with the sell-side advisers. Often, bidders will be invited to put their questions in writing for review in advance of management meetings. Management meetings will usually be attended by representatives of the seller or its advisers, both to ensure that questions do not go beyond the pre-set pattern and that appropriate answers are given to questions, and also to record the questions asked, as this may help to shed light on the questioner's real concerns.

Similarly, plant visits will usually be accompanied to prevent any unauthorised approach to employees.

4.9 Second-round bids

The remaining bidders in the auction process will submit their final offers together with their mark-up of the draft sale documents by no later than a specified date set out in the process letter.

As with the first-round bids, the second-round offers will usually not be framed in such a way that they are capable of giving rise to a legally binding contract merely by an act of acceptance by the seller, but at this stage the seller will look very carefully at the terms offered by the various bidders. It will not necessarily wish to accept the highest price, because the terms offered may have a cost attached to them, even though the stated consideration may be the highest.

4.10 Evaluation

Following consultation with the advisers, the seller will usually look to assess whether, based on these responses, the relevant bidders intend to conclude, or are likely to be capable of concluding, a sale at the price offered, or whether there are terms or conditions which make the likelihood of a successful conclusion of a transaction more remote. Thus, an uncomplicated sale on an unconditional basis without a price adjustment mechanism, but with a clean break, may be more valuable to the seller than seeking a better price from a sale which is subject to onerous conditions that may be difficult to satisfy, either in the short term or possibly even at all, or may be subject to potentially extensive price adjustments later.

Before deciding on the preferred bidder, the seller may try once more to play the bidders off against each other and obtain an increase in the value of the offers received or improvement in the terms offered. This process may take a few days.

When the seller has ultimately made its choice, it will nevertheless want to keep the preferred bidder under pressure, using the presence of other bidders that have completed their own due diligence as an incentive to the preferred bidder to make concessions on price, terms or timing.

(a) Final negotiations

Once a preferred bidder has been selected, a period of exclusivity will often be negotiated and agreed. This is usually the high point of the transactional balance of power for the seller. Once exclusivity is granted – often, but not inevitably – the competitive tension is reduced. During the exclusivity period, the seller and its advisers will seek to maintain the momentum to finalise the negotiations and execute the transaction with the preferred bidder, since it is usually difficult to revive negotiations with a second bidder if there have been protracted discussions with a preferred bidder that have broken down. The seller and management, with the assistance of their advisers, will therefore typically ensure that further queries are answered promptly and that efforts by the preferred bidder to introduce new points and/or delay the process are firmly resisted.

4.11 Legal risk

While there are significant commercial risks to initiating an auction process, running a formal auction process can add legal risk for the seller and this will need to be appropriately managed. Prospective sellers seeking to engage in this type of process should ensure that they seek advice early in the process in order to manage this risk.

(a) Financial Services and Markets Act 2000

The seller and its advisers will carry out due diligence before the information memorandum is distributed to bidders, to avoid any risk of a breach of Section 397 of the Financial Services and Markets Act 2000 (misleading statements).

Breach of Section 397 of the Financial Services and Markets Act is a criminal offence, the maximum penalty being up to seven years in prison, and any investment agreement entered into in reliance on the information memorandum will be unenforceable. As with prospectuses for public issues, if reports or forecasts are attributed to third parties in the information memorandum, their consent to their names being used will need to be obtained.

(b) Contractual risk

At each stage in the process, the seller will need to ensure that it does not inadvertently bind itself to a contract with any of the bidders. Therefore, sellers will take care to ensure that all documentation, including the process letter, is framed in such a way as to avoid this and heavily caveated to ensure that disappointed bidders cannot seek to rely on this in a breach of contract action. In general, the greater the level of formality in the auction process, the higher the risk of this will be.

In a similar fashion the seller, in drafting documentation relating to the auction – and in particular the process letter and other documents governing the running of the process – will be keen to avoid binding itself to an obligation to consider the bids which are submitted. Again, the risk of this will be greater in more formal processes, where the seller risks inadvertently binding itself to its own process.

Although English courts will not generally recognise an obligation to negotiate in good faith, in the context of an international transaction it will be important to bear in mind that where any of the parties involved is a foreign entity, or any part of the negotiations may be deemed to be conducted outside the United Kingdom, there may be a risk that such an obligation will arise in another jurisdiction. A seller which is conducting an auction with overseas bidders (or where any of the assets are located in another jurisdiction) should consider the need for local counsel at an early stage.

(c) Confidentiality

As mentioned elsewhere in this chapter, the principal rationale in choosing to run an auction sale process is to capitalise on the competitive tension among bidders by effectively playing one bidder off against another. Bidders will generally be careful to ensure that the offers and mark-ups that they provide to the seller are confidential and in particular will not be shared with other bidders. This is generally contrary to the seller's desire to leverage the benefits of competition, and an over-eager (or ill-advised) seller may risk breaching confidentiality obligations if it takes competitive bargaining too far. While this risk can be managed to a certain extent by the seller implementing clear rules in the auction process, bidders that do not believe that their bid information will be kept confidential will be reluctant to put forth bids in the first place. Advisers, and prudent sellers, will also be alert to the reputational risk that any breach – or even perceived breach – of confidentiality will bring.

(d) Fraudulent misrepresentation

A further risk arises out of the same desire on the part of sellers to leverage the benefits of competition, particularly at the negotiation stage. Sellers may wish to maintain or even enhance the level of competition by leading a bidder to believe that the seller has received an offer from another party on materially better terms, in the hope that the bidder will seek to match those terms. Equally, the seller may know that statements being made (eg, in a presentation to bidders) are untrue. Aside from the confidentiality risk mentioned above, this gives rise to a serious possibility of fraudulent misrepresentation (even if, in the example of the misleading presentation, no warranty is given in the sale and purchase agreement on the presentation). Therefore, this is clearly an area that sellers and their advisers should avoid. A number of cases illustrate the hazards of failing to do so. The most recent high-profile case in this area, taken by Terra Firma against Citigroup (currently on appeal) in relation to the EMI transaction, also highlights the public relations and reputational risk which such an action involves for sellers and advisers, even if it is ultimately unsuccessful.

5. Conclusion

Despite the advance organisation required by an auction process, the consumption of management time taken in dealing with multiple bidders, the consequent distraction from management's 'day job' of actually running the business, the increased professional advisers' costs, the distraction and the risks of undertaking what could ultimately be a failed process, the attractions of an auction process remain strong. Sometimes an 'off-market' deal may be more appropriate and sometimes processes will be pre-empted; however, it is unlikely that the auction process is going to go away. For all its unpopularity with private equity houses that are looking to buy assets, the auction process remains very popular with private equity houses that are selling assets – and that perhaps tells you all you need to know.

Partial exits

Tom Evans
Kem Ihenacho
Clifford Chance LLP

---

1. Introduction

This chapter discusses the disposal by a private equity house of a material part of an investment by way of either a sale by the portfolio company of certain assets (and liabilities) or a sale by the private equity house of a portion of its investment in the portfolio company. First, we deal with key issues arising on the disposal by a portfolio company of material assets. We refer to the 'retained business' and 'retained group' as the business and collection of entities, respectively, which the portfolio company retains following the partial exit transaction; the 'target business' and 'target group' refer to the business and entities being disposed of by the portfolio company. Second, we consider briefly matters relevant to the disposal by a private equity house of part of its investment in the portfolio company.

Before embarking on a discussion of the key details relevant to a partial exit, it is worth considering the context in which the partial exit takes place. By its nature, a partial exit will not be the final significant transaction in relation to a portfolio company: the retained business or shareholding in the portfolio company is still to be disposed of. The natural inclination of the portfolio company or private equity house when disposing of a target business or part of its investment in the portfolio company, respectively, will be to maximise the value received for the partial exit transaction. However, the terms of the partial exit transaction may affect the terms and value of the final exit by the private equity house from the portfolio company. For example, consider giving comfort in the form of warranties and indemnities to the third-party buyer as part of the partial exit transaction. The grant of the warranties, while serving to maximise the value of the target business, will be a burden on the retained business. The creation of contingent liabilities for the retained business has the potential to depress disproportionately the consideration paid by a buyer for the retained business; it may impair distributions being made at a later date.

The usual reason for a portfolio company to dispose of material assets is to realise value from a part of its business which is distinct or may be made distinct from the business that it retains. For the private equity house, by 'breaking up' the portfolio company, the expectation is that the value of its component parts sold separately will, by the time that the private equity house exits the portfolio company entirely, be greater than the whole. By dividing the portfolio company into distinct business entities, the private equity house may:

- attract prospective buyers which would not be interested in the consolidated group;

- liberate or be perceived to liberate managers who have expertise in the particular market relevant to the relevant business;
- remove any perceived or actual impediments derived from other businesses carried on by the portfolio company; and
- permit the remaining businesses to focus on their own core competencies.

An example may be a large conglomerate manufacturing and distributing food and tobacco products. In those circumstances both businesses involve manufacturing and are consumer focused, and require extensive distribution networks and an appreciation of how to incentivise retailers and consumers to purchase their products. Nevertheless, both businesses operate in distinct markets, with distinct supply chains and differing regulatory and reputational concerns, some of which may conflict.

The reasons for a partial sale by a private equity house of its investment in a portfolio company are varied:

- Business combination – the partial exit may be part of an acquisition by, or 'merger' of, the portfolio company, the consideration for the acquisition being the sale of, or the issue of, new interests in the existing portfolio company. An example is the combination of the AA and Saga by private equity houses CVC and Permira and Charterhouse, respectively, in the United Kingdom.
- Mitigating risk – a private equity house may wish to realise a significant portion of its investment in, but wish to retain an exposure to, the relevant portfolio company. This may be driven by the private equity house's plans at the outset of the investment (eg, through syndication) or as a result of later identifying a suitable partner for the investment.
- Forced disposal – as part of a restructuring, a creditor may be offered an equity interest in the portfolio company as an incentive to compromise on amounts owed by the portfolio company. Restructuring transactions are not considered further in this chapter.

2. Disposals by portfolio companies of material assets

2.1 Structuring and preparation

A portfolio company may dispose of a single material asset, the identification, confirmation of title and transfer of which may be relatively straightforward. It becomes more complicated where the portfolio company wishes to dispose of a particular business, which will comprise various assets and liabilities, each of which needs to be identified, its owner verified and the method of transfer to a buyer determined.

(a) What is being sold?

Conceptually, it will usually be clear what is being disposed of by the portfolio company; in the above example it is likely to be either the tobacco business or the food business. The component parts of the tobacco business or food business will be less apparent:

- Will motor vehicles used to transport tobacco or food or both be included in the sale?
- Should the target business continue to benefit from preferential terms with logistics companies which are dependent on volumes derived from both the target and the retained business?
- How will premises used by both businesses be allocated?
- What rights will the respective businesses have to occupy those premises following the transaction?
- Will a business be able to continue to use plant used by both businesses?
- Who will bear the burden of taxation and liability for defective products manufactured or distributed by the target business prior to completion?

It will be necessary to identify those assets and accompanying liabilities which comprise the target and retained businesses so that these may be divided with certainty and with minimal interruption to each business. A business will generally comprise a combination of:

- contracts – the benefit of contractual rights (together with the burden of contractual obligations);
- machinery and fixed plant;
- real estate – freehold properties, leasehold properties, licences or other rights to occupy or use land or premises;
- IP rights – patents, trademarks, designs, copyrights, domain names and know-how;
- motor vehicles;
- office equipment and records;
- stock – raw materials, partly finished and finished goods;
- trade debts and credits with third parties;
- any claims against third parties; and
- goodwill.

(b) Who holds which assets and liabilities?

Having determined the assets and liabilities comprising the target business, it will then be necessary to establish which member of the portfolio company group holds title to those assets. This seems self-evident; however, as businesses evolve, the member of the group initially carrying on a particular business in a particular market may change. For example, consider a subsidiary established in a developing market which initially acts on behalf of the entire group; once this market expands, further legal entities may be formed or take on responsibilities in the relevant market, but the assets held and liabilities incurred by the first established member of the group may never be transferred to subsequent legal entities carrying on business in the relevant market. Ultimately, the directors of the original member of the group in the market are comfortable that, given the support of the corporate group in which it exists, there is no need to incur cost to transfer the assets and/or liabilities to the member of the group now carrying out the relevant business. Identifying who holds title to the assets and liabilities comprising the target business is nevertheless significant, as only the holder will be able to transfer title effectively.

Useful resources to assist with identifying the legal owner of an asset or liability are as follows:

- party details of written contracts;
- any asset registers; and
- publicly available information such as IP registers and land registries, together with the accounts prepared for each member of the group.

(c) *Share or asset sale?*

Once the owners of the assets and liabilities comprising the target business have been identified, it will then be a case of determining from the portfolio company's perspective whether the disposal of those assets and liabilities is best structured as a share sale or an asset sale, or a combination of both. An additional factor in the case of a partial exit will be that some members of the portfolio company group may hold assets and liabilities for both the retained business and the target business. There are three key options for the transfer of the assets and liabilities of the target business to the buyer:

- Direct transfer of assets and liabilities – the existing holder transfers the assets and liabilities relating to the target business to the third-party buyer. The assets and liabilities held by the existing holder used by the retained business are retained by that retained group member. This approach means that there is a single transfer of assets and liabilities, without the need for a pre-sale reorganisation.
- Transfer of new holder – the existing holder transfers the assets and liabilities relating to the target business to another (potentially newly formed) group member. The interests in this group member are then transferred to the third-party buyer.
- Transfer of existing holder – this is the reverse of the second option: the existing holder retains the assets and liabilities relating to the target business and transfers the assets and liabilities relating to the retained business to another member of the group. The existing holder is then transferred to the third-party buyer.

In each of the second and third options, a common mechanism for increasing the likelihood that the risk of any asset or liability resides with the selling group member is for it to indemnify the counterparty for any loss arising from such asset or liability.

A significant factor affecting the structure for the disposal will be taxation.[1] From a legal perspective, there are a number of considerations:

- Certainty as to retained assets and liabilities – where the existing holder is transferred to the third-party buyer, only specific assets and liabilities identified in any pre-sale transfer or which transfer by law (eg, employees and associated liabilities pursuant to legislation implementing the EU Acquired Rights Directive)[2] will reside with the retained group. Except in exceptional

1 See the chapter on tax.

circumstances (eg, some environmental or pensions liabilities), unknown or latent liabilities will generally remain the responsibility of the existing holder (ie, these will transfer to the third-party buyer). Conversely, where a buyer purchases a member of the group to which specific assets and liabilities are transferred (particularly if that group member is newly incorporated), unless specifically transferred or transferred by operation of law, all other liabilities (and assets) will remain with the retained group.

- Related party transactions – any transfer of assets and liabilities within the portfolio company group will need to be made for value which is defendable in order to minimise the risk of any administrator or liquidator that is subsequently appointed challenging the transaction.
- Logistical burden – transferring assets and liabilities intra-group prior to completion and transferring only shares on completion is likely to ease the burden on completion and be more efficient. Subject to any parameters negotiated between the portfolio company and third-party buyer, the terms of the intra-group transfer may be determined by the portfolio company and documents effecting the transfer prepared by the portfolio company with limited input from the third-party buyer.

(d) Are any consents required under debt and equity finance documents?

Consents may be required for the disposal of the target business and any associated pre-sale reorganisation under the terms of existing debt and equity finance arrangements.

The terms of third-party debt finance made available to the portfolio company are likely to include provision for certain pre-agreed disposals:

- Disposals which are considered immaterial from a net asset, earnings and/or turnover perspective – provided that the disposal does not itself, and does not in combination with other disposals within a given period, exceed thresholds reflecting agreed levels of materiality (often referred to as 'baskets'), the consent of the relevant lenders will not be required.
- Pre-agreed disposals which are permitted outside of the baskets referred to above – any pre-agreed disposals are usually drawn from the business plan for the portfolio company shared with lenders prior to acquisition. If the disposal of the target business is not permitted under the terms of the debt financing, consent will need to be sought from the relevant lenders and the timing for receiving such consent factored into the deal timetable.

Typically, the majority equity investor and any significant minority investor(s) will be required to consent to any disposal in excess of permitted thresholds. In the case of the private equity house which will usually be instigating the partial exit, this will not be a significant issue. If additional equity investors have a consent right, such consent (potentially subject to conditions such as minimum price) will usually be sought before launching any partial exit process.

2 Directive 77/187/EEC, as amended by Directive 98/50/EC and consolidated in Directive 2001/23/EC.

2.2 Separation issues

(a) Transitional services

Irrespective of how distinct the target business is from the retained business, there are likely to be some areas where its operations are integrated with the retained business. Typical areas for integration across a corporate group include logistics services, IT services (eg, support, maintenance, data processing, personnel, payroll and accounting), general administrative services and the right to occupy/share premises. In the period immediately following completion of the partial exit, the retained group or the target group may be unable independently – or, in the case of the target group, with the assistance of its buyer – to provide these services, as the capacity to do so has been respectively transferred or retained by the portfolio company.

Therefore, the buyer and portfolio company may agree that for a period following completion, the retained group or target group will supply to the other the relevant services, until such time as the other has established a basis upon which it can source them itself. The terms under which services are provided are usually recorded in a transitional services agreement or transition agreement.

Generally, a transitional services agreement will not provide a completely satisfactory solution for the recipient of the services. The supplier of the services will generally not be a professional service provider and therefore often will not accept an obligation to meet the service levels that the recipient would expect of a usual service provider. Therefore, there is usually a clear incentive for the recipient of the services to conclude the transitional arrangements promptly. Key considerations for any transitional services agreement are as follows:

- Regulated services – where the services to be performed are regulated and require the supplier or recipient to be licensed or to meet certain prudential or fit and proper person requirements, the appropriate components for any authorisation will need to be provided for in the agreement (eg, disaster recovery, record keeping and access requirements).
- Consents – if the provision of the services requires the use of products or services supplied by a third party, the consent of that third party may be required (eg, in the case of a lease, a tenant will often be precluded from granting any interest in the relevant premises to any third party).
- Data protection – to the extent that the provision of services requires the provision or use of personal information, the provider of the information will need to be satisfied that the restrictions applied to the recipient of the information are appropriately robust such that it may comply with applicable privacy regulations.
- Solicitation of employees – given that employees of the provider will be providing services to the recipient during a period when the recipient is attempting to establish its own capacity to do so, there is an innate risk that employees may be solicited by the recipient.
- EU Acquired Rights Directive – there is a risk that employees who provide the services to the recipient will transfer to the recipient or a replacement service

provider upon the expiry or termination of the transitional service period by operation of the relevant local law implementing the EU Acquired Rights Directive. A recipient will be keen to avoid taking on the risk of any such employer-related liability.

- Facilitating exit – the recipient will generally be eager to set up its own capability, retain professional service providers or, if acquired by a corporate group, utilise the support of the acquiring corporate group to provide the services governed by the transitional services agreement. Therefore, it will be important that the agreement details and binds the provider to carry out the necessary steps to facilitate the recipient's ultimate independence from the provider. For example, in the case of IT systems, this is likely to involve the export of data and the training of personnel to interrogate and use the relevant systems.

(b) Intra-group agreements

Distinct from transitional services, which will be supplied for a limited period, there may be arrangements between the retained business and the target business which are intended to survive completion. These previously intra-group arrangements will exist with varying degrees of clarity, with the need to document them in any detail driven largely by the need to evidence compliance with applicable laws and regulations (eg, transfer pricing restrictions). As the retained business and target business will no longer be under common control following the transaction, in most cases it will be desirable for these arrangements to be clarified and their terms recorded. Common examples of these arrangements are as follows:

- Agency arrangements – members of the target group may act as agents for members of the retained group, or vice versa, distributing, selling or acquiring goods and services on behalf of the respective principal. Defining the scope of the agency relationship (ie, the products and/or services in relation to which one person can bind the other) and the terms of remuneration will be key.
- Shared premises – this arises where a member of the retained group or the target group is the lessor or owner of a premises and both the target business and retained business intend to use the premises for a significant period following completion. Of relevance will be any restrictive covenants applying to the use of and creation of interests in the premises.
- Use of plant and machinery – the target business and retained business may share the use of plant and machinery. Depending on the title to such assets, toll manufacturing or contract manufacturing arrangements may need to be put in place to secure adequate manufacturing capacity and to share the burden of maintenance and replacement of the relevant equipment.

In addition to rights granted and services provided by members of the retained group to members of the target group and vice versa, the finances of both may be integrated. Depending on existing arrangements, cash-pooling arrangements may be in place between group members and inter-company loans may exist between members of the respective groups. The cash-pooling arrangements will need to be adapted to reflect the disposal of the target business. It is unlikely that either the retained group or the target group will want inter-company loans between the two groups to remain outstanding following completion, in which case the loans will need to be repaid, assigned, capitalised or otherwise dealt with within applicable corporate law restrictions and considering taxation implications.

Finally, there may be guarantees or other sureties given by a member of the retained group to secure the obligations of a member of the target group, and vice versa. These guarantees may be cash collateralised, supported by a letter of credit from a financial institution or both. Commonly, guaranteed obligations are given for the following:

- Debt financing made available to a group member – typically, members of a corporate group which have material assets, turnover or earnings will be required to guarantee the obligations of other obligor members under the terms of debt finance made available to the group.
- Trading and licensing arrangements – material suppliers to a member of the group may require that the obligations of the group member be guaranteed by another member of the group, in order to strengthen the financial covenant of the contracting group member. This is particularly the case with suppliers or licensors which are paid in arrears for products delivered, services performed or intellectual or other property used.
- Leases – it is common for landlords to buttress the financial covenant of the tenant group member with a guarantee from another group member.
- Certain insurance arrangements – again, where a significant deductible exists under an insurance policy, particularly in the case of public liability insurance or product liability insurance, a group member may be required to guarantee the obligations of the insured group member.

If a guarantee is given by a member of the target group or the retained group in respect of an obligation of a member of the other group, then for the potential liability and risk of the guarantee to sit with the group which also receives the benefit of the underlying arrangement, a new guarantee will need to be entered into. For a new guarantee to be agreed between a member of the relevant group and the third party, time will need to be spent discussing with the third party the terms of the guarantee and the financial covenant of the new guarantor party; any bank guarantee or other support from a financial institution will need to be agreed with the relevant financiers. To the extent that arrangements cannot be transferred prior to completion, pending a replacement arrangement being put in place, it is usual for the group receiving the benefit of the guarantee to indemnify the entity giving the guarantee for any loss arising from the guarantee being called.

(c) *Releasing and renegotiating security*

The buyer of the target business will expect to receive from the seller the assets of the target business free from any encumbrance. If the portfolio company borrows funds from a third party, arrangements will need to be made to release any security supporting the obligations under the terms of the debt finance. The lender(s) to the portfolio company will generally agree to release security over assets of the target business following payment of any amounts as provided for under the loan documents. Given the timing sensitivity of lenders, depending on the jurisdiction, on completion either security will be released or, where particular formalities are required, an obligation to undertake those formalities will be delivered. The mechanics of release vary by jurisdiction and legal counsel in each jurisdiction will need to confirm the validity of the release and attend to any necessary filings. For the retained group, depending on the terms of security required in connection with the debt finance, additional security may need to be granted over further assets, or potentially by additional members, of the retained group, such that any minimum asset, revenue and/or earnings coverage thresholds are met.

(d) Intellectual property

For the purposes of a partial exit, the intellectual property of a portfolio company can be divided into two categories:

- Intellectual property to be used by either the retained business or the target business, but not the other – generally, to the extent not already owned by a member of the relevant group, the relevant intellectual property will be assigned. If the intellectual property is licensed to third parties, an assignment of such a licence will be required for the third party to continue validly using the intellectual property. In case of intellectual property licensed to the portfolio company, a similar analysis applies, subject to any restrictions on assignment or change of control.
- Intellectual property to be used by both the retained business and the target business – a typical approach would be for the retained business to retain ownership of the intellectual property, or the head licence, and to grant the target business a licence or sub-licence (subject to any restrictions under the terms of the head licence).

(e) Splitting contracts

A member of the portfolio company group may procure goods or services from a particular supplier on behalf of the group, rather than individual group members negotiating separate arrangements with the same supplier. In the example of the tobacco and food conglomerate referred to above, both businesses may utilise a significant volume of transport capacity, which may be procured on a whole of business and global basis. Given the aggregate value to the supplier of the combined procurement of transport capacity, the terms applicable to the combined group arrangement may be preferential to those available if the individual businesses, or members of the separate groups, contracted separately with the relevant suppliers.

To continue the supply of goods or services following completion of the partial exit, a retained group member or target group member, depending on the identity of the original contract counterparty, may need to enter into a parallel arrangement with the third party. To the extent that any preferential terms are contingent on the combined volume of both the target group and the retained group, subject to the terms of the relevant agreement, it may be beneficial for both the target and retained groups if the relevant contract counterparty procured the goods or services on behalf of both the retained group and target group, subject to suitable waivers of liability and cost sharing.

The usual approach for customer contracts is to enter into new contracts so that the terms of these relationships may develop in confidence and as necessary without the need to involve members of the other groups. If commercially desirable, if an agreement relates to both the retained business and the target business, certain rights and obligations under the existing agreement may be novated to a member of the relevant group or a member of the relevant group may be sub-contracted to perform the relevant obligations.

(f) Retirement benefits

A particular issue that may arise on dividing assets and liabilities as between the target business and the retained business is liability for defined benefit pension schemes for current and former employees. If the target business maintains defined benefit pension schemes which relate solely to the target business, then, subject to usual concerns of ongoing liability in relation to any underfunding,[3] the expectation would be that the relevant pension scheme for employees of the target business would transfer with the target group. However, where defined benefit schemes apply across the portfolio company, the portfolio company will ideally wish to transfer the obligation to pay at least some of the benefits attributable to the target business (and the underlying assets accumulated by the portfolio company for that purpose) to the buyer. The buyer is likely to resist such transfer of liabilities and assets (and therefore risk), but equally the portfolio company will not wish to retain all of the pensions risk in respect of retirement benefits already built up itself. Where employees and former employees from the retained business and the existing business are members of the same defined benefit scheme and a split of pension liabilities is agreed, provision will usually be made for:

- the buyer to set up a new scheme providing replica benefits;
- payment by the trustee or administrator of the existing scheme to the trustee or administrator of the new scheme of an amount equal to the assets accrued in respect of the employees (and possibly former employees) of the target business, usually as calculated by an actuary in accordance with agreed principles or, in some jurisdictions, a formula prescribed by law;
- acceptance by the trustee or administrator of the new scheme that it is responsible for the liability to pay the retirement benefits in respect of each employee (and possibly former employee) of the target business; and
- potentially, transitional arrangements in case the buyer cannot establish the new scheme prior to completion of the partial exit.

Where the transaction means that one or more companies will be exiting a UK

3 See the pensions chapter in the sister publication to this book, *Private Equity: A Transactional Analysis*, where these issues are considered in detail.

defined benefit pension scheme, the exiting company will typically be liable to make a payment to the scheme to address its share of any underfunding in the scheme. It may be possible to negotiate payment of a reduced amount with the trustees of the pension scheme. Typically, a buyer will seek indemnity protection in respect of any such liability arising on the transaction.

(g) ***Taxation implications***

Taxation considerations on a partial exit are detailed in the chapter on tax.

2.3 Sale documentation

In the acquisition documentation chapter in *Private Equity: A Transactional Analysis*, key terms of acquisition documentation on private equity transactions are considered. The process for an initial public offering of securities is detailed elsewhere in this book. Those considerations will generally be relevant on a partial exit in a similar fashion to a full exit and so are not repeated here. However, the proposed consideration mechanism for a private sale, the allocation of post-completion risk, restrictive covenants and treatment of misallocated assets warrant particular consideration in the context of a partial exit.

(a) ***What is the most appropriate consideration mechanism?***

Whether a locked box mechanism (the features of which are explained in the acquisition documentation chapter referred to above) will be appropriate for a partial exit will depend on how integrated or distinct from a financial perspective the target business is from the retained business. Where, for example, our tobacco and consumer goods businesses use the same debt finance facilities, cash-pooling arrangements, office premises and distribution networks, and the same legal entities carry on activities for both businesses, it will be more difficult to establish a set of accounts which are rigorous enough to permit a buyer to determine a definitive price for the target business on a standalone basis. It may also be difficult to identify any leakage from the target business following the date of the accounts on which the locked box purchase price is calculated. Where these uncertainties exist, a buyer is likely to be more comfortable with a more traditional completion accounts mechanism, which permits the buyer to confirm the assets and liabilities of the business following completion. On the other hand, where, in our example, the tobacco and consumer businesses are carried on by separate legal entities and the integration between the businesses is limited or its terms well documented, a locked box may be more easily accepted by a buyer.

(b) ***Allocation of post-completion risk***

To the extent that any warranties or indemnities are given by members of the retained group, care will need to be taken to ensure that these obligations do not unnecessarily impede the return of funds to shareholders or disproportionately depress the value of the retained group. Where a significant obligation is agreed to by a retained group member, the directors will need to be satisfied, considering the likelihood of such risk arising, that the group member has sufficient assets available to satisfy the obligation. For a member of the retained group disposing of a significant portion of its assets, it may be prudent in the minds of the directors to retain some or all of the proceeds from the disposal until the potential liability under the transaction documents has expired. Equally, when the retained group is ultimately sold by the private equity house, any impact on the value and terms of the subsequent transaction arising from potential liability for warranty and indemnity claims from the initial disposal will be assessed by potential buyers.

(c) ***Restrictive covenants***

In the example of the tobacco and consumer goods business, there is unlikely to be a significant degree of overlap between the retained and target businesses. However, in other transactions there may be a higher risk of competition following completion of the partial exit. For example, consider a retained and target business that are distinct only in respect of the geographic markets in which they operate or which use similar manufacturing techniques, although historically for different customers. In these circumstances the terms of the restrictive covenants will be particularly important for both the target and retained groups to continue to operate their businesses competitively following completion, and should be reflected in the sale and purchase agreement and any relevant IP licences.

In addition, the retained business will be keen to maintain a distinct corporate identity from the target business and will not wish to be exposed to the risk of any adverse events caused by the target business affecting the goodwill of the retained business. Accordingly, the target business may be required to change any names which may be identical or confusingly similar to those used by the retained business.

(d) ***Misallocated assets***

As the assets comprising the target business are likely to be held by a variety of members of both the retained and target groups, it is possible that some assets or liabilities used exclusively by the target business may be inadvertently retained by the retained group, or vice versa. To accommodate this potential, it is common for the transaction documents to include an obligation – commonly known as a 'wrong pockets ' provision – to procure that where an asset held by the buyer or a member of the target group relates exclusively or predominantly to the retained business, then for a period following completion, the buyer shall procure that the target group transfers the asset to the seller and vice versa. Consideration may or may not be paid for the transfer, and any taxation accruing as a result of the transfer is ordinarily payable by the retained group in the case of a transfer tax, or vice versa.

2.4 Application of proceeds

On realising the proceeds from a partial exit, the portfolio company must decide on the application of those proceeds. Typical considerations for application of the proceeds are as follows:

- Third-party lenders – to the extent that the portfolio company borrows from third-party debt finance providers, either by a positive covenant to pay to the debt finance provider amounts realised on a disposal of assets outside of the ordinary course or by a negative covenant against payments by the parent of the banking group to its shareholders, funds will usually be applied first to repay or part-repay debt finance. To the extent that there are senior, mezzanine and/or junior debt providers, the arrangements for application of any such proceeds will have been negotiated at the time of entering into the transaction according to the agreed priority of these creditors.

- Working capital – subject to any requirements under the debt and equity funding documents and under the relevant fund documents of the private equity house, all or a portion of the proceeds may be retained by the portfolio company for use in other parts of its business. The terms of the debt finance made available to the retained group may require that such proceeds be reinvested in the relevant business within a particular period.
- Equity investors – to the extent that funds are available, payments may be made to shareholders or their related parties on instruments invested in the portfolio company. In considering the application of proceeds, and in particular the extent to which proceeds may be retained by the portfolio company, the constitutional documents for the relevant fund should be consulted to determine any obligation to repatriate any proceeds on realisation of the value of the target business.

2.5 Management incentive scheme

In the case of a typical equity-based incentive scheme there are two key concerns for any management incentive scheme on a partial exit:

- What will the entitlement of managers be on a partial exit?
- Will the management incentive scheme provide an appropriate incentive to management of the retained business following completion?

On the first of these concerns, whether managers will be entitled to realise any return on their participation in the management incentive scheme will depend on the particular terms of the scheme. The terms of the scheme may provide that an employee who is employed by the target group and who therefore transfers from the portfolio company is treated as a good leaver and paid the applicable good leaver price for his or her equity. Where a manager in those circumstances would be treated as a bad leaver, a discretion may be exercised to treat him or her otherwise. Alternatively, depending on the timeframe during which the private equity house intends to exit the retained business and the willingness of the managers of the retained business to permit managers to participate in the equity growth of the retained business following completion, managers of the target business may be permitted to retain some or all of their investment in the portfolio company.

For managers who are employed by the retained group, whether any return is payable on a partial exit will depend on:

- the materiality of the disposal in the context of the portfolio company as a whole;
- whether the proceeds derived from the disposal are sufficient to repay all prior ranking and entitled creditors; and

- the desire for the private equity house to keep managers adequately incentivised until a full exit.

Such prior ranking entitlements will include any third-party debt providers and most likely the vast majority of the private equity house's investment in the portfolio company, which will typically be by way of shareholder loan or preference shares. Managers of the retained business may receive no return from the scheme on a partial exit where proceeds are not paid in respect of ordinary shares. Even where funds are paid on shareholder instruments, the desire for the private equity house to retain management's financial exposure to the portfolio company may mean that managers' returns in respect of the partial exit are not realised until a full exit. Where managers have invested in shareholder loans or preference shares, together with their ordinary shares (ie, as part of the 'institutional strip' or 'hard equity'), payment may be made on these instruments in the same way as they would be made to the private equity house.

3. Disposals by a private equity house of part of an investment in a portfolio company

The second type of partial exit briefly discussed below is the disposal by a private equity house of a portion of its investment in a portfolio company. Depending on the terms agreed with other investors, a private equity house may be permitted to transfer to a new investor a portion of its shares and other instruments in the portfolio company. An alternative structure is for the private equity house to transfer its entire holding in the portfolio company to a new entity in which it has an interest, together with the new investor. The latter structure might be used where the private equity house and another investor wish to combine their respective investments by contributing them to the new entity; in this case each will have a smaller proportionate interest in a larger, combined business.

3.1 Transfer permissions and rights

Depending at which level within the corporate structure the private equity house intends to transfer instruments, the transfer may be subject to restrictions set out in a shareholders' agreement or constitutional documents of the relevant entity. Common rights and obligations which may apply to such a transfer are set out below. Whether these apply is likely to depend on the proportion of the private equity house's investment being transferred:

- Tag-along right – a transfer of shares or other instruments by the private equity house may give rise to a right for minority shareholders (whether management or other minority shareholders) to transfer all, or a proportionate amount, of their investment in the portfolio company to the new investor.
- Right of first offer – before transferring any of its investment in the portfolio company, the private equity house may first need to permit other existing investors to make an offer for some or all of their *pro rata* proportion of the instruments proposed to be transferred to the new investor, the existing

investors naming their price and any other terms. The private equity house may accept or reject each such offer and, in respect of those instruments for which such offers are made, may transfer those instruments for no less than what was offered by the relevant existing investor for an agreed period.

- Right of first refusal – before the transfer to the new investor takes place, an existing investor may have the right to acquire some or all of its *pro rata* proportion of the instruments to be transferred for a price which at least matches that offered by the new investor, and on the same terms. Such a right may deter the new investor from entering into the transaction if other shareholders can ultimately cut across the negotiations if they offer an equivalent price.
- Drag-along right – the private equity house may be able to force minority investors to deliver to the new investor all or a proportion of their investment in order to deliver the intended number of shares and other instruments to the new investor.
- Syndication – the private equity house may be permitted to transfer a portion of its equity to third parties without the restrictions imposed by the above rights within certain prescribed limits as to the proportion of equity to be syndicated and the time during which such a transfer may be made.

If the involvement of minority investors in the partial exit remains unclear prior to launching the transaction, the potential timing requirements to comply with notice and other terms of the respective rights set out above will need to be factored into any deal timetable.

3.2 Ongoing governance arrangements

As part of the disposal by the private equity house of a portion of its investment, the rights and obligations of the private equity house and the new investor following completion will need to be agreed. Depending on the portion of the investment held by the new investor, there may be implications for the corporate governance of the portfolio company and the new investor will wish to protect its investment going forward:

- Corporate governance – the disposal by the private equity house may mean that it no longer holds the required threshold of shares or other instruments required to carry out certain corporate actions. For example, to amend the articles of association of, or to admit new shareholders to, a Luxembourg *société à responsabilité limitée*, commonly used as a holding company for a private equity investment, the approval of a majority of the shareholders holding three-quarters of the shares is required.
- Board representation – the new investor may wish to participate on the board tasked with determining the strategic direction of the portfolio company. Whether such participation will be by way of nominating a director or an observer for appointment to the board or by receiving board papers will depend on the significance of the new investor's investment in the business.
- Restrictions on transfers – the existing transfer restrictions applicable to

investors other than the private equity house (eg, management) may need to be adjusted to reflect the differing characteristics of the new investor (eg, if the new investor is a financial investor, transfers among its group may need to be permitted).

- Tag-along right and drag-along obligation – whether the private equity house and the new investor have the benefit or burden of tag-along and drag-along provisions (or any other share transfer right or obligation, such as a right of first offer or right of first refusal) will need to be determined.
- Rights on new issues – will the consent of the new investor be required for new share issues or will it have have pre-emption rights on a new issue?
- Consent rights – will the consent of the new investor be required for other material actions of the portfolio company?

As with other transactions where rights to exercise control over the portfolio company are altered, consideration will need to be given by both the new investor and the private equity house as to whether approval should be sought from, or notice given to, any antitrust or industry regulators. In addition, if the portfolio company has a defined benefit pension scheme in the United Kingdom, the usual consideration will need to be given to whether the transaction would have a material detriment on the likelihood of accrued scheme benefits being received under the scheme, and whether any clearance from the Pensions Regulator should be sought. The relevant factors to be taken into account regarding UK defined benefit pensions schemes are set out in the pensions chapter of *Private Equity: A Transactional Analysis*.

3.3 Implications for agreements with third parties

As with any transfer of shares in an ultimate holding company, it will be necessary to consider whether the transfer of instruments by the private equity house will create any rights for a third party under existing arrangements. For example, a right to termination or other redress may be expressed to arise on a change of control; whether such a right is created will usually depend on the shares, board representation and contractual rights transferred or granted to the new investor. Of particular significance will be any mandatory pre-payment obligation under the terms of the debt financing made available to the portfolio company and the key commercial contracts.

4. Conclusion

Partial exits will be a significant event in the life of a portfolio company. While ideally realising an immediate benefit from disposing of significant assets, there is potential for the terms of any partial exit to affect the ultimate exit from the portfolio company. Balancing the desire to maximise the value of the target business at the time of the partial exit with the value of the retained business will be key in delivering optimal returns to investors.

Private equity house spin-outs

Amy Mahon
Clifford Chance LLP

1. Introduction

This chapter seeks to explain some of the key considerations on a spin-out of a fund manager, from the perspective of both the management team and the disposing institution. These spun-out fund managers may then themselves become the subject of a private equity exit (eg, a sale or an initial public offering (IPO)), as discussed in other chapters of this book. The past few years have seen an increase in the number of fund management teams exiting from a larger fund management business or a bank. For example, HSBC spun out its private equity fund management business in Asia (HSBC Private Equity (Asia)) to form the new firm Headland Capital Partners, and in 2011 it spun out its infrastructure and real estate fund management business in the United Kingdom, forming Infrared. In 2009 Bridgepoint Private Equity acquired the private equity business of Hermes. In August 2010 private equity firm Ridgemont Equity Partners spun out of Bank of America. In February 2011 Phase4 Ventures, a venture capital arm of global investment bank Nomura, spun out from its parent with financing provided by HarbourVest Partners. Barclays is also exiting its private equity business Barclays Private Equity. There are a number of reasons driving this trend.

2. Reasons for spin-outs

The Volcker Rule, which forms part of the Dodd-Frank Wall Street Reform and Consumer Protection Act 2010, prohibits banking organisations from engaging in proprietary trading and from sponsoring or investing in private equity (and hedge) funds, subject to limited exceptions. This rule is likely to result in a number of US bank-backed private equity (in the broadest sense, including infrastructure) funds and hedge funds being spun out of those banks.

Increased regulatory capital demands on banks from Basel III and Solvency II (among other regulations) and the increased levels of regulation of private equity funds (eg, under the Directive on Alternative Investment Fund Managers) may also encourage fund managers to exit from banks in line with the broader strategy of many of these banks to exit from non-core businesses. Some funds within larger fund management businesses are also seeking independence: for example, in March 2011 the Blackstone infrastructure team announced its intention to separate from the private equity firm.

The terms 'fund spin-out' and 'fund manager spin-out' are used to describe a range of transactions. This chapter focuses on exits of fund management businesses by institutions, such as banks or larger fund management businesses, by way of a sale of the business to its management team.

3. Structure of the disposal

3.1 Assets being sold

The business being sold is the fund management business and the assets are usually the entities that are the managers and the general partners and other vehicles fundamental to the fund management business (eg, custodians or other holding vehicles). An alternative structure to the transfer of the fund management vehicles themselves would be for the management contracts and other rights and obligations of the fund documentation to be assigned or novated to the buyer group, which would comprise one or more newly formed managers and general partners. Carried interest, typically in the form of equity interests such as limited liability partnership interests or limited partnership interests or shares (depending on the jurisdiction and structure of the fund), will also need to be transferred to the relevant recipients in the buyer group.

Fund management is a people business and the other major asset (although legally regarded as a liability) is the employees, who may or may not be employed by the target company (or companies) to be acquired. If they are employed by one of the corporate entities being sold, employment contracts will transfer automatically with that corporate entity. Alternatively, as is often the case, the employees may be employed by a retained company within the seller's group. If so, the employment contracts of those employees that are wholly or mainly assigned to the business will transfer by operation of law under the Transfer of Undertakings (Protection of Employment) Regulations (TUPE). Goodwill, track record, office equipment, books and records are also important assets of the business and, if not housed within the target entities, will need to be transferred specifically to the buyer as well.

The assets forming the business will be sold with full title guarantee free from encumbrances, although this covenant can be difficult for a seller to give for assets that are not shares or partnership interests, and may be varied for certain categories of asset.

3.2 Parties

For the purposes of this chapter, we have assumed that the seller is a bank or another large institution. It may also be an existing fund manager (eg a pension fund, a hedge fund or a private equity fund manager) seeking to exit from a particular part of its fund management business. The buyer will be a vehicle owned by the senior managers of the business. Many spin-outs are structured similarly to any other management buy-out, although typically there will not be an institutional investor making an investment alongside the management team. Therefore, the management team will form the acquisition vehicle (or vehicles) which will acquire the business.

Certain fund management businesses or platforms may be sold to other fund management businesses. These transactions add an extra layer of complexity, with a number of regulatory affiliation issues to be considered. Due diligence of both businesses must be carried out. For example, most fund documentation will permit management of only one fund with the same investment policy; therefore, merging with a manager vehicle that will continue to manage its own legacy funds may require consent from investors in both funds.

3.3 Drivers of structure

While it is typically most straightforward to achieve a transfer by way of sale of the shares (or other equity interests) constituting the business, the structure of the transaction will often be driven by due diligence that determines which structure will give rise to the lowest number of third-party consents required. Inevitably, as a result of the transaction, some consents or amendments to existing arrangements will be necessary. Consequently, the aim will be to adopt a transaction structure which avoids consent being required from counterparties where there is likely to be resistance or where the consent will require an additional commercial incentive to be forthcoming. To the extent that consent from the investors in the relevant funds is required, there is always the concern that investors will use the consent requirement to extract a benefit in the form of fee reductions or other more attractive fund terms, particularly if the fund is not performing well. Therefore, the deal will be structured to minimise the impact on investors and the number of changes required to fund documentation.

At the portfolio level, 'captive' funds of banks or other institutions are more likely to have a number of express links to the selling bank or institution, which may result in consent being required from lenders or other counterparties at the portfolio company level. For example, change of control provisions in the equity or debt arrangements could trigger pre-emption rights under the shareholders' agreement at the portfolio company level or pre-payment of the debt. Pre-emption rights on a change of control are unusual in a straightforward leveraged deal, but are common on consortium transactions. If triggered, pre-emption rights could add timing issues and force an unwanted exit or sell-down of a particular asset; consequently, most transactions will seek to avoid this by structuring around any such matters or obtaining advance consent from the other shareholders. A change of control provision in the debt arrangements would be resolved by obtaining lenders' consent, but lenders may use this opportunity to renegotiate lending terms or margins, particularly in the current market.

Tax planning will also drive the structure to be adopted, not just in relation to corporate tax issues, but in relation to the transfers of carried interest to minimise the crystallisation of tax liabilities.

3.4 Consideration

The consideration structure will be similar to most other acquisitions and therefore a 'locked box' consideration mechanism will frequently be used. This mechanism involves the price paid by the buyer being agreed at signing based on the cash-free, debt-free, tax-free value of the business (with an assumed 'normalised' level of working capital), at a fixed date (often called the 'effective date') determined on the basis of a balance sheet from that date, with the buyer having the economic benefit of the business from that point in time. This is achieved by including restrictions on the 'leakage' of value to the seller from that effective date to the date of closing by including covenants relating to the conduct of the business and an indemnity in respect of payments (being value leakage) to the seller's group that are not permitted as ordinary course legitimate payments from the business. Often, interest is payable on the purchase price from the effective date because the buyer has the economic benefit of the business from that date, but the seller is funding it.

The alternative, often seen as more favourable to the buyer, is to have the price based on the estimated value of the business at completion, usually being an estimate of debt and cash levels and working capital, and also often including an allocation for bonuses and benefits. This estimated price is paid at completion and is then adjusted upwards or downwards after completion to reflect the actual position at completion by way of a completion accounts adjustment. This involves the preparation and agreement of completion accounts after completion to determine the actual net assets, profits, debt and cash levels and working capital in the business at completion to determine the adjustment. If a completion accounts mechanism is used, there will be a negotiation as to who prepares the first draft completion accounts, but this will often end up being the buyer, as it usually has full access to the information after completion. Usually, the mechanism allows the seller to revise the accounts, and if the parties fail to agree them, the matter is usually referred to an expert for determination.

As a regulated business, the new business will have minimum regulatory capital requirements and will need working capital to operate the business. Therefore, this capital will need either to be left in the business being acquired or to be funded by the buyer. Occasionally, there may be a mechanism for equity to be subscribed to satisfy regulatory capital requirements. To the extent that the business has excess cash above this minimum regulatory capital requirement and the amount of normal working capital required, the parties may prefer the seller to strip out this excess cash prior to the sale. This can be achieved by including in the sale and purchase agreement a mechanism to distribute cash to the seller prior to completion. If a locked box consideration mechanism is used, this distribution will be 'permitted' leakage to the seller and capped. This avoids the cash-constrained management team having to fund the acquisition of excess cash in the business.

The consideration for the acquisition will usually be some multiple of management fee. Carried interest is more difficult to value and its allocation more difficult to agree. Its valuation and apportionment after completion will be one of the most contentious commercial issues on the transaction and often financial advisers will be engaged on both sides to facilitate agreeing the valuation. A number of sale and purchase arrangements on fund manager disposals will include deferred consideration mechanics where the payment of consideration is staggered such that the management team has the opportunity to earn the fees to enable it to fund payment. Deferred consideration mechanisms can also be structured as an earn-out, whereby future payments to the seller depend on future profits or success of the business: for example, they can be linked to future fund size, which (under most fund terms) has a direct impact on the management fee earned by the fund manager for managing the fund.

Many spin-outs will have a limited element of leverage, depending on the value of the business being acquired. If debt funding is being used to fund the purchase price, the seller will need comfort that the funding will be available on completion by having visibility over the terms of the equity and debt funding. The buyer will need to ensure that there is no gap in funding as between the equity funding and the debt funding and the obligation to pay the purchase price under the terms of the sale and purchase agreement.

4. Preliminary considerations

The buyer and the seller should give some thought to a number of preliminary matters at the outset of the transaction.

4.1 Conflicts

One of the key preliminary issues to consider on any management buy-out is the potential and actual conflicts that arise in relation to the management team. Very often on a fund spin-out, the management team will have no equity ownership in the business itself (although it may have some equity or options in the seller and will have various entitlements to carried interest), but it will be an indirect buyer of the business, typically buying 100% of the business together through a newly formed acquisition vehicle in which each senior manager has an equity interest. On the one hand, they are employees who currently run the business and are very knowledgeable about the business; on the other, they have a direct financial interest in the buyer seeking comfort from the seller, which has benefited from the profits of historic ownership and will benefit from payment of the purchase price. As buyers, the managers are directly interested in the terms of the sale and purchase agreement. As employees, they will owe a duty of care to their employer, which is the seller or the target. In addition, a number of managers may be directors of the target companies and, as such, owe duties to the target companies. The general partner and manager vehicles owe fiduciary duties to the investors in the fund and consequently the directors of those vehicles must consider the investors' interests. A number of the managers will also be 'keymen' under the terms of the fund documentation – meaning that they must devote an agreed proportion of their time to management of the business of the fund, failing which, typically, the investment period of the fund is suspended. These tensions and competing interests mean that the management team is pulled in many different directions. It is important to agree upfront how these conflicts will be managed.

From the seller's perspective, it is important to remind the management team of its duties of confidentiality, and to ensure that there is a coordinated approach to informing investors of the possible change of control in such a manner as to cause minimal disruption to the business.

For companies incorporated in England and Wales, under Section 175 of the Companies Act 2006 a director has an obligation to avoid situations in which he or she has an interest which may possibly conflict with the interests of the company. Therefore, the transaction may put the directors who are members of the management team and have their own personal interests in the buyer in a conflict situation, given their duties to manage the target business having regard to the interests of the shareholders. It is thus important to have the conflicts of the directors with interests in the transaction authorised by the directors of the target company in accordance with Section 175 of the act and the articles of association of the target company (assuming that the articles permit such authorisation). For this purpose, only directors of the target company who are not interested may vote and count in the quorum as required by Section 175(6) of the act. Directors must declare their interests in the transaction to the other directors in accordance with Section 177 of the act. Similar provisions will apply in many other jurisdictions. The directors of the general partner and manager vehicles will need to ensure that the terms of the fund documentation are complied with (including keymen provisions), and that the fiduciary duties owed by such entities to the investors in the fund are observed.

4.2 Confidentiality

While a deal is being negotiated, until there is some certainty, it will be important to ensure that all parties keep the potential transaction confidential. Rumours and market leaks about a potential spin-out may give rise to uncertainty about the fund's future, affecting the fund's ability to enter into transactions. Agreeing a leak strategy will be essential if the seller is listed and is a sensible precaution on any spin-out. Most listed companies will be obliged to disclose any transaction that is likely to have a significant effect on the price of the listed instruments. Issuers listed on a regulated market in the United Kingdom may well need to disclose information about the transaction if it is of a kind that a reasonable investor would be likely to use as part of the basis of its investment decision. Disclosure and Transparency Rule 2.5 permits the delay of such disclosure so as not to prejudice the issuer's interests if the omission would be unlikely to mislead the public, recipients of such information owe the issuer a duty of confidentiality and the issuer can ensure the confidentiality of such information. This position must be monitored so that an appropriate announcement can be made at an appropriate time – for example, on signing heads of terms or a binding sale agreement.

A coordinated strategy in relation to disclosure to limited partners will be important to ensure that a thoroughly considered proposal is put to limited partners which they can understand fully. Equally, the timing of the announcement will be important. If at any point it is contrary to the interests of the limited partners not to be aware of the potential transaction, the general partner and/or manager will have a duty to inform the investors. Consequently, the timing of any spin-out should be carefully planned to ensure that appropriate communications can be made at annual investor meetings and that disclosure is made prior to any major fundraising.

5. Due diligence

A key feature of the transaction is the due diligence to be carried out, principally by the legal, accounting, financial/valuation and taxation advisers. In addition, advisers may need to conduct due diligence on pensions and insurance matters, and possibly executive remuneration. From the legal perspective, a change of control analysis must be carried out at two levels:

- at the level of the fund itself, by checking the fund documentation to determine what consents may be required to the change of control and whether any amendments to the fund documentation are required to reflect the changes occurring as a result of the transaction; and
- at the level of the portfolio, by checking the arrangements relating to the equity and debt funding of the portfolio assets, as well as other major contracts (eg, with regulators or concessionaires) which may also contain change of control provisions that need to be waived.

Many fund arrangements will not include change of control provisions, but will include keyman obligations which require the participation of certain named individuals in the management of the fund. Often with bank-sponsored funds, these simply require the involvement of senior employees of the bank rather than, or in addition to, named individuals, and therefore these provisions may also be triggered as a consequence of the spin-out. Funds sponsored by an investment bank will occasionally include change of control provisions requiring an ownership link to the bank, or may include other obligations ensuring access to the deal pipeline of the bank, for example. These will require either ongoing covenants from the selling bank to ensure that those obligations can be complied with or amendments to the fund documentation.

At the portfolio level, there are often banking arrangements where the lenders require an ongoing link to the seller (particularly where the seller is owned by a large bank or a broader funds management platform which has given the lenders comfort in respect of the portfolio company), and in infrastructure portfolio companies there will often be project arrangements which require the portfolio company to have a link with the seller as the ultimate controller of the fund that owns the portfolio company. While funds typically avoid giving parental guarantees, occasionally funds with a parent bank will put in place parent guarantees. Such guarantees will need to be identified in due diligence and alternative arrangements put in place to replace them.

One consideration for both the buyer and seller early in the process when appointing advisers is who should conduct the due diligence and which parties will have reliance on such due diligence. Since both parties will need to be comfortable that the necessary consents and obstacles to the transaction have been identified and dealt with, both parties will require reliance on much of the due diligence with appropriate reliance terms and liability caps. The buyer will usually have a more extensive scope, covering the usual areas of employment, pensions, tax, finance and an analysis of any other material contracts. Certain information may be more easily accessed by one or other party – often the management team – and the buyer will typically prefer to conduct the due diligence exercise as it will want to frame the scope of the exercise. However, as the management team will have an intimate knowledge of the business, the scope of due diligence may be narrower than in a corporate acquisition.

The seller may also require due diligence to be carried out to support any warranty and indemnity protection that it is giving – particularly in relation to litigation, employment liabilities and tax, for example.

5.1 Regulatory approvals

A thorough analysis of the regulatory and antitrust approvals required for the transaction must be carried out. See below in relation to conditions.

5.2 Pensions

Pensions will be an important part of the transaction and due diligence exercise, particularly where the employees participate in a defined benefit pension scheme (as distinct from a defined contribution scheme). As the business is being carved out of a larger group, it is relatively unusual for the pension scheme to be taken over in full by the buyer. Where a pension scheme is taken over by the buyer, those companies in the buyer's group which are participating employers will be bound by the obligations imposed on them by the pension scheme's rules and by statute. The buyer's group as a whole will be exposed to the Pensions Regulator's 'moral hazard' powers under the Pensions Act 2004; clearance might be sought from the Pensions Regulator by way of comfort that its powers will not be exercised as a result of circumstances connected with the acquisition. Where a company leaves the pension scheme, as might often occur on a spin-out where a number of employer companies are sold to the buyer, a statutory debt may be imposed under Section 75 of the Pensions Act 1995. Unless the trustees agree to the payment of a reduced amount, the amount payable is equal to the company's share of the deficit in the pension scheme calculated on the expensive buy-out basis (ie, the deficit which would exist if the benefits were secured through the purchase of annuities and deferred annuities from an insurance company). Careful analysis will need to be conducted to determine whether a Section 75 debt arises, its likely size and whether attempts should be made to agree a reduced payment with the trustees. There may also be circumstances where it is appropriate to obtain Pensions Regulator clearance (bearing in mind that a company being sold will have exposure to a pension scheme retained by the seller for up to six years after sale under the Pension Regulator's moral hazard powers). If the scheme is a defined contribution scheme, it will generally be easier to deal with. On a business transfer, whether the scheme operated by the seller is a defined benefit scheme or a defined contribution scheme, the buyer will need to comply with the requirements for providing acquired employees with a minimum level of pension provision. The buyer may also be liable to replicate the seller's defined benefit pension terms payable on redundancy or more generally on early retirement, even where the buyer does not operate a defined benefit pension scheme. The buyer might seek contractual protection in relation to such 'Beckmann' liabilities.

5.3 Employment issues

A full employment legal review exercise must be carried out. If the transaction is structured by way of a share sale, the employees will transfer their full entitlements and contracts in place. The buyer will need to understand the cost of these benefits for the purposes of its business plan. If the transaction is structured by way of an asset sale, the employees will transfer by TUPE, again with their benefits needing to be replicated, although most rights arising from occupational pension schemes (with some exceptions)[1] can be excluded from this requirement. Of course, a newly formed management-backed vehicle may be unable to replicate all of the benefits that the seller (eg, a listed investment bank) can offer: share/option schemes, defined benefit pension schemes and gym membership can be difficult for a new business to replicate. Thus, there will need to be variation of existing employment contracts (in the case of a share sale) and consultation on the measures to be adopted (in the case of an asset sale). TUPE consultation obligations should be built into the deal timetable.

6. Conditions

Spin-outs can often have a high level of conditionality, given the requirements for third-party and regulatory consents, as well as complicated separation arrangements which cannot be implemented prior to having a binding acquisition agreement. Depending on the size of the transaction and the nature and turnover of the parties involved, an antitrust approval will often be required as well. The acquisition agreement will typically contain the usual provision that both parties will use reasonable endeavours to achieve the satisfaction of the conditions.

The Financial Services and Markets Act 2000 requires individuals or corporate bodies wishing to acquire control of a firm authorised by the Financial Services Authority (FSA) to seek prior approval from the FSA under Section 178 of the act. These new controllers of the authorised manager/general partner entities must obtain FSA approval in order to become the owners and controllers of those entities. Failure to notify or obtain approval is a criminal offence under Section 191 of the act and subject to a fine. The rules look up through the chain of ownership to identify any persons that may have control over the 10% or more interest held in the parent company of the target manager/general partner companies. For these purposes, an individual is deemed to be an undertaking and accordingly, where the buyer is backed by individuals with an interest of 10% more, they will need to obtain prior FSA approval to be individual controllers of the authorised entities.

Notification to the FSA must be in writing and is often referred to as a Section 178 notice. It constitutes a cover letter to the FSA incorporating the high-level details and summary of the proposed restructuring and the proposed controller for which approval from the FSA is sought. The authorised entities themselves must notify the FSA in writing if a person obtains control of them and this notification can be dealt with in the same cover letter.

The FSA has 60 business days from receipt of a valid application to respond. It will determine whether to approve the acquisition of control unconditionally or subject to conditions. It will consider the suitability of the proposed controller, its financial soundness, its reputation, its ability to comply with the FSA prudential requirements and the likely influence that the proposed controller will have on the

---

1 Certain early retirement benefits may be an exception – see *Beckmann v Dynamco Whicheloe Macfarlane* [2002] 64 PBLR and *Martin v South Bank University* [2003] 85 PBLR.

authorised entity. If the FSA believes that it requires further information, it must submit its request for this information within 50 working days of receipt of a complete application. Depending on the complexity of the application, a response is usually received in 30 to 40 days. Once the change of control has actually occurred, the authorised entities and the controllers will need to notify the FSA, typically by a simple letter.

Of course, in many spin-outs, the business operates in several jurisdictions and many jurisdictions will have similar regulation and licensing regimes. A thorough analysis must be conducted by legal counsel in the relevant jurisdictions to identify what approvals must be obtained and the appropriate applications and filings made.

7. Allocation of risk and responsibility

7.1 Bargaining position

The main source of contention on a spin-out, as with many disposals, is the allocation of risk and liability as between the seller and the buyer. On the one hand, the buyer has run the business and has knowledge of the business. Many fund management businesses operate with relative autonomy within a bank, making most of the operational and strategic decisions themselves. Remuneration and compliance matters are typically run centrally; but at a micro level, individual performance compensation (whether it be basic salary, option awards, bonus or carried interest) is often determined by the senior managers as between the team itself. Similarly, tax at a corporate level will often be run centrally, but the tax planning of the vehicles and the carry schemes will usually have been implemented by the management team. Therefore, there is an inherent conflict in asking the parent bank to provide warranty and indemnity protection to the buyer in respect of a business which the bank has allowed the management team to run. The buyer will argue that the bank has had the benefit of the business historically, has had overall oversight and control of the business and is being paid value for the business, and that the seller should therefore provide meaningful protection to the buyer as it would on any other disposal.

Much of the allocation of responsibility will turn on the relative bargaining position. In this regard, a bank caught by the Volcker Rule will be in a weaker position than a bank exploring the options to dispose of a non-core business line. There is also an interesting dynamic in a number of spin-outs whereby the seller will have some residual franchise concerns to ensure that the standalone business can survive and continue managing existing funds. This is particularly the case where, as often happens, the seller will have a large investment in the fund or funds managed by the general partner and manager being sold, and therefore it will want to ensure that the business is properly financed, serviced and authorised to enable it to continue its business and effectively manage the seller's investment.

7.2 Warranties and indemnities

Most spin-outs will include a tax indemnity in respect of unpaid tax similar to that found on a corporate transaction, although there are exceptions to this rule. As with most secondary transactions, where a private equity house is disposing of a part of its fund management business, it will heavily resist assuming a large contingent liability such as a tax covenant and a retention may need to be agreed or the buyer may need to proceed without a tax indemnity. Careful consideration of the personal tax arrangements of the individual managers will be required, as neither party will wish to have responsibility for an adverse tax ruling in relation to the individual managers' position. In particular, the transaction will need to be structured to avoid crystallising a taxable gain on the part of the managers where possible.

Most acquisition agreements will include a provision that the buyer and seller may not make a claim directly against employees or former employees in connection with a warranty claim. This will protect employees of a target business from being sued by the seller in the event that the buyer brings a warranty claim. In many spin-outs this principle may also need to be extended to the portfolio companies and their employees and officers, to the extent that any warranty protection is given which relates to the portfolio businesses.

7.3 Buyer knowledge

It is important to deal upfront with the issue of buyer knowledge and the seller will seek to ensure that it does not provide protection in respect of any issue which is known to the buyer. The principle for many spin-outs is that the buyer cannot make a valid claim in respect of matters of which it is aware, unless such matter is covered by a specific indemnity. Furthermore, given the ability of the senior management team to control operational matters, the seller will also seek to exclude liability for any action taken by or at the direction of or with the informed consent of the management team. This principle will often flow through the entire agreement, applying to indemnities and, if a locked box consideration mechanism is used, to any indemnity for the costs, expenses, losses and damages arising as a consequence of the leakage (although the leakage itself must be returned by the seller to the target).

7.4 Covenant strength of buyer

There is also a need for some reverse protection from the buyer. The buyer will typically not have good covenant strength and therefore a guarantee from the carry vehicle or a retention of purchase price may be required.

8. Ongoing covenants

8.1 Non-compete

A key feature of the commercial deal will be for the seller to covenant not to compete with the buyer's business for a fixed period. There will typically be carve-outs for any retained business that is currently being carried out alongside the business being exited, and carve-outs for other usual operations of the bank which may be linked to private equity itself – for example, lending to portfolio companies or other fund managers, or participation in other private equity-sponsored vehicles as part of a co-investment. Investing in competitor funds can be contentious. In the climate of Volcker, banks that are bank holding companies are unable to invest in private equity funds in any event, but they will nonetheless be reluctant to limit their flexibility to invest in other funds, and banks that are not bank holding companies will not have this limitation. The outcome of this commercial debate will often depend on the extent to which the new business is reliant on the seller as its main sponsor. For more established funds, this will be much less of a problem. Setting up a competitor fund manager with a similar investment policy to the spun-out fund will clearly be prohibited.

8.2 Use of name

The use of the seller's name in connection with the buyer or its business will be prohibited from completion of the transaction. Consequently, advance preparation prior to completion will need to be carried out to ensure that the business can function fully under the new names with effect from completion of the transaction. A transitional period of usage will be heavily resisted by the seller (particularly if it is a bank), and therefore name changes will need to be implemented as part of the separation planning between signing and completion.

8.3 Use of track record

There may also be debate over the extent to which the bank can continue to use the track record of the team that has been spun out. This is part of the protection which the new business needs to ensure that the bank does not compete with it, yet many banks will consider this a shared track record and may wish to use it for other fundraising and client marketing purposes.

8.4 Non-solicit/no rehire

The buyer will want to ensure that the selling bank does not seek to rehire its employees and the bank may also want protection that the new business will not poach any staff remaining behind with the seller. Typically, these businesses are standalone, but there may be some overlap in, for example, compliance, legal, human resources and tax divisions. Also, to the extent that a number of redundancies are agreed as part of the sale, the party that picks up the cost of these redundancies (usually the seller) will want to ensure that the buyer does not subsequently rehire those individuals and so will seek reimbursement of any severance amounts.

8.5 Other sale and purchase terms

Other parts of the sale and purchase agreement will be broadly similar to those in any other acquisition. The agreement will contain standard covenants for actions between signing and completion, although a good deal of cooperation may be needed by both parties, particularly in relation to separation matters and regulatory consents. Access to books and records for a period following completion will need to be included. A 'wrong pockets' provision is also likely to be an important provision for a spin-out, as with any carve-out of a business from a larger business. This provision obliges the seller to transfer to the buyer any asset which is subsequently identified as being predominantly required for the target business, but which was not transferred by the sale and purchase agreement. There is also a reciprocal arrangement in respect of assets transferred to the buyer which are predominantly required by the retained business of the seller.

9. Transitional services and separation issues

As with any sale of a non-core business, significant separation issues must be considered. Assuming that regulatory approvals are obtained (see above), a compliance function will need to be put in place and HR and treasury teams will need to be established, as well as new premises and an IT system. If there is insufficient time to replicate these services before the transaction completes, a transitional services agreement will need to be put in place for a transitional period, until the standalone business has replicated these services. It is often difficult from a compliance perspective to permit the new business to operate from the same premises as the bank and therefore new premises should be prioritised.

10. Conclusion

In the current regulatory environment, and with increased pressure on banking institutions to free up their balance sheet, it is likely that there will be a pipeline of fund manager spin-outs over the coming years. These are complex transactions involving a myriad of legal issues for which specialist legal advice should be sought.

Private equity-sponsored IPOs

Stuart Boyd
David Holdsworth
John Lane
Linklaters LLP

This chapter considers the elements of an initial pubic offering (IPO) that a private equity sponsor will need to consider prior to launching an IPO in respect of one of its portfolio companies. In particular, the following items are discussed:

- process;
- debt structure;
- liability issues for a private equity sponsor;
- key commercial terms for private equity sponsors;
- pre-IPO investments; and
- IPOs as part of a dual track process.

1. Initial considerations for private equity sponsors

As with any exit, on an IPO exit a private equity sponsor will be focused on ensuring that it is delivering a cash-on-cash return for its investors so that it can create a track record of successful exits for its next round of fund raising. This cash-on-cash return will be judged not only in absolute terms, but also on the time taken from initial investment to realisation of the investment. Accordingly, on an IPO the certainty of cash returns and timing of the process will be key considerations for the private equity sponsor.

An IPO is arguably more susceptible to market conditions than a trade sale and the IPO process is generally longer than one would expect for a trade sale. It is also a more public process, so the perception of an unsuccessful IPO may have more of an impact on the sponsor's exit options for the portfolio company than would be the case with a more private trade sale process.

However, the certainty of exit and timing of exit are not the only criteria by which an exit will be judged. For example, IPOs allow (and indeed prospective investors in the IPO and the underwriting banks will generally require) the private equity sponsor to retain a significant stake in the portfolio company. This may be attractive where there is a need to realise some return on invested capital at the same time as a desire to benefit from further upside in due course. In other cases the partial exit may be seen as a disadvantage as compared to a trade sale.

A key benefit of an IPO is that for companies that are well prepared for IPO and are attractive to the public capital markets, there is an opportunity to achieve a higher valuation as compared to a trade sale.

Before embarking on an IPO process, the private equity sponsor will therefore consider whether the portfolio company in question is suited to an IPO and how an

IPO compares with other exit options. Once the decision is taken to proceed with the IPO, these wider considerations will remain relevant to the private equity sponsor and a key focus of the private equity sponsor will be to ensure, to the greatest extent possible, predictability of the pricing and the timing of the IPO.

2. Process

2.1 Pitches and management of the IPO process

Private equity sponsors, with their experience of exits and focus on returns for investors, typically take an active role in structuring and managing the IPO process. This will often include running a competitive process to appoint the financial adviser/lead underwriting banks. Agreement on a wide range of commercial terms is often made a condition to appointment. After the appointment of advisers, the private equity sponsor will look to be closely involved in the process and will typically have, and will express, its views on a range of matters that flow through to the timing and terms of the IPO.

2.2 Availability of financial information and financial reporting systems

The proposed timeline for the IPO will be a key focus, given the need to deliver returns to the private equity sponsor's investor base.

One of the factors determining the timeline for any IPO will be the availability of financial information on the group to be listed. The financial information that is required will vary depending on the market on which listing is being sought, but at the most basic level the financial information will need to provide investors with an accurate guide as to the historic performance of the group and a metric against which the future performance of the group can be measured. In the United Kingdom, a premium listing would require unqualified audit reports for three years representing 75% of the value of the business, although the practice would usually be to show 100% of the business going back three years.

In relation to a private equity-owned business, the matter can be complicated if the group to be listed has been formed through the combination of various different businesses. Where this is the case, it will be critical to establish what financial information is available, what the accounting policies are, under which those financials have been prepared and how that information is going to be presented in the prospectus.

In many cases the solution will involve consolidated financial information being presented alongside self-standing financials on parts of the group which were acquired over the three-year track record. The self-standing financials will be presented up until the date of the acquisition by the main group company. *Pro forma* financial information (effectively showing what the position would have been if the acquisition had occurred at a specified date) may also be disclosed; indeed, in some cases it may be required.

If such information is not readily available, producing it to a standard that can be used for a prospectus is extremely time intensive. An initial workstream will therefore involve clarifying with the reporting accountants that appropriate financial information will be available or agreeing a clear timeline for production of such information.

Any large-scale IPO is likely to involve an offering in the United States, a consequence of which is that the underwriting banks will require the reporting accountants to provide 'negative assurance' in relation to changes since the last audited financial information. This negative assurance comfort takes a prescribed form, the relevant governing regulation being Statement on Auditing Standards No 72 (SAS 72). SAS 72 also provides a definitive cut-off of 135 days from the last audited accounts as a threshold beyond which the accountants will be able to provide the comfort that is required. Accordingly, when developing the timeline for the IPO, the '135-day' rule will need to be considered to ensure that the appropriate comfort will be available.

This requirement for audited financial information and comfort thereon, coupled with the need for the equity markets to be 'open', means that there are likely to be only specific windows in any given calendar year during which IPOs can be successfully launched. Given the importance of timing to private equity sponsors, such constraints will need to be factored into the planning process. Additional work being identified late in the process can result in a window being missed, which can delay the IPO by six months or more; this will have a significantly adverse effect on the private equity sponsor's internal rates of return.

The underwriting banks will also want to ensure that the financial reporting procedures that the group has in place are sufficient to enable it to meet its continuing obligations post-listing. A private equity portfolio company is likely to have strong reporting systems due to the information and regular provision of such information that is required by private equity sponsors and the lenders that have provided leveraged finance to the portfolio company. However, this does not necessarily mean that the systems will be sufficient to ensure compliance with post-IPO continuing reporting obligations. In the United Kingdom, one of the banks will be making a declaration to the UK Listing Authority (UKLA) as sponsor that the issuer can meet such obligations. It will require the reporting accountants to report on the reporting procedures of the group and provide comfort that they are sufficient to meet the relevant requirements. Again, any highlighted deficiencies will need to be remedied, which can result in delays to the listing.

Finally, financial due diligence will be required to ascertain that the listed group will have sufficient working capital following the IPO. As discussed below, this will involve an analysis of the debt position of the listed group post-IPO. In the United Kingdom, in the context of a premium listing (see "Choice of market" below), a specific confirmation that the working capital of the group will be sufficient for the 12 months following the IPO must be given in the prospectus. Accordingly, a specific report will be prepared by the reporting accountants which tests the working capital position of the to-be listed group against agreed sensitivities (ie, a reasonable worst case).

2.3 Appropriate management team

While a strength of any successful private equity-owned business will be its operational management team, this team will undoubtedly need to be bolstered with additional members to ensure that the business, once listed, meets the regulatory and corporate governance requirements of the relevant market. Investors will also expect the highest standards of corporate governance, and so as a minimum the business to be listed is likely to require additional non-executive directors to be appointed to the board of the listed entity.

The UK Corporate Governance Code requires at least half of a premium listed company's directors, excluding the chairman, to be independent non-executives (at least two for 'smaller companies' – those below the FTSE 350). Non-executive directors appointed by the private equity sponsor (or other investors) will generally not constitute 'independent' directors for this purpose because they were originally appointed by a substantial shareholder.

The private equity sponsor will also need to consider, together with its advisers, whether the management team needs any additions to ensure that the group has a management structure which will be acceptable to investors in the IPO and thereafter will be able to comply adequately with its additional reporting and investor relations obligations that come with a listing. While this is driven partially by eligibility requirements (eg, a listing in London will require one of the financial advisers (known as a sponsor) to provide a confirmation to the UKLA that the group will be able to meet its continuing reporting and other obligations post-listing), market sentiment regarding the management team will also be important. As noted above, underwriting banks will typically look to the reporting accountants to provide comfort that the management team and its systems are sufficient to meet the continuing obligations for the group post-IPO.

Conversely, of course, given the involvement of management in any IPO process, the private equity sponsor will also need to ensure that the management team are committed to the IPO process as without them, it will not be possible to launch a successful IPO.

2.4 Structure of the IPO

The factors that will be taken into account in deciding on the structure of the offering, and the market on which to commence trading, are common to non-private equity IPOs. These will include the size and nature of the company and its business, the breadth of shareholder base that is being sought and the likely level of demand for the company's shares.

Clearly, the amount of money to be raised from the IPO and the parties that are raising that money will also be critical. It is here that the views of the group to be listed on the one hand, and the private equity sponsors and the other selling shareholders on the other, may differ. The private equity sponsor (and other selling shareholders) will be keen to maximise their cash return through the IPO exit, but the working capital needs of the group to be listed and investor sentiment must also be borne in mind.

In terms of what these mean for structuring the IPO, the basic question is whether the listing will involve the issue of new shares by the company (to the dilution of the existing shareholder base) – known as a primary IPO; or the sale by existing investors of the shares – known as a secondary IPO. Clearly, the former results in the listed group receiving proceeds, with the latter resulting in proceeds being received by the shareholders.

These two basic structures are not mutually exclusive. Indeed, in most listings the IPO commonly involves both the issue of new shares and the sale of existing shares.

The precise split between primary and secondary will be a key discussion point at the outset of the process and through the final stages of pricing the IPO. Driving these discussions is the fact that, once listed, the group will be expected to stand on its own and therefore investors will want to know that the proceeds being raised by the group will be sufficient to allow it to maintain, develop and grow its business to produce returns in the future. As discussed below, the working capital position and debt position of the group post-listing will feature heavily in this analysis. Investors may also want to feel that the private equity sponsor is not cashing in and de-risking itself from the business, and so the level of 'free float' (ie, the percentage of share capital in public hands) will also be a key discussion point for the structuring of any IPO. Both these factors can lead to pressure for capital to be raised by the company by the issue of new shares, rather than sale of shares by the private equity sponsor and other shareholders.

Even where the decision is taken that all money to be raised in the IPO will be primary (ie, through the issue of new shares), the private equity sponsor and other selling shareholders may be asked by the underwriting banks to commit to sell up to an agreed number of shares if so requested by the underwriting banks. This option (known as the 'over-allotment option') for the underwriting banks allows them to call for shares (known as the 'over-allotment shares') to cover short positions held by the lead underwriting bank following trading activity undertaking by it to help stabilise the price of the listed securities post-IPO. This practice is common in several jurisdictions and represents a carefully controlled exception from anti-market manipulation legislation, such practice typically being permitted only for a limited period post-IPO.

2.5 Choice of market

Choice of market will be determined by a number of factors, including access to potential investors, the valuation of similar companies listed on the exchange, liquidity, the entry requirements and the level of continuing regulation and disclosure required. The size of the required free float (ie, the percentage of the share capital post-IPO that will be in public hands) will also play a part.

In a large number of EU markets, the free float requirement of 25% is a firm limit, dictated by EU legislation (in the form of the Consolidated Admissions and Reporting Directive). There is some flexibility on the larger deals in London with the consent of the UKLA to reduce the free float limit down to approximately 20%. In contrast, in Hong Kong the free float requirement is formally also 25%, but structures have been developed which would allow an issuer potentially to reduce substantially the amount of the free float that is initially required (eg, recent Hong Kong IPOs have had free floats of 10%). There is a greater flexibility still for non-US issuers listing on the NYSE, which facilitates the sponsor selling off its position partially, over time, or completely. As the sponsor may hold a significant stake post-IPO, it will want various controls over the business and management that are not standard or available for Euro listings.

To list in the United Kingdom, companies have a choice of a Main Market listing on the London Stock Exchange (premium or standard listing), admission to AIM or admission to the Professional Securities Market (PSM). A premium listing on the London Stock Exchange sets the highest eligibility bar, carries the most onerous continuing obligations, but also carries the greatest prestige and is the only market which will result in FTSE Indices inclusion (if the FTSE Indices criteria are met), thereby ensuring that the potential investor base is the greatest. A standard listing on the London Stock Exchange requires similar levels of disclosure to obtain the listing, but the eligibility criteria are less onerous (eg, a three-year track record is not required; nor is a working capital statement).

New applicants for a listing on the standard segment of the Main Market will have to publish a prospectus, so the same level of preparatory work will be required for a standard as for a premium listing. In contrast, a prospectus may not be necessary for admission to AIM. This is because institutional-only offers can be made on the basis of an admission document drawn up under the AIM Rules and approved by a nominated adviser. However, in other important respects the AIM Rules for Companies impose greater regulation on issuers, including the requirement to have a nominated adviser and comply with certain continuing obligations, such as the requirements to notify or obtain shareholder consent for certain types of transaction. The standard listing option is therefore less onerous in terms of continuing obligations than an AIM quotation.

A standard listing is most likely to be attractive in two contexts. First, for some new applicants, particularly those from emerging markets, the global depositary receipt (GDR) route may be the most suitable. GDRs, which are typically sold only to professional investors, may be listed on the standard segment of the Main Market (the alternative is a listing on the PSM). Second, the standard listing route may also be attractive as a short-term measure until issuers can meet the eligibility requirements for a premium listing and can step up to that status, as the standard listing regime is based on the minimum standards applicable under EU law.

2.6 Pre-IPO reorganisation

The capital structure of a private equity-owned group is likely to be complex and will require significant amendments prior to listing.

While the capital structure will have been designed to align management with the private equity sponsor and any other institutional shareholders, the economics of the various constituents will vary significantly and will most likely involve different instruments and securities for tax, governance and other reasons.

This complex structure will need to be simplified pre-IPO and will typically involve either the insertion of a new holding company or the conversion of various instruments into a single class of equity, with the percentage ownership being determined by the economic entitlements that each party has in the group. Of course, this is further complicated by the fact that, due to ratchets, waterfalls and so on, the economic entitlement of any stakeholder is uncertain until pricing of the IPO, which is at the final stage of the IPO process. Therefore, it may be unclear when the preliminary prospectus is produced:

- exactly what the size of the exit will be at different points in the valuation spectrum;
- which of the group of selling shareholders will sell at what point in that spectrum;
- if there is insufficient demand from the market to satisfy all required sales, who will have priority to sell and who will effectively be deprived of the opportunity to sell (if there is insufficient demand or scaling back); and
- to what extent the management team are receiving a large cash payment on exit and to what extent they will have a significant stake post-IPO – both key factors for investors, as they determine how incentivised the management team will be post-IPO.

In addition to restructuring the capital structure to ensure it is suitable for listing, the shareholders may also wish to extract value with a pre-IPO dividend. Such dividends are common, but must be fully disclosed in the investor materials, particularly the prospectus. In determining the quantum of any such dividend, careful consideration will need to be given to ensure that it will not be perceived by investors as leaving the group undercapitalised and/or with an inappropriate level of leverage, and will not prejudice the working capital position of the group post-IPO.

The private equity sponsor, the portfolio company and their advisers will therefore need to ensure that the capital restructuring of the group is planned, described in the marketing materials and implemented in such a manner that is tax efficient for both shareholders and the group. The disclosure will also need to be sufficiently clear and informative such that investors can understand the economic interests of each of the stakeholders, those stakeholders' proceeds from the IPO and their stake in the company post-IPO, without drawing attention away from the investment case for the company.

2.7 Documentation and due diligence

The principal document in any IPO from a legal perspective will be the prospectus. The precise requirements for the prospectus will depend on the market(s) on which the securities are to be listed and the jurisdictions in which the securities will be offered. However, the requirements are becoming increasingly standardised, particularly in Europe, where European legislation means that the listing requirements for the principal markets across Europe are largely aligned.

The management team will be critical to producing the prospectus and a considerable amount of their time will be required not only to provide information to the relevant advisers (through a data room end diligence/drafting sessions), but also to provide input into the document so that the company and its 'equity story' – which seeks to articulate the reasons for an investment and set reference points for valuation of the business – are appropriately presented. The underwriting banks will also want to carry out due diligence on the company to ensure that all relevant information has been included in the document and to ensure that the description in the document is accurate and not misleading.

Several other marketing materials will also be produced, principally presentations to analysts and potential investors. As in any other IPO, these will 'tell the story' of the IPO, but will need to be consistent with the prospectus.

The degree to which the private equity sponsor will have input into these documents will vary, but its involvement will tend towards oversight of the process and input into the presentation of the 'equity story', rather than specific input on the more detailed description of the business and IPO proposal, save to the extent that the materials relate to the private equity sponsor itself.

3. Debt structure post-IPO

Any private equity portfolio company that is considering an IPO exit is typically more heavily leveraged than entities coming to market from different backgrounds. Institutional investors have recently been looking closely at levels of leverage for IPO companies and will increasingly expect a significant reduction in levels of leverage on IPO. Accordingly, one of the key elements to successfully launching the IPO will be striking the balance between the application of proceeds to reduce debt to a level acceptable to public market investors, while allowing the private equity sponsor to realise enough on the IPO to make it worthwhile for it to proceed with the deal.

While the negotiation of any restructuring will take place early in the process of an IPO, it will typically be implemented immediately prior to the IPO. To the extent that proceeds from the IPO will be required to repay any debt, this will need to be disclosed fully in the listing document.

In conjunction with considering the leverage of the group post-IPO, the working capital position of the group post-IPO will also need to be considered. In addition to satisfying investors that the position of the group is sustainable, in the United Kingdom there is also a regulatory angle which must be considered, as any company seeking a premium listing on the London Stock Exchange must include a statement in the prospectus that it will have sufficient working capital for at least 12 months from the date of the IPO. The bank acting as the sponsor to the listing application will in turn be expected to give a working capital confirmation to the UKLA. For the purpose of this confirmation, the bank will require the company to prepare projections demonstrating a clean working capital position for 18 months from the listing, with sufficient headroom to allow comfort to be given by reporting accountants that sufficient working capital will be available to the group even in a 'reasonable worst-case' scenario.

Any leverage package will therefore need to be structured to allow the group sufficient headroom over the period.

In addition to looking at the level of leverage and the interaction with working capital, other aspects of the debt position of the group will need to be considered, including the need to re-set the debt covenants and recast them to reflect that the group will be listed post-IPO.

4. Liability issues for private equity sponsors

On any IPO, the underwriting banks will require an underwriting agreement between the issuer, the banks and the selling shareholders.

This underwriting agreement will lay down the terms of the agreement between the company, its principal shareholders and the underwriters of the IPO. It contains the respective obligations of the company to issue new shares, the shareholders to sell its shares and the underwriters to procure purchasers or subscribers for the shares or purchase or subscribe themselves. In consideration for these obligations on the underwriters (in addition to the agreed fee), the underwriters will require representations and warranties from the company, and the investor as selling shareholder, and may also require them from its directors. They will also require a full indemnity from the company and may also require indemnities from others.

While the direct liability of the private equity sponsor is likely to be limited relative to the company, the private equity sponsor will of course have indirect liability to the extent that it retains a stake in the company post-IPO. Due to that alignment with the company (and management), the private equity sponsor will often take an active interest in the negotiation of the obligations (eg, representations, warranties and indemnities) of the issuer under the underwriting agreement.

In relation to any liabilities as seller, the key for the private equity sponsor will be to avoid long tail liabilities which are inherently inconsistent with its fund structure, where generally proceeds are immediately passed on to the limited partners upon receipt – that is, proceeds received on a successful IPO exit will not be held by the private equity fund, but rather will be distributed to the limited partners to lock in any rate of return arising on the exit.

So what protections will private equity sponsors be prepared to provide to underwriters? Broadly speaking, the norm is that only a narrow range of warranties will be provided – limited to title, capacity and authority. Typically, private equity sponsors will also accept that they have to provide undertakings and warranties concerning compliance with selling restrictions and securities laws. These categories of representations and warranties and undertakings are relatively easy to negotiate and the private equity sponsor can generally get comfortable on the risk attaching to these potential liabilities, as they are broadly equivalent to what would be required on a trade sale or, in the case of compliance with selling restrictions/securities laws in connection with the IPO, are generally within the control of the private equity sponsor.

The difficult negotiations tend to relate to additional representations and warranties addressing matters concerning the accuracy of disclosure in the prospectus or the past relationship between the private equity sponsor and the issuer.

Where a private equity sponsor is selling as part of the IPO, the underwriting banks may also expect indemnities from the private equity sponsor. These indemnities are likely to be more limited than the indemnity to be provided by the company.

The starting point for many private equity sponsors will be that they do not give indemnities as they are inherently at odds with the structure of their fund. However, where an indemnity is narrowly drawn to cover, for example, simply breach of the warranties, this becomes a legal debate as to whether the breach of warranty should give rise to a contractual claim (which under English law would require the underwriting bank to mitigate any loss etc), as opposed to a right to claim for payment under the indemnity.

Where an indemnity is given, a private equity sponsor is likely to ask that the liability of the private equity sponsor under any warranties or indemnities (except potentially matters going to title to shares or where there has been any wilful default or fraud) be limited to its net-of-tax proceeds from the IPO.

Market practice on such indemnities varies considerably between jurisdictions.

5. Key commercial terms

In addition to the process-related decisions to be taken and the liability issues for the private equity sponsor, a number of commercial terms will need to be agreed during the process of the IPO. In many cases the issues are common between private equity and non-private equity IPOs.

5.1 Costs and expenses

The underwriting agreement will also deal with the allocation of costs and expenses to be reimbursed to the underwriters by the company and the private equity sponsor/selling shareholders, and with the payment of commissions by the company and the private equity sponsor/selling shareholders to the underwriters.

5.2 Lock-up

The underwriters will require the private equity sponsor (and each selling shareholder) to agree to enter into a lock-up agreement in relation to its retained stake, either as part of the underwriting agreement or in a separate agreement. The period of the lock-up tends to be one of the principal areas of negotiation, as its length is a very important issue to the private equity sponsor. If the private equity sponsor cannot achieve its full exit at the outset, it will want to know what its flexibility is either to distribute the shares in specie after the IPO to fund investors or to sell down in the market subsequently for cash. Of course, it will want to be free of the shackles of lock-up as soon as possible following the IPO.

Determination of the period will be a commercial decision. Typically, it ends up at 180 days or six months post admission of the shares, although lock-up periods of between six and 12 months have been seen. Less than six months is of limited value to the underwriters and over 12 months may be considered to fetter the private equity sponsor unduly.

In the usual way on any IPO, the lock-up is a broad prohibition on disposal of any part of the retained holding or transactions having an equivalent effect, including derivative transactions. Transfers for internal purposes may be permitted, as may transfers that are required post-IPO to complete any capital reorganisation or to settle obligations under the over-allotment option. These arrangements will be of significant importance to the investor community and accordingly will be disclosed in the prospectus/listing document.

The terms of the lock-up will also provide for potential waiver by the underwriters. Such a waiver may be granted if the share price has performed well and the underwriters believe that a disposal of further shares will not be adversely received by the market.

In addition to the lock-up, in some cases the underwriters may attempt to impose orderly marketing obligations on the investor for up to a further 12 months after expiry of the lock-up. Such obligations may require consultation with the underwriter prior to any disposal and involvement of the underwriter in the sale process. In some cases the underwriter may push for tranches of the investor's holding to be released for sale periodically. Such obligations would need to be considered in light of the circumstances of the particular IPO and the views of the underwriting banks as to what the market will require. There is no legal requirement for such provisions, however, and so the discussion is a purely commercial one.

An obligation may be placed on the company to assist with any subsequent sale of shares. This is because a prospectus may be required (if the sale involves a non-exempt offer) to facilitate the sale. This can be distinguished from the practice in the United States, where once a Securities and Exchange Commission registration has been established, the involvement of the company in any transfer of a significant number of shares will not be required.

5.3 Employee incentive schemes

As discussed above, any pre-IPO incentive schemes are likely to need to be restructured as part of the capital restructuring of the group immediately prior to IPO, and typically new post-IPO schemes will also be adopted. These post-IPO schemes will be in a form customary for a publicly listed company and acceptable to the market. Full disclosure of the schemes will be required in the prospectus.

The incentivisation schemes for private equity portfolio companies can, where valuations are at the higher end of expectations, be extremely remunerative for management teams. In drawing up the new post-IPO schemes, the private equity sponsor, together with the financial advisers, will need to strike a balance between rewarding and incentivising employees while not incurring criticism from institutional investors where such post-IPO schemes are viewed as unduly diluting the value of the investors' participation.

5.4 Relationship agreement

An important question will be the degree of influence that the private equity sponsor can exercise over the company once it is listed. With a substantial continuing stake in the listed entity, the private equity sponsor will want to treat the IPO event as an opportunity to realise gains, but will also want – as far as can be reconciled with the listed environment – to continue to manage the company in essentially the same way as it has historically been managing the company. There is often a natural conflict here with the regulatory requirements and market expectation on an IPO. For example, under the eligibility rules for a London premium listing, the company must be able to demonstrate that it is an independent company and that arrangements are in place to prevent abuse by any controlling shareholder of its controlling position. Public shareholders will also expect to be properly looked after and appropriate standards of corporate governance to be put in place. This inherent conflict is generally dealt with in the United Kingdom through a relationship agreement.

The core of that agreement will be a provision that requires the shareholder to allow the company to continue to operate independently and to ensure that dealings between the company and the shareholders will be on arm's-length terms.

However, relationship agreements are also used to grant the private equity sponsor certain rights in relation to the company post-IPO to provide it with a degree of control over the company. Such rights include board appointment rights for the private equity sponsor post-IPO and access rights to information post-IPO. It may also be the document under which the private equity sponsor seeks to secure additional commercial protections, such as the right to prevent any subsequent share issues (in order to prevent the private equity sponsor being diluted) and the level of involvement that the private equity sponsor can require from the company when the private equity sponsor looks to sell down its shares in a subsequent sale.

These rights are often contingent on a specified shareholding being maintained, with rights reducing if the shareholding drops below thresholds. For example, a private equity sponsor may have the right to nominate two directors if it holds more than 20% of the share capital, one director if it holds more than 10% of the share capital and no such nomination rights if the shareholding drops below 10%.

Any sharing of information with the private equity sponsor will need to be made subject to the company not breaching its continuing obligations, and the private equity sponsor will need to consider its position under insider dealing and market abuse rules to the extent that it receives material unpublished information under such a provision.

The other commercial term on the relationship agreement that is often raised is to whether the private equity sponsor will provide a non-compete undertaking as between it and the company. While such a provision is not uncommon (or necessarily resisted) where the significant shareholder is a trade investor, a private equity sponsor will typically be far more concerned not to have give such an undertaking. It is likely to place a higher value on having complete freedom to make such investments in whatever sector account it wishes, without restriction.

6. Pre-IPO investments

A common feature of private equity exit IPOs since 2008 has been investment by third parties in the group around the time of the IPO. Such investment can take a number of different forms, including simple equity, convertible bonds, high-yield bonds or hybrid securities. Such structures have advantages for investors, as they offer the upside of equity-like returns with downside protection through the debt-like qualities of the instruments.

The timing and rationale for such investments can also vary significantly – from the cornerstone investor shortly before the IPO which is effectively aligning itself with the private equity sponsor to the strategic investment alongside an IPO (but outside the formal IPO process). This latter situation has benefits for the group, as it may guarantee (conditional on the IPO succeeding) a portion of the total cash that must be raised and, as the investment is outside the IPO process, fees and commissions are not payable on any such amounts.

The pricing of such investments will obviously be critical, as while a discount may be offered, it will also need to be disclosed in the prospectus and may have an impact on the price that public market investors are prepared to pay.

In terms of issues to be managed, conflicts of interest are the most obvious – a private investor in one of these (private) placements might be looking to get substantially more access to management and underlying information; it might want to do its own due diligence, look at material contracts and have access to management. Public investors in the IPO, in contrast, will receive only the prospectus and the benefit of a road show presentation.

In circumstances where there is a pre-IPO investment, it will therefore be necessary to consider:

- how to defend that the IPO investors did not get less information than the private investor; and
- the implications for the private investor in respect of its ability subsequently to deal in the open market in the shares, once the issuer is listed.

7. Relevance of fund structure

As noted at the outset, this chapter assumes that a single portfolio company is being listed. However, it is possible to look at alternative structures where either the whole or part of the private equity fund is listed.

7.1 Private equity – whole fund listing

Although it has been done, the listing of the whole portfolio of a fund which was originally set up as a traditional closed-ended fixed life private equity fund is (and is likely to remain) an uncommon event. These funds are generally set up with the express intention of disposing of their assets (on a one-by-one basis, and with proceeds and liabilities strictly ringfenced among assets) and returning capital to investors over a fixed term.

While IPOs of individual fund assets are a long-established method of disposing of investments (and fund documents expressly provide that distributing listed and freely tradable stock post-IPO is a substitute for returning cash to investors), documents would require substantial amendment in order to produce a listing of the whole fund and most fund documents do not contemplate this approach.

The general expectation of private equity investors for receiving back their money within a fixed timeframe and some scepticism about the advantages of holding these types of assets for more than the medium term are likely to mean that the listing of whole funds remains unlikely.

7.2 Private equity funds – partial portfolio IPOs

While company-by-company IPOs are normal, they do not normally come with a manager attached or with the fees that accompany this structure. It is therefore likely that investors would need to perceive there to be some extra value out of buying a portfolio managed in this way. This may be the case (eg, the old 'country funds') where the investments are of such a specialist nature, either by sector or by geography, that the manager's expertise is seen to be a big value add, even in the case of a long-term hold.

8. Dual track process

It is possible for the potential IPO of a portfolio company to be run in conjunction with other exit routes. Running more than one process in parallel is often referred to as a dual track process. This typically involves the IPO process and a trade sale being run in parallel, but other exit routes (eg, strategic investments, refinancings with dividend extractions) can also be run in parallel, giving rise to triple track processes. It is also possible to lead effectively with one route (ie, an IPO) and, shortly before completion of the process, for the portfolio company to be effectively offered to private investors to determine whether a better and more certain price can be obtained.

Where the processes are run in parallel, the principal advantages of such structures is that they allows the private equity sponsor to maintain competitive tension in any M&A auction process as, irrespective of how competitive the auction is, the IPO will always act as an alternative which can be used by the private equity sponsor to create tension.

Conversely, alternatives to the IPO hedge the private equity sponsor's risk to volatile equity markets, meaning that the IPO cannot go ahead at the price that it is looking for.

There are also potential synergies, as a prospectus or listing document prepared for an IPO can be used as an effective disclosure document for the trade sale process (perhaps obviating the need for vendor due diligence or an information memorandum), and clearly any data room that is compiled is likely to be suitable for both processes.

The key discussions on the dual track process will be the extent to which the IPO documents have been finalised and the extent to which the private equity sponsor and/or management team are willing to stand behind and/or warrant the contents of the document.

To ensure that a genuine parallel process works effectively, a dovetailed timetable will need to be produced to ensure that documents are available at the appropriate stages of both tracks, to ensure that both remain viable. However, no matter how much planning goes into the timetable, the workload for the management team is likely to be significant, so the risk of insufficient time being spent on the day-to-day operation of the business is real.

In terms of advisers, the prevalence of dual and triple track processes has resulted in an increasing number of independent financial advisers being appointed by private equity sponsors. These advisers will be incentivised to achieve an exit, but crucially will not form part of the underwriting syndicate on the IPO.

A final point to note is that dual track processes can result in the IPO being viewed as a fall-back to a failed M&A process. Clearly, any such perception in the market will have a negative impact on price, and so the 'story' to investors will need to be managed carefully where the process involves more than one track. Similarly, the buy-in from financial advisers to a genuine dual-track will be required, as they will not wish to incur reputational damage with investors where they are perceived to be marketing an IPO that is never likely to occur (because a trade sale is the more likely result).

Financing issues on private equity exits

Stuart Brinkworth
Chris McLaughlin
Hogan Lovells International LLP

1. Introduction

For private equity sponsors, the issue of debt finance is of paramount importance and nearly always influences key decision-making processes, including the timing and structure of private equity transactions. The availability, size and cost of debt finance can have a direct impact on the ability of private equity sponsors to achieve successful exits by way of sale or of their portfolio companies to raise additional finance to recapitalise.

The events between 2007 and 2009 in particular made these issues more pronounced. The huge reduction in liquidity in the debt markets that began in Summer 2007, followed in 2008 by the worst banking crisis in modern history (epitomised by the collapse of Lehman Brothers and the Icelandic banks, together with the bail-out of several European banks) and in 2009 by the onset of the worst economic crisis since the Great Depression of the 1930s, created a unique 'perfect storm'. For leveraged finance, this perfect storm had a profound effect. According to data provider Thomson Reuters, leveraged loan issuance in Europe fell from a peak of $314.6 billion in the first half of 2007 (immediately before the credit crunch) to $35.5 billion in the first half of 2009 after Lehman Brothers collapsed. Unsurprisingly, this had a huge impact on deal activity within the private equity market. In 2009 UK exits fell to only 253, valued at just £2.5 billion. This followed the record number of 423 exits in 2007, valued at £24.1 billion, and 336 exits in 2008, valued at £9.9 billion (source: cmbor.com/Barclays Private Equity/Ernst & Young).

Although liquidity in the banking market improved from 2010 onwards (corresponding to an upswing in the number and value of private equity exits), the ability of potential purchasers to raise finance, the amount that can be raised and the nature and type of that finance have been and remain in a state of flux.

This chapter explores a number of financing issues which vendors may need to consider when planning an exit and also considers recapitalisations as an alternative means of generating a return on a private equity sponsor's investment prior to an exit.

2. Certain funds

Although a vendor may not necessarily concern itself *per se* with how a prospective purchaser is going to fund the acquisition of the business asset that it is selling (so long as the purchaser can complete the purchase as soon as possible after becoming the preferred bidder), where that purchaser is going to use some form of debt finance, the vendor should be concerned with how likely it is that the proceeds of that debt finance will actually be available to complete the acquisition – a concept commonly known as 'certain funds'.

There are two aspects for the vendor to consider here. First, has the purchaser secured a commitment from its lenders to provide finance to assist it in making the acquisition? The answer to this lies in the nature of the financing documentation delivered by the purchaser to the vendor as part of the bid process (the so-called 'commitment or bid pack'). Second, how watertight is that funding commitment – what else does the purchaser need to deliver to the lenders and just how easy would it be for those lenders to refuse to lend at closing? The answer to this question depends on the exact wording within the debt documentation itself.

2.1 Background to certain funds

The practice and concept of certain funds are derived from public market acquisitions. For example, in the United Kingdom, under General Principle 5 of the City Code on Takeovers and Mergers, a bidder making an offer for a public company listed on the London Stock Exchange where cash forms at least part of the consideration for that offer will be required to show that it "can fulfil in full any cash consideration". This is underpinned by Rule 24.7 of the code, which requires a bidder's financial adviser to confirm that the bidder has sufficient cash resources available to it to meet this requirement.

In the context of loan documentation for the acquisition of a public company, this effectively means that:

- all of the financing documentation must be signed and effective at the point when the offer is announced;
- all of the conditions precedent to signing must have been satisfied;
- all of the conditions for drawdown must have been satisfied as of the date of announcement or, to the extent that they remain outstanding, must be wholly within the bidder's control to deliver; and
- during the period between the offer being announced and the date on which the debt facilities will be required to be drawn, the ability of the lenders to refuse to lend must be kept to a limited set of circumstances (see below for a more detailed discussion).

Although the code does not apply to private M&A transactions, the principle of a purchaser having to demonstrate its ability to fulfil cash consideration when submitting a final bid for a private business is one which has become market practice among private equity vendors. Commentary on this subject tends to focus solely on what conditionality is contained in a loan agreement for the drawdown of funds. However, before even getting to that stage, consideration must be given to the nature and level of the commitment in the first place. Accordingly, 'certain funds' is a point for consideration from the submission of final bids through to the drawing of funds under a loan agreement.

Before Summer 2007, at the peak of the last cycle of the private equity market, certain funds became a key consideration, particularly in auction processes.

Competition between potential buyers of businesses and between lenders competing to lend to those purchasers during that period fuelled a drive:

- on the part of sellers, to eliminate both lending risk (the risk of lenders refusing to lend to bidders) and execution risk (the risk of the loan documentation process holding up the sale process or causing it to fail); and
- on the part of bidders, to make their bids as compelling as possible as a means of distinguishing themselves from other bidders on grounds other than price.

These dynamics resulted in the emergence of new techniques, such as the use of interim loan agreements (discussed below), as a certain funds tool.

2.2 Commitment aspect of certain funds in the bidding process

As mentioned above, a key issue in any sale process is the level of funding commitment that is delivered by the bidders when final bids are submitted. The vendor's advisers will not always prescribe a particular form of funding commitment in the invitation to submit final bids and, even when they do, bidders may see this as a minimum and not an absolute requirement. Notwithstanding the inconsistency in process, in practice it should always be a requirement of private equity vendors that sources of external finance be subject to certain funds. The problem for both vendors and bidders is that 'certain funds' has no single meaning. Given that certain funds in a private M&A context is not subject to any regulatory regime, and in particular because there is no cash confirmation process (unlike with offers for public companies), certain funds can come in all different shapes and sizes. However, generically, there are three different levels of financing commitment.

(a) The unfundable certain funds bid (aka 'uncertain funds')

We have named this type of certain funds as 'unfundable' simply because at the time of the bid, the bidder has not signed a loan agreement or entered into any other documentation under which funds can be drawn. Instead, the bidder simply delivers a commitment letter signed by its lenders, together with a term sheet (which is often short form), showing the terms that have been agreed between the parties. Therefore, the bid is subject to the bidder and its lenders agreeing the final terms of, and entering into all of the financing documentation required for, that bid.

This type of bid is extremely common in smaller mid-market deals, where bidders (and indeed their lenders) do not want to spend huge amounts of time or incur large upfront costs negotiating lengthy term sheets or interim loan agreements (and want to keep abort costs to a minimum should the bid ultimately prove unsuccessful).

This type of bid demonstrates that the bidder has reached agreement in principle with its lenders for the required debt finance for its bid, but has not reached an agreement on documentation. This is really the minimum that a vendor should expect to be delivered to demonstrate that the bidder will be able to fund the acquisition.

When reviewing this type of arrangement, the vendor should ensure that the commitment letter contains confirmation from the lenders that they have final credit approval for the facilities and have satisfied all of their due diligence requirements in relation to the bid (eg, financial, legal and commercial due diligence). The sole level of conditionality to providing that finance should be the entering into of loan documentation based on the term sheet which is attached to the commitment letter when the bid is submitted (and, of course, satisfaction of all conditions precedent to the availability of the facilities).

This type of bid scores extremely low on the certain funds scale and, in reality, it is difficult to describe this as certain funds. This type of bid carries with it a high level of execution risk and will almost certainly result in a delay of weeks before the parties are ready to exchange contracts on the sale and purchase agreement, because final financing will not be available until full documentation has been negotiated and exchanged between the bidder and its lenders.

The degree to which the term sheet contains an upfront agreement on all terms incorporated into the financing package varies enormously. Generally speaking, the longer and more detailed the term sheet, the more comfortable that the vendor can be as to the purchaser's execution risk to which it is exposed, but this is not always the case.

(b) *The fundable certain funds bid*

While the unfundable certain funds bid has obvious cost and time advantages pre-bid, the funding and execution risks associated with it post-bid led to the development of fundable bids which included 'fundable commitment letters' or 'interim financing arrangements' (IFAs).

Put simply, a fundable commitment letter is a commitment letter attaching a (usually detailed) term sheet, which binds the lenders to lend the facilities on the basis of those short-form terms, even if full finance documents are not signed by the closing date.

On the other hand, IFAs are structured so that, in addition to a commitment letter and term sheet delivered as part of a final bid, the bidder delivers an interim loan agreement, which is capable of immediate execution and (subject to satisfaction of limited conditions precedent) drawing. With the arrival of IFAs, fundable commitment letters have all but disappeared from the market, particularly given the advantage to drawing against a definitive loan agreement.

The interim loan agreement fulfils two purposes:

- It acts as a form of bridge finance, in that it allows the preferred bidder to fund the debt element of its bid before the full loan documentation is entered into; and
- It acts as a documentation bridge, meaning that the vendor does not have to worry about whether the preferred bidder can enter into full documentation before the planned closing date or the impact that the full documentation process will have on the timetable, as the preferred bidder can close and fund under the IFA. Bidders also like this option because it frees up valuable time to enable them to focus on the due diligence for and terms of the acquisition.

As a result, this type of bid scores high on the certain funds scale. This notwithstanding, IFAs are not used exclusively in all areas of the leveraged market;

they are most commonly used in much larger deals, particularly where some underwriting aspect is involved. They are less common in mid-market deals due to the limited availability of finance below €30 million of earnings before interest, taxes, depreciation and amortisation (EBITDA), and are almost never used at the smaller end where sponsors do not want to incur the costs involved.

The interim loan agreement is similar to a bridging agreement. There are no financial covenants and, where drawn, it is repayable within a short timeframe (usually 30 days – see further below). However, an interim loan agreement differs from a bridge agreement in the events of default, representations and warranties, and positive and negative undertakings. As the interim loan agreement is very much a certain funds tool, it usually contains only those events of default, representations and warranties, and positive and negative undertakings which would constitute a certain funds drawstop under a full loan agreement (see section 2.3). A bridge agreement, on the other hand, often contains those provisions seen in a full loan agreement.

Although the interim loan agreement is legally capable of being drawn, it is almost always the intention between the purchaser and its lenders that the full loan agreement be entered into prior to closing, and that funding take place under that agreement rather than the interim loan agreement. A statement to this effect is usually contained within the commitment letter and is the basis on which lenders become comfortable offering an interim loan agreement in the first place. It is also because of this that lenders will rarely offer an IFA on a deal that will have no gap between signing and closing, as it would almost certainly mean funding under an interim loan agreement rather than under the full loan agreement (which, given the limited events of default, representations and warranties, and positive and negative undertakings, lenders are naturally reluctant to do).

Notwithstanding a lender's strong preference to fund under the full loan agreement, occasionally funding does occur under the interim loan agreement where, for instance, the full loan agreement has not been finalised before the closing date because conditions to completion under the sale and purchase agreement have been complied with earlier than anticipated (eg, antitrust clearance). Where the interim loan agreement is drawn under, there will usually be a requirement to repay that loan within 30 days of it being drawn (ie, with a drawing under the full loan agreement).

When examining an IFA that has been submitted as part of a bid, the vendor should be concerned with the same issues as referred to above (ie, whether the lenders have confirmed in the commitment letter that they have received full credit approval and satisfied all of their due diligence requirements). In addition, the vendor should ensure that the commitment cannot terminate if the preferred bidder does not enter into the long-form loan agreement before the intended closing date. The commitment letter will usually express this as an intention of the parties, but with no consequence if it fails to materialise (the lenders will rely on the fact that the purchaser will have to refinance amounts drawn under the interim loan agreement within 30 days of drawing and therefore will have to enter into a full loan agreement by that date). Finally, the vendor needs to ensure that any backstop date for the commitment (after which the preferred bidder loses its right to require the lenders to enter into the interim loan agreement) is far enough away to enable the transaction to complete on its intended timetable, preferably with some room for manoeuvre.

Generally, the term sheet submitted along with this type of bid is more detailed than that submitted with an unfundable bid. This is driven from both a lender's and a bidder's perspective to ensure more certainty and efficiency in the outcome of the final documentation process, given that each will be locked in once the bid is submitted. However, so long as the interim loan agreement is structured such that it is fully available, the vendor need not concern itself with how developed terms are between the bidder and its banks, since it is the commitment and interim loan agreement which provide the comfort on certain funds.

(c) The fundable fully documented certain funds bid

The final form of certain funds bid, which has become more common since the credit crunch but still remains an exception, is for a bidder to submit its bid with fully negotiated long-form loan documentation rather than an interim facilities agreement. The bid pack will either comprise a commitment letter with the loan agreement attached or include a copy of the executed loan agreement itself.

This trend has arisen as bidders, in increasingly competitive auction processes largely brought on by the shortage of quality business assets being sold, have sought to gain competitive advantages over other bidders. While on the face of it this approach eliminates all of the execution risk from a transaction (given that there are no outstanding documents to be agreed in the post-bid process), it significantly increases abort costs for bidders, since they will have incurred almost all of the costs and expenses involved in obtaining debt finance for the deal before becoming the preferred bidder (including negotiating any mezzanine or other subordinated funding documents and any intercreditor agreements, and agreeing the forms of all conditions precedent).

Market participants have questioned whether, from a vendor's perspective, anything is to be gained from this approach over a bid which includes an IFA. With an IFA, the bidder can still demonstrate fully available funds to complete the purchase from the vendor, and on that basis it is difficult to see how this style of bid scores any higher on the certain funds scale. Banks are also reluctant to go down this route (particularly if they are not offered an abort fee), as it means committing a great deal of time and resources to a bid that has only a partial chance of success.

That said, those that have adopted this route have pointed to it as a differentiating factor often adopted by bidders that have made up their mind at an early stage of a process that they want to be viewed as the leading bidder and to demonstrate how serious they are about completing the purchase. It is also viewed as the primary means of counteracting the risk of an all-equity bid from a rival bidder (as it gives the same low level of execution risk as an all-equity bid) or as necessary if attempting to pre-empt an auction process. However, although this approach has a certain commercial rationale, the advantages from a certain funds perspective are grounded more in (vendor) perception than reality (giving the impression of a greater and ultimate level of certainty of funding that actually perhaps does not exist). Of course, this approach still does not guarantee success on a bid where, for instance, the bidder is not the highest bidder (see section 2.4).

2.3 Conditionality of the finance

As explained at the beginning of this section, once the level of commitment has been gauged, it is important for the vendor to explore how watertight that funding commitment is (ie, whether the conditionality is contained in a term sheet or whether it has been incorporated in a fundable commitment letter, IFA or a full-length loan agreement). This is because ultimately the certainty of funding comes down to the ability of the lenders to refuse to lend. It is this aspect which is traditionally referred to as 'certain funds' and falls into two categories – drawstop events and conditions precedent to drawdown.

Drawstop events (ie, a limited set of circumstances in which lenders can refuse to lend) should apply only where there is a gap between exchange and completion, and where there is no financing condition under the sale and purchase agreement. Where there is a financing condition, lenders are reluctant to grant certain funds (since the purchaser has an out if financing is not made available on or before the closing date). However, where the purchaser retains any liability for failing to meet its financing condition, it will insist on certain funds language being included in the financing documentation.

Only limited representations and warranties, undertakings and events of default in the financing documentation (whether an interim or full-length loan agreement) should be capable of enabling the lenders to refuse to lend the acquisition debt at closing. Generally, these include:

- occurrences of certain events of default (generally, non-payment, insolvency, unlawfulness and invalidity, cessation of business, expropriation and repudiation);
- breaches of certain 'major' restrictive undertakings (including restriction on mergers, negative pledge, disposals, indebtedness and loans and guarantees); and
- breaches of certain major representations and warranties (usually limited to status, binding obligations, non-conflict, power and authority, and validity and admissibility in evidence).

In addition, the lenders will usually be entitled to refuse to lend where there has been a change of control of the bidder's acquisition vehicle or a termination event under the sale and purchase agreement, or where it is unlawful for a lender to lend.

From the vendor's perspective, it is essential to ensure that all of these drawstops apply only to the preferred bidder (or rather, its bidco group) and not to the target group. In saying that, it is becoming more common for lenders also to include as a drawstop event the insolvency of any member of the target group. If a term sheet or IFA is to be replaced with a full financing package before closing, the vendor should also ensure that the full loan documentation contains certain funds provisions which match (or at least are no less certain than) those contained in the term sheet or IFA. Vendors often overlook this as the focus on certain funds tends to end once a preferred bidder has been selected. The level of conditionality must always remain the same from final bid to drawing of funds.

As regards conditions precedent, the essential test is whether all of the conditions precedent are either satisfied or wholly within the control of the preferred bidder. One of the key areas of concern for both bidders and the vendor is to keep the conditions precedent to drawing at a minimum. Because of this, matters such as taking security over the business assets being sold (particularly where multiple jurisdictions are involved) are usually pushed back to conditions subsequent, leaving the financing relatively clean from onerous conditionality.

Often, the bidder will require its lenders to deliver a form of conditions precedent satisfaction letter, which will confirm that all conditions precedent to the signing of the interim loan agreement have been met and that the documentary conditions precedent to the drawing of the interim loan are in agreed form. This letter is usually addressed to the bidder only, but will be capable of disclosure to the vendor on a non-reliance basis.

2.4 Certain funds in context

Given the variety of approaches to certain funds, the reality for vendors is that the degree of certainty of funding either offered or required differs from deal to deal and is really a function of a number of factors.

For instance, if a seller is selling to a single purchaser in an off-market transaction or finds that an auction process has not generated the level of competition that it had hoped for, certainty of funding may not be of primary concern (eg, compared to achieving a successful sale regardless or achieving the price that it is looking for, even if it means a more uncertain process).

Even when a seller has been able to run a competitive process, pragmatically it may take the view that it accepts a bid, for example, based on a commitment letter and term sheet over a bid which is based on a fully agreed loan agreement because the bid price of the former is higher. In reality, there is no golden rule and much depends on the vendor's overall feel for the credibility, deliverability and assumed risk of a particular bid, of which certain funds is only one consideration.

Ultimately, certainty of funds may really become an issue only where two or more bids are hard to differentiate between on value (and perhaps other terms), meaning that the vendor will then look at which is the more deliverable from a financing and execution perspective as a means of differentiating between them. This creates a real quandary for bidders, since the differentiating nature of certain funds can be viewed as mainly retrospective, so the decision as to what level of certain funds to submit with a bid can be a tough one.

The type of debt product being used may also be a factor. For example, in the case of high-yield bonds, which have to date dominated the larger end of the private equity market post-credit crunch, achieving certainty of funding may be more problematic than bank debt. This is because few sponsors are willing to take on bond market risk by entering into bridge-to-bond financing for acquisitions which could form part of certainty of funding on a bid. Where the vendor is in a strong position (due to a competitive process), it may be able to take this risk out of a transaction by requiring the purchaser to fund the acquisition price in an all-equity deal (therefore pushing the risk of debt financing wholly onto the purchaser) – although the larger the transaction, the more difficult this becomes.

However, where there is a sole purchaser for whatever reason, it is highly unlikely that the purchaser itself will be prepared to take bond market risk. In these circumstances the vendor may have to either enter into a long exclusivity process to enable the bond process to reach conclusion or enter into a sale and purchase agreement that has some form of bond financing condition. Alternatively, the vendor may find a way of bridging the divide itself (eg, by agreeing a vendor loan note that is repayable from the proceeds of a high-yield bond). All of these scenarios create a great deal of certainty of funding and execution risk for the vendor, particularly if:

- the issuer of the high-yield bond (the holding company of the business asset being sold) would be a debut issuer in that sector;
- the business asset itself is not a well-known business; or
- there are signs that appetite in the high-yield bond markets may be softening.

Therefore, it is clear that certainty of funds is a key consideration for a vendor, but not the only consideration and not the main consideration in all circumstances.

3. Staple finance

3.1 Staple finance explained

One way in which a vendor can reduce the risk of certainty of funding for an exit is to put in place a 'stapled' finance package. 'Staple financing' in the context of private equity transactions refers to a pre-arranged financing package put together by the vendor and its financial advisers, which can be used by the preferred bidder to fund the debt element of its purchase of the business asset being sold. The term derives from the practice of 'stapling' the financing terms on offer to the information memorandum or other materials being used to solicit bids for the business asset being sold.

The principal advantage of staple financing from the vendor's perspective is that it ensures the availability of debt financing for all available bidders, which should create a more competitive auction process and increase the chance of achieving the best possible sale price. The financing terms on offer can take the form of a commitment letter and short-form terms, a full-length term sheet or even a fully documented loan agreement.

3.2 When is a staple a staple?

Similar to certain funds, 'staple financing' is often a term used loosely to describe a variety of situations. Generally speaking, there are two forms of staple.

(a) The 'hard' staple

A 'hard' staple refers to an arrangement where one or more staple banks have agreed detailed terms with the seller and issued a credit-approved commitment letter capable of being accepted by the preferred bidder, subject only to documentation. While a hard staple would most likely be the preference for a vendor (given the certainty of funding that it offers for potential bidders), they are not that common, for the following reasons:

- Most bidders will view a staple as a starting point for negotiations rather than an end product. They are often aimed at the lowest common denominator and therefore can often be beaten in terms of quantum, price or other terms. At the height of the pre-credit crunch market, when debt was freely available and competition for banking mandates fierce, hard staples were rarely taken up because they just could not compete with the market. Indeed, banks would do everything that they could to avoid being a staple bank, as it was a sure way of not winning the lead arranger mandate on a deal.
- Sponsors prefer to work with their existing banking relationships and will not want to have new lenders forced upon them. Larger sponsors generally also work with their own 'house' banking terms and so will be reluctant to accept an arrangement that deviates materially from those terms.
- In truth, banks feel a great deal of antipathy towards hard staples. They force a bank to commit huge internal resources right at the start of a process where there is no certainty of outcome. Moreover, the banks may have to create several 'trees' internally so that the bank can speak to multiple bidders, each in isolation from the other. In the post-credit crunch world, where banks have slimmed-down leveraged finance teams, resources can become stretched quite quickly – and all for a deal that may not reach completion and a financing proposal that the banks know has a relatively small chance of being utilised.
- Banks will not want to commit funds to an unidentified preferred bidder. It is often said that hard staples provide a potential bidder with debt that it would otherwise have been unable to raise – banks take the view that there is probably a reason for that and they will want to be happy with the identity of the preferred bidder that they are backing.

Notwithstanding the above, hard staples are achievable. In areas of the market where there is a limited availability of financing (eg, for deals where EBITDA is below €30 million), the lack of competition for debt will increase the likelihood of a hard staple being taken up, particularly with business assets in sectors that are not attractive to all lenders (eg, media, retail and healthcare).

(b) The 'soft' staple

A 'soft' staple represents a much broader set of arrangements and reflects, in practice, any set of circumstances that is not considered to be a hard staple. Here, the staple banks have met with management, reviewed a draft information memorandum, perhaps reviewed vendor due diligence (where available) and extracts from the operating financial model of the business and, based on that, expressed a view to the vendor as to the likely quantum and pricing that they are willing to offer. The banks will also be willing to express a 'house' view on quantum, pricing and terms to potential bidders; but, unlike with a hard staple, will make no firm commitment to lend. Any offer of financing will be indicative only and will almost certainly be subject to final credit approval and the identity of the preferred bidder. The banks also will not establish trees until the final stages of the bidding process (when there are fewer bidders to deal with).

The soft staple differs from the hard staple in that it is more of a process than a product and has several advantages:

- From the vendor's perspective, it brings some degree of comfort as to the availability of debt finance and a successful outcome to the auction process;
- It enables the vendor to gauge an early indication of an achievable price (based on likely debt-to-equity ratios);
- The early-stage engagement between banks and management and the availability of financial information and vendor due diligence can flush out potential credit issues at an early stage, giving the vendor the best possible chance of resolving those issues before the end of the auction process or at least ensuring that the bidders are bidding on the best possible information;
- Banks do not have to commit huge resources at the start of the process and can wait until the final-round bidders have been identified before forming internal trees and choose to support only those bidders that they wish to support;
- Because the soft staple process runs from pre-bid to final bid (compared to a hard staple which is all but finished before initial bids are submitted), and because of the gradual nature of the process itself, it is much easier for bidders to introduce their own lending relationships into the process; and
- The longer gradual process also means that it is easier for bidders to structure their own debt packages, based on their own house terms, based on their business plan for that business asset, rather than accepting a generic staple deal that, in trying to appeal to everyone, ultimately appeals to no one.

It is because of these reasons that soft staples are invariably taken up.

Whether participating in hard or soft staples, vendors should be aware of the dangers of exclusive financing arrangements. It is not uncommon for arrangers of staple financing to attempt to block lenders on the staple from providing finance to bidders outside the staple. This is usually effected through the confidentiality letters that lenders are often asked to sign to gain access to the relevant information when considering whether to participate in a staple. While lenders themselves will often pick on such provisions (and almost certainly ask them to be removed), the vendor itself should ensure that its advisers are not attempting to provide for a staple on an exclusive basis, since there is nothing to be gained overall by a vendor seeking to restrict the availability of debt finance in relation to a bid for one of its assets, particularly when liquidity restrictions still affect the market.

3.3 Roll-through financing as a staple alternative

Although not strictly a form of staple financing, one practice which has arisen as a direct consequence of the credit crunch is the roll-through of existing debt by a purchaser. Here, rather than arranging new debt finance for the purchase of a business, the purchaser persuades the existing lenders to waive their right to repayment, which usually arises on a change of control, and continue with the current financing arrangements (which are usually those put in place by the vendor when it originally acquired the business).

Lenders will typically agree to this type of arrangement where the target business is not highly leveraged (so recently recapitalised businesses are not that suited to a roll-through), and where the leverage on a future refinancing would be greater (and certainly not less) than the current leverage of debt in the business (meaning that the roll-though lenders are not taking refinancing risk). These types of arrangement are typically quite short term in nature, with the lenders usually only waiving their change of control pre-payment right for up to six months.

The roll-through lenders will usually charge the purchaser a fee for the roll-through, with a portion of that fee being redeemable against any future fees payable to the roll-through lenders should they participate in any subsequent refinancing of the business (thereby incentivising the purchaser to refinance with the roll-through lenders). The roll-through lenders may also charge an increased margin for the roll-through period and will also want to be comfortable with the identity of the purchaser, although this is often more of a consideration on the refinancing rather than on the roll-through itself.

From the vendor's perspective, this type of arrangement is a neat alternative to staple financing. There are usually no vendor cost implications (since any costs are picked up by the purchaser), and the time and effort saved in dealing with potential staple banks are considerable. It is also a neat solution to any certain funds issues that may arise on the sale process and usually a consent letter from the roll-though lenders is all that is required from a documentation process. Notwithstanding its clear advantages, the roll-through is certainly not the market norm and it remains far more common for lenders to be repaid on a change of control. Nonetheless, the possibility of a roll-through is one aspect that a vendor should consider when looking at a potential purchaser's viable debt options.

4. Vendor financings

The capital structure of an acquisition is not always solely a matter for the purchaser. When financing is scarce or there is a disparity between the vendor's and purchaser's price expectations, pressure to come up with innovative financing solutions is shared equally between vendors and purchasers.

The lack of available bank debt for leveraged buy-outs in 2009 and 2010 meant that there was often a disparity between the price that a vendor expected to achieve and that which the purchaser was prepared or able to pay. As banks restricted themselves to conservative leverage multiples, private equity sponsors were forced to increase their equity cheques to bridge the gap between bank debt and vendor expectations. However, purchasers were prepared to go that extra mile only if the vendor was prepared to go with them. In the market turmoil that followed the global financial crisis, vendors of all asset classes were being told that deals could be carried out only if they were prepared to accept significant deferred consideration or provide a vendor loan into the acquisition structure. While this has obvious drawbacks for a vendor looking to exit an investment, these must be weighed against an improved offer price and possible tax efficiencies.

A distinction should always be made between deferred consideration and a vendor loan note. Deferred consideration is likely to be an unsecured short-term liability of the purchaser, which may or may not be subject to performance criteria of the target company. Although a liability of the purchaser, it is unlikely to be hardwired into the capital structure and bank lenders would expect it to be settled in full within a relatively short timeframe post-completion of the acquisition. Alternatively, a vendor loan is likely to form part of the ongoing capital structure for the life of the investment (or until its redemption) and occupy the space between bank debt and investor equity.

The bank lenders to an acquisition will wish to see any vendor financing treated as equity: from their standpoint, it should be unsecured, fully subordinated under an intercreditor agreement, have no cash pay element and be repaid only upon an exit. However, the larger the vendor contribution to the capital structure, the more likely it is that the vendor will ask for some protections similar to those afforded to the bank debt. Therefore, it is not uncommon to find a vendor loan note which shares in the bank security (but participates in recoveries only following a payment in full of the bank debt) and receives a cash coupon subject to a bank's right to turn this off on occurrence of a default, akin to a 'mezzanine payment stop'.

A vendor's appetite for a vendor loan will depend on how eager it is to sell the relevant business and how willing it is to assume a debt position. It is no coincidence that the most common providers of vendor financing in recent times have been financial institutions seeking to dispose of 'non-core' operations. Throughout 2009 and early 2010, banks were keen to raise capital and shift non-core assets. The vendor loan was an indispensable tool to assist in shifting unloved assets for the best price possible. Vendor loans are also common in management buy-outs at the smaller end of the deal spectrum, where access to bank finance can be difficult.

It is fair to say that a vendor loan holds considerably less attraction to most private equity sellers. A private equity seller will normally want to exit an investment completely and return funds to its investors. The longer that it remains tied into an investment, the more likely that its rate of return will suffer, so it will be very reluctant to offer vendor financing as part of a disposal. If there is a significant funding gap, the seller is much more likely to look to management to bridge that gap or to roll over some of its existing equity into the new investment and continue to participate as a traditional private equity player.

Many of the large private equity players have established significant debt funds in recent years and it is not impossible that certain funds could choose to use this capability to assist in exiting deals where finance is proving hard to find.

5. Issues around IPO exits

5.1 Overview of IPO exits

There was considerable expectation at the start of 2011 that the public equity markets would provide opportunities for private equity firms to exit maturing investments. Everyone had been there before. At the start of 2010, although debt for leveraged buy-outs was still proving difficult to come by, the equity markets had made excellent progress from the lows of 2008. Advisers had been appointed and private equity investors were confident that certain of the better-known investments could avail of the equity rally. However, by early summer, many of these hotly tipped initial public offering (IPO) candidates (including New Look, Travelport and Merlin) had withdrawn from the process.

Although IPOs are certainly the most high profile of private equity exits, they remain less common than a trade sale or, in the United Kingdom at least, a secondary buy-out. An IPO tends to be an option for larger investments with a recognisable profile. The equity markets have viewed certain recent IPO candidates with scepticism, emphasising that they are not to be seen as a dumping ground for pre-credit crunch vintage leveraged buy-outs. Nevertheless, there has been an increasing number of success stories (eg, Amadeus, HCA, Pandora and AZ Electronic Materials), which suggests that the equity markets are willing to back private equity-led IPOs. Preqin, the market information provider, has reported that 17% of global private equity exits in 2010 came from IPOs. This number surpasses pre-credit crunch levels, with an increase of 12% on 2006 and 29% on 2007.

IPOs undoubtedly provide an opportunity to private equity funds to deliver existing investments. However, they may not allow for the complete exit preferred by private equity. Equity investors want to know that the private equity investor continues to have 'skin in the game'; therefore, they will be expected to retain a significant stake in the business post-IPO. This partial exit, combined with the huge costs, additional reporting and fiduciary duties post-IPO, means that private equity funds may continue with a sale process during preparation for an IPO. The sale process can provide a fallback should the equity markets prove unresponsive; while the potential listing price can serve to maintain price tension with potential purchasers. Some recent studies have speculated that companies acquired after filing for an IPO command a higher sale price.

Any company which completes a listing should emerge with a considerably healthier balance sheet. The company's debt documentation may require its original leveraged buy-out facilities to be repaid in full with the proceeds of the listing; however, it is very common for these pre-payment provisions to be subject to a descending ratchet, depending on the leverage of the company post-IPO. In such circumstances the company may need to pre-pay only a percentage of listing proceeds, with the remaining proceeds available for the general corporate purposes of the group. In reality, the newly de-levered group is unlikely to maintain its leveraged buy-out financing and will seek financing terms which better reflect its new credit rating. The company has the choice of securing new financing or negotiating revised terms with its existing lenders. However, certain companies will benefit from 'qualifying IPO' provisions in their leveraged buy-out debt documentation which pre-approve revised debt terms on completion of a listing.

5.2 Concept of a 'qualifying IPO'

Essentially, a 'qualifying IPO' is a partial exit by way of an IPO that does not trigger a change of control, but triggers a change in the financing terms. This type of provision, which is rarely seen in mid-market transactions, has become increasingly common at the larger end of the market. Post-IPO, the financial sponsor should continue to hold at least 30% of the ordinary share capital of the company (although this number can vary between 25% and 35%, depending on the jurisdiction of incorporation and/or listing), down from the usual 50%. The result of a qualifying IPO is to move from a leveraged facility agreement to something closer to an investment-grade facility agreement. Therefore, it is key that the IPO has sufficiently de-risked the group, which is usually determined by a post-IPO leverage test.

A typical qualifying IPO clause will give effect to many of the following amendments – although the number and extent of the amendments will depend on quite how 'investment grade' the company really is:

- Margin – the margin will be reduced to levels which better reflect the new profile of the company.
- Financial covenants – these are likely to be restricted to just a leverage and interest cover covenant, and may well be set at a single level from the date of the IPO.
- Information covenants – the requirement to provide monthly facilities and annual budgets may be removed.
- Disapplication of certain covenants – private equity sponsors will often seek to disapply restrictions on mergers, holding company activities, treasury transactions, cash management and bank accounts, and obligor to non-obligor transactions.
- Increase of baskets – private equity sponsors will typically ask for a doubling of any annual or over-the-life permission baskets, with particular focus on permitted acquisitions, permitted disposals, permitted financial indebtedness, permitted guarantees, permitted joint ventures and permitted loans.
- Dividends – both the private equity sponsor and investors will expect greater flexibility on dividends, and it is common to see dividends permitted subject to an annual limit or leverage ratio.
- Security and guarantees – the sponsor may request that security over the operating assets be released and the lenders rely solely on share pledges.

The great advantage of these provisions is that the company need not incur the cost of arranging new post-IPO facilities or the delay and difficulty of seeking the leveraged syndicate's consent to wholesale changes to the banking documentation. Typically, decisions on release of security would be a 'super-majority lender' (somewhere between 80% to 90%) decision and any reduction in margin or waiver of a mandatory pre-payment would be expected to require unanimous lender consent. Therefore, on large syndicates, the presence of a qualifying IPO clause can save significant time and money. Furthermore, even if not a long-term solution, the revised facilities can buy the company time to complete the IPO before it seeks more attractive financial terms once it has bedded into its new post-IPO environment.

Without these provisions, the company is likely to require the consent of all lenders to move its financing terms closer to investment grade. If there is a particularly large syndicate of lenders, this can prove challenging. Given the broad range of institutions which now invest in the secondary leveraged market, there may not be a 'one size fits all' approach to seeking lender consent. Certain lenders may be focused on credit risk and others on their investment rate of return. In order to avoid a situation where a minority lender has a veto over the company's request, most large leveraged finance facilities of the 2005 to 2007 vintage contain a 'yank the bank' provision, which allows sponsors to replace non-consenting lenders on certain key votes. Ideally, the 'yank the bank' provision would apply to all lender decisions only where the vast majority of other lenders had already provided their consent. This level tends to be around 80% to 90% of lenders' participations, but can be set lower. Sponsors can then arrange for the non-consenting lender to transfer its participation at par to another more supportive lender. This mechanism often favours arrangers and key relationship banks, as they can provide a backstop facility to replace any dissenting lenders.

6. Recapitalisations

All of the above scenarios envisage some form of exit by the vendor. However, an exit may not always be a viable option for a private equity owner due to market conditions (ie, a more conservative exit environment); or indeed it may not wish to exit the business at that time where, for instance, it feels that expected future growth may provide a better exit opportunity at a later date. Historically, in this situation private equity owners have been able to consider a recapitalisation of that business asset as an alternative to a full exit.

6.1 What is a recapitalisation?

In private equity terms, a recapitalisation (often referred to as a dividend recapitalisation or leveraged recapitalisation) is a way of extracting value from a business without having to exit formally that business. It is achieved by replacing equity value with additional leverage, meaning that the shareholdings arrangements generally remain untouched. Recapitalisations differ from refinancings in that in the latter, while the business is re-leveraged to the same extent, there is no 'cash out' to the equity holders.

From a private equity owner's perspective, a recapitalisation is a means of delivering cash proceeds to limited partners in much the same way as an exit. It also has the advantage of de-risking the private equity investment (as a return has already been achieved) at a time when a formal exit is not viable. Unlike an exit, a recapitalisation has the added advantage of not only delivering a return, but also extending the exit horizon at the same time. In this regard, a recapitalisation can increase the overall return on a business asset, as the proceeds on a recapitalisation and subsequent sale can often exceed the value obtained through a pure sale.

Recapitalisations generally occur where the business asset has de-leveraged through repayment of the acquisition finance used to acquire it by scheduled amortisation and voluntary and mandatory pre-payment (ie, via the operation of a cash sweep), and where the business asset has itself increased in value through a growth in EBITDA and/or being valued at a higher valuation multiple than when it was purchased (although see below for a discussion on this). Thus, the private equity owner can re-leverage the business asset against the improved EBITDA and extract cash value from the business at that point.

Notwithstanding the above, recapitalisations do have some disadvantages: they depress the cash-on-cash multiple and, depending on the type of debt used, they can also lock the private equity owner into a more expensive debt package (eg, where mezzanine debt is used), with a higher interest burden and potentially lengthy non-call features or expensive redemption premiums.

6.2 Recapitalisations pre-credit crunch

Prior to the credit crunch, achieving a recapitalisation was a fairly easy process for private equity owners and lending to recapitalisations formed a large part of the leveraged finance market and accounted for a high proportion of debt lent to private equity-owned businesses. There were a number of reasons for this:

- The extremely favourable economic conditions at that time meant that EBITDA growth was easily achieved over relatively short timeframes;
- The competitive nature of the private equity market meant that valuation multiples were ever increasing which, combined with easily attained EBITDA growth, meant that the implied value of equity investments (ie, the current enterprise/market value) increased significantly;
- Competition within the lending markets also led to lending multiples (the quantum of debt being lent as a multiple of EBITDA) increasing year on year, while at the same time margins reduced along with arrangement fees, meaning that private equity-owned businesses could borrow more for less cost; and
- Lenders allowed private equity owners to extract a full return on risk capital based on the implied equity value of the business (which was constantly increasing), rather than the cash value of the initial investment (which remained the same), and allowed them to do so more than once during the lifetime of the investment.

Thus, private equity owners could play the debt markets to achieve a full return (and more), while retaining a business that would continue to increase in value at that time.

6.3 Recapitalisations during/post-credit crunch

Following not just the credit crunch, but also the banking crisis and recession, a different set of dynamics evolved that changed the nature and achievability of recapitalisations. In particular:

- the recession brought an end to the continuous trend of year-on-year growth which had fuelled EBITDA and implied value growth on which recapitalisations prior to the credit crunch had been based;
- the lack of liquidity in the debt markets meant that margins and deal fees rose, while leverage multiples dropped sharply, making it hard to raise high

levels of debt and making the interest burden vastly more expensive, even when replacing debt on a like-for-like basis (ie, senior debt replacing senior debt); and

- lenders were reluctant to see private equity owners 'taking money off the table' at a time of economic uncertainty, thereby removing any incentive for the owner to continue to support a business because it had already achieved its return in cash terms.

Given these changing dynamics, it is hardly surprising that there were very few recapitalisations during this period.

6.4 Recapitalisation going forward

At the time of writing, there are signs that the pendulum has started to swing back, albeit slowly, in the direction of an environment that is more favourable to recapitalisations. Margins are starting to reduce once again, largely due to an increase in competition for senior debt – particularly among collateralised loan obligation funds – and a reduced number of senior debt deals due to the current prevalence of high-yield bonds over senior debt. High yield itself has also given an opportunity for larger deals to recapitalise, particularly as high-yield leverage multiples are generally higher than those for senior debt and high-yield investors are much less sensitive about how the proceeds of a recapitalisation are used.

That said, deals that were closed pre-credit crunch (on high leverage multiples and low margins) and of insufficient size in debt terms to access the high-yield bond market are unlikely, in the short term at least, to be able to re-lever to a level that makes a recapitalisation viable (in terms of an increased overall debt quantum) or cost effective (in terms of increased interest cost and fees).

While the dynamics surrounding recapitalisations may well be showing signs of changing, the crux for private equity owners, particularly in the mid-market, is not only whether lenders will again let them extract full value from a business, but also what will be the basis of that value. Lenders in mid-market deals do not seem, for the moment at least, to be buying back into the concept of implied equity value and instead are focusing on the cash equity value of a business (ie, the amount of cash equity that a private equity owner has paid into the business). If this remains the case, the basis for mid-market recapitalisations will be vastly reduced compared to the pre-credit crunch era and compared to the larger end of the market, where capital market options offer greater flexibility. Moreover, many lenders now take the view that even where they are willing to support a mid-market recapitalisation, they will do so only if the private equity owner maintains a 30% to 40% cash equity cushion in the business. If this remains the case, it would seem that the cult of the perpetual recapitalisation is over for mid-market private equity houses, as will be the concept of a recapitalisation as an alternative to a full exit.

Winding-up

Philip Hertz
John MacLennan
Gabrielle Ruiz
Clifford Chance LLP

1. Introduction

This chapter focuses on exits by way of a sale by the investment holding company of an operating group and the impact of insolvency and winding-up on that investment vehicle. The sale could arise for any number of reasons. It might be a trade sale, an auction or a secondary buy-out, or it might form part of a portfolio sale or a sale 'forced' by the secured lenders which have partly financed the original buy-out in circumstances where they would otherwise enforce their security over the operating group. Whatever the type of sale, the issues arising from the holding company's insolvency and winding-up will be the same. Investors in the holding company (ie, the private equity backer, management and possibly others) might, and frequently do for tax and other reasons, sell their shares in the holding company directly. In such cases the themes and issues highlighted in this chapter may well hold good and remain of relevance and concern, although this will depend on the type of entity that holds the shares and the relevant laws governing its insolvency. However, given the scope of this chapter, only English law and its application to companies are specifically addressed.

1.1 Why are insolvency law and related considerations of concern on exit?

Insolvency law and related considerations are of concern on exit for two principal reasons:

- For the exit to mark the end of a successful investment, there is a need to ensure that it is not soured by leaving the otherwise solvent holding company for the investment – whose board of directors might include personnel employed or engaged by the private equity investor (referred to in this chapter as 'investor directors')[1] – insolvent as a result or in consequence of the exit.
- The exit itself might have been precipitated by or be in circumstances where the operating business, and with it the holding company, is in a financially distressed situation (ie, it is insolvent or close to insolvency).

For convenience, the former scenario is referred to as 'non-distressed' and the latter as 'distressed'.

1 Such directors are often referred to as 'nominee' directors, with the private equity investor having the right, as part of the arrangement governing its investment and allowing it to keep a check on its investment, to nominate one or more directors to the board of the holding company.

In each scenario, where possible, the common aim is to give the holding company a 'solvent burial' – that is, to ensure that it is a solvent as opposed to an insolvent winding-up. This is important because of the myriad issues, both legal and commercial, that flow from insolvency and an insolvent winding-up for the holding company, its directors, its private equity investor and a purchaser (see section 3).

2. Winding-up

2.1 Overview

The Insolvency Act 1986[2] and associated rules govern the winding-up of companies. The purpose of the winding-up of a company is to ascertain its liabilities, get in and realise its assets and then apply the proceeds of realisation *pari passu* in satisfaction of its (unsecured) liabilities. A liquidator is appointed to conduct the winding-up.

A winding-up may be commenced, among others, by the company's members or by the court. Where it is commenced by a company's members, it is referred to as a 'voluntary' winding-up. Where it is commenced by the court, it is often referred to as a 'compulsory' winding-up.[3]

2.2 Solvent winding-up

To commence what is commonly referred to as a 'solvent' winding-up following a sale of the operating group, the directors of the holding company will have to swear a statutory declaration of solvency. Assuming that they can do this and the declaration is made, then if the holding company's members commence a liquidation by passing a special resolution that the company be wound up voluntarily, the voluntary winding-up will be a 'members' voluntary liquidation'.[4] Along with the special resolution, the company's members will also pass an ordinary resolution appointing one or more liquidators. Although, in theory, a solvent winding-up can be commenced by the court, this is unusual and, in practice, a solvent winding-up will be commenced voluntarily after careful planning by the holding company and its private equity investor.[5]

A statutory declaration of solvency is a statement that the directors, having made a full enquiry of the company's affairs, are satisfied that the company will be able to pay its debts in full with interest within a maximum period of 12 months starting

---

2 The Insolvency Rules 1986.

3 The terms 'winding-up' and 'liquidation' are synonymous and used interchangeably. The other key insolvency proceeding under English law of relevance in this context is administration. The primary objective of an administration is to rescue the company as a going concern. If this is not possible, then the administration may be conducted for the purposes of achieving a better result for the company's creditors as a whole than would be the case if the company were wound up. This is effectively a 'winding-up' through administration. Issues that flow from an insolvent winding-up are also likely to apply in the event that a company enters into administration. Where the consequences and issues arising from administration differ from the winding-up regime, they are noted in this chapter.

4 Section 90 of the Insolvency Act.

5 Section 124 of the Insolvency Act permits the company to apply to the court for its winding-up on the range of grounds set out in Section 122 of the Insolvency Act. These include the ground that the company has resolved by special resolution that it be wound up by the court. This particular ground is rarely used in practice and, in the context of a planned winding-up of an investment holding company following a successful exit, it would be usual for the company to be wound up voluntarily.

from the commencement of the winding-up (which is on the passing of a members' special resolution for the winding-up). The declaration, which must be sworn by at least a majority of the directors, is supported by a statement of the company's assets and liabilities, and must be made no more than five weeks before the passing of the members' special resolution. The careful diligence and planning that the directors will need to undertake in order to assess whether such a declaration can be made will have to take into account not only the company's actual liabilities, but also, as the declaration covers a future period, its prospective and contingent liabilities. Therefore, in structuring and agreeing the terms of the exit sale, the directors of the holding company will also need to consider carefully the liabilities that will be incurred as a result. To make the declaration, the holding company need not necessarily be 'solvent' in its own right. If a third party has agreed to meet its liabilities, presumably on non-recourse terms to the company, the directors may well conclude that they are able to make the declaration. Realistically, it is likely to be only the private equity investor that could be expected to provide such support if necessary; but the terms of the particular investment fund's constitution may prohibit such support and there may also be issues of commercial precedent which make this undesirable, bringing the structure and terms of the exit sale into sharp focus. A director found to have sworn the declaration of solvency without reasonable grounds will be liable to imprisonment, a fine or both.[6]

2.3 Insolvent winding-up

Perhaps surprisingly, there is no definition of what it means to be 'insolvent' in the Insolvency Act. However, a winding-up will be regarded as an 'insolvent' liquidation if it takes one of two forms. The first is a voluntary winding-up commenced by special resolution of the company's members in circumstances where the directors have not made a statutory declaration of solvency. A voluntary winding-up in such a case is a 'creditors' voluntary liquidation'.[7] Although the members may appoint, by ordinary resolution, one or more persons to act as liquidator, a creditors' meeting must be held within 14 days of the commencement of a creditors' voluntary liquidation; at that meeting the creditors may vote to appoint a liquidator of their own choosing in its place (the creditors' interests being paramount on account of the insolvency).[8]

The second winding-up option – which may be instigated not only by the company's members, but also by others, including its directors and its creditors[9] – is a compulsory winding-up by the court on the grounds that the company is unable to pay its debts. 'Inability to pay debts' is defined in Section 123 of the Insolvency Act. It includes the two classic formulations of 'insolvency' under English law:

- 'cash-flow' insolvency, where a company is unable to meet its debts as they fall due; and

---

6 Section 89(4) of the Insolvency Act.
7 Section 90 of the Insolvency Act.
8 In practice, the company and creditor meetings are usually held on the same day, with the company meeting being held first. See Sections 98 to 100 of the Insolvency Act.
9 Section 124 of the Insolvency Act.

- 'balance-sheet' insolvency, where the value of a company's assets is less than the amount of its liabilities, taking into account its contingent and prospective liabilities.[10]

Although there are important differences between a creditors' voluntary liquidation and a compulsory winding-up on grounds of inability to pay debts, the effects of each which are of concern in the context of the matters addressed in this chapter are the same, and as such are referred to collectively as 'insolvent winding-up'.

2.4 Insolvent winding-up and EU law

The impact of EU law on English insolvency law has been profound. One of the many important developments has been in the area of cross-border insolvency, with the entry into force of the EU Insolvency Regulation (1346/2000). The EU Insolvency Regulation allocates and regulates insolvency jurisdiction between EU member states[11] in relation to the insolvency of entities other than (among others) insurance undertakings and credit institutions.[12]

While the impact on English insolvency law of the EU Insolvency Regulation and the detail of the regulation are relatively complex, two key points should be noted in the context of the winding-up of an investment holding company following a sale:

- As the EU Insolvency Regulation is concerned only with the allocation of insolvency jurisdiction between the courts of member states, it has no bearing on the commencement or conduct of a company's solvent winding-up by way of a members' voluntary liquidation and does not impose the law governing such a winding-up. As a matter of English law, the law of the jurisdiction of a company's incorporation or registration will be the proper law governing its solvent winding-up.[13]
- Where a holding company is insolvent and has either its centre of main interests (COMI)[14] or an establishment[15] in England, then it could be subject to an insolvent winding-up in England either by the court or pursuant to a creditors' voluntary liquidation. Therefore, it should not be assumed that

---

10 In light of recent case law (*BNY Corporate Trustee Services Limited v Eurosail-UK 2007-3BL plc* [2011] EWCA Civ 227) the 'balance-sheet' description is misleading in that the test, the details of which are outside the scope of this work, is not based on a simple snapshot of the balance sheet. It requires some assessment of future prospects.

11 Excluding Denmark, which has opted out of the EU Insolvency Regulation. Therefore, references in section 2.4 to 'member states' should be taken to exclude Denmark.

12 The excluded entities are subject to separate regimes and legislation.

13 Brussels and Lugano Conventions, Articles 16(2), 53; Civil Jurisdiction and Judgments Act 1982, Section 43(2); EU Council Regulation 44/2001, Article 22(2); SI 2001/3929, Sch 1, para 10.

14 'COMI' is not defined in the EU Insolvency Regulation, but there is a rebuttable presumption that it is in the same jurisdiction as the registered office and it is generally understood to correspond to the place where the business conducts the administration of its interests on a regular basis and is ascertainable by third parties (paragraph 13 of the preamble to the EU Insolvency Regulation).

15 'Establishment' is defined by Article 2(h) of the EU Insolvency Regulation as being any place of operations where a company carries out a non-transitory economic activity with human means and goods. In general terms, companies that are holding vehicles in the strict sense are unlikely to have an 'establishment' and will have only a COMI, although each case will turn on its own facts.

English insolvency law and its effects are irrelevant because the holding company is registered or incorporated outside, or has its seat somewhere outside, the United Kingdom. If the group or holding company has connections with the United Kingdom – be they operations, creditors (suppliers, financiers or otherwise) or customers or directors who are based and work in the United Kingdom – then careful consideration must be given as to whether the holding company has its COMI or an establishment in England.[16]

3. Impact of Insolvency Law and an insolvent winding-up on exit

3.1 Relevance of insolvency to exit

Insolvency law and related considerations will be of concern and relevance to the holding company, its directors, its private equity investor and a purchaser on exit in the following scenarios:

- Non-distressed scenario – although the holding company is not in a financially distressed position, it becomes insolvent as a result or in consequence of the sale, and therefore could become subject to an insolvent winding-up following the sale.
- Distressed scenario – the holding company is in a financially distressed position at the time of sale and might therefore be subject to an insolvent winding-up.

The principal matters of concern for these parties that flow from the holding company's insolvency under either scenario and its subsequent insolvent winding-up can be grouped under four main headings:

- inability to distribute proceeds – an inability on the part of the holding company to distribute sale proceeds to its private equity investor so as to allow a timely realisation of its investment;
- director liability – potential liability for the directors of the holding company (including any investor directors) in the event of an insolvent winding-up;
- unwind of sale – the possibility of the sale being unwound; or
- disclosure – the potentially adverse effects for the directors of the holding company personally and for the business of its private equity investor because of any disclosure made or required to be made about the insolvency and the winding-up.

Each of these issues is addressed in section 3.3 below. Any one of them may be sufficient to jeopardise the overriding aim of the private equity investor – namely, a

---

16 In addition, companies with their COMI outside of the European Union may be wound up in England under:
- Part V of the Insolvency Act where, among other things, they have a sufficient connection with the United Kingdom; and
- Section 426 of the Insolvency Act at the request of a court in a relevant country of territory (these are prescribed by statutory instrument and include the Cayman Islands, Gibraltar, Hong Kong, Ireland and the Virgin Islands) exercising insolvency jurisdiction in respect of the relevant company.

clean and quick exit. Accordingly, by ensuring that the holding company is left in a solvent state following the sale, it should be possible not only to secure the goal of the private equity investor, but also to avoid the damaging effects and adverse consequences of an insolvent winding-up for the holding company, its directors, a purchaser and the private equity investor alike. The means of achieving a solvent winding-up of the holding company in both a non-distressed and distressed scenario are considered in sections 4.1 and 4.2, respectively.

Before considering each of the principal issues of concern, the position of a holding company that is otherwise insolvent prior to a sale, and why and how it might become insolvent as a result or in consequence of the sale, is addressed.

3.2 Non-distressed holding company

If a holding company is otherwise solvent, then while the reasons for avoiding insolvency are clear, it may not be immediately clear why the company should become insolvent as a result of a sale. However, practice and experience show that the grounds upon which a holding company becomes insolvent as a result or in consequence of a sale might well include the following (or a combination thereof):

- The amount of liabilities incurred by the holding company under the sale and purchase agreement (eg, under warranties and indemnities) and generally as part of the sales process by reason of adviser fees and the like exceeds the value of its assets, including the purchase price.
- During the life of the investment, the holding vehicle has incurred or become subject to liabilities, either of its own or connected with the operating business, which will remain extant after the sale but which it will be unable to satisfy or provide for from the proceeds of sale and any other assets that it may have. Liabilities that it has incurred might include amounts due under directors' service contracts, for advisory services, for shared services with the operating business or for financial support provided to subsidiaries by way of guarantee. Liabilities to which it might be subject could include liability for any deficit in a defined benefit pension scheme maintained by one of its subsidiaries.[17]
- The proceeds of sale are distributed to shareholders so that the holding company is then unable to meet its actual, contingent or prospective liabilities incurred as part of the sale.

However, the fact that an otherwise solvent holding company might become insolvent post-exit on these grounds, a combination thereof or indeed other grounds is not to say that the company should find itself in this position; quite the contrary.

(a) Insolvency as a result of sale

Before entering into any sale, the directors of the holding company will, among other things, need to consider carefully the terms of the sale and the position of the

---

17 Under the Pensions Act 2004, a company connected with another company that operates a defined benefit pension scheme can in certain circumstances become liable for any funding deficit in that scheme.

company following the sale, taking into account all of its liabilities and how those liabilities will be provided for or satisfied. The latter assessment may require a detailed and considered analysis of the company's financial position, together with appropriate legal, financial or other advice. The board of directors will then need to decide whether, in light of its statutory duties to the company under the Companies Act 2006,[18] entering into the sale is a correct and proper course of action.

While every case will turn on its own facts and circumstances, in practice, the situations in which the directors of a holding company could properly decide to enter into a sale as a result of which the company becomes insolvent are likely to be rare. If the directors were to embark on such a course of action in the absence of extenuating circumstances, it may result in the breach of one or more of their statutory or other duties owed to the holding company, with the attendant prospect of personal liability as a result and, in some cases, the unwinding of the transaction.

(b) *Insolvency following distribution*

Again, in practice, there are likely to be few if any circumstances in which the directors of the holding company could or should resolve to distribute the proceeds of sale so that the company is then left without funds to discharge its liabilities.

3.3 Key areas of concern

(a) *Inability to distribute*

A key commercial concern for the private equity investor will be to receive its share of the proceeds of sale quickly and realise its investment. Where the holding company is insolvent or close to insolvency, this will be difficult, if not impossible, regardless of whether the distribution is proposed to be made by way of dividend, share redemption, buyback or otherwise. This is because of the rules prohibiting:

- an unlawful return of capital;[19]
- an unauthorised reduction of capital;[20] and
- an unlawful distribution (ie, a distribution in the absence of distributable reserves).[21]

A detailed analysis of these rules is beyond the scope of this chapter. However, suffice to say that if the holding company is insolvent or potentially insolvent, it is very unlikely that its directors could or should make any distribution to its shareholders or enter into any transaction with substantially the same economic effect as a distribution.

(b) *Directors' duties and liabilities*

The directors of a holding company owe statutory duties to that company (and not

---

18 See section 3.3(b) below.

19 See *Aveling Barford Ltd v Perion Ltd* (1989) 5 BCC 677 and Sections 845, 846 and 851 of the Companies Act.

20 See *Trevor v Whitworth* (1887) LR 12 App Cas 409 and Section 641 of the Companies Act.

21 See Sections 830 to 835 of the Companies Act.

shareholders, creditors or others) pursuant to Sections 170 to 177 of the Companies Act.[22] Briefly, these duties are:

- to act within their powers (Section 171);
- to promote the success of the company (Section 172);
- to exercise independent judgement (Section 173);
- to exercise reasonable care, skill and diligence (Section 174);
- to avoid conflicts of interest (Section 175);
- not to accept benefits from third parties (Section 176); and
- to declare an interest in proposed transactions and arrangements (Section 177).

These duties may be enforced by the company against the directors or, in certain instances, by the shareholders of the company on the company's behalf through a derivative action (Sections 260 to 264 of the Companies Act). In the event that the company is wound up or goes into administration, the liquidator or administrator may bring a claim for breach of statutory duty in the name of the company in respect of any breach that the company could have pursued prior to the winding-up or administration. The remedies in case of breach of these duties by a director of the holding company include damages and, other than with respect to a breach of duty to exercise reasonable care, skill and diligence, the setting aside of a transaction that is the subject of the breach.

The directors of a holding company that is insolvent or close to insolvency will also owe various duties and obligations over and above their statutory duties under the Companies Act. Breach of these duties and obligations may result in personal liability for the directors and, in certain cases, criminal liability. An overview of each of these duties and obligations as they apply to the directors of a private company[23] follows.

Common law duty to act in the best interests of the company: One duty of directors that has not been replaced by the statutory duties under Sections 171 to 177 of the Companies Act[24] applies when a company is insolvent or close to insolvency, and requires the directors to act in the best interests of the company by maximising its value and, in doing so, to have regard predominantly, but not exclusively, to the interests of the company's creditors.[25]

---

22 These statutory duties are owed by shadow directors as well as *de facto* and *de jure* directors (see footnote 29). They replace most, but not all, of the various common law, equitable and fiduciary duties to which directors were subject prior to the entry into force of these sections of the Companies Act (Section 170(3)). However, the statutory duties are to be interpreted and applied in the same way as the common law rules and equitable principles that they replace, and regard is to be had to those rules and principles when interpreting these statutory duties (Section 170(4)).

23 Directors of a public company may also face liability in respect of a serious loss of capital (Section 656 of the Companies Act). Also, where the shares in a public company are listed and have been admitted to trading on the London Stock Exchange, the directors may also face liability under the Financial Services and Markets Act 2000 in connection with information provided to the market and market abuse. While holding companies in a typical buy-out structure will be incorporated as private rather than public companies, public companies may be found in structures where there has been a 'public to private' acquisition by the private equity house or listing is considered a likely exit from the outset.

24 It is preserved by Section 172(3) of the Companies Act.

This duty recognises that when a company is insolvent or close to insolvency (or becomes insolvent in consequence of the breach of this duty), it is the company's creditors and not its shareholders that should properly be regarded as the owners of the company, since it is their money which is at risk, and as those that should be protected against acts which might diminish the company's value. A liquidator of the company[26] may bring a claim against the directors in the name and on behalf of the company. The loss recoverable by way of a claim for damages will be the loss of the company and not loss suffered by individual creditors. From the perspective of the private equity investor, this shift is stark when set against the general statutory duty of directors to the company under Section 172 of the Companies Act that applies outside the zone of insolvency. Section 172 requires that the directors act in a way that they consider, in good faith, would be most likely to promote the success of the company *for the benefit of its members as a whole*. It is this shift in interest from shareholders to creditors that frequently leads to investor directors finding themselves in a position of conflict.[27]

Wrongful trading: Pursuant to Section 214 of the Insolvency Act, the liquidator of a company[28] may apply to the court for contributions towards the assets of the company from any person who is or was a director of the company[29] from the point at which that person knew or ought to have concluded that there was no reasonable prospect of avoiding insolvent liquidation. It is a defence to an action under this section for a director to show that, from the point that he or she knew or ought to have known that insolvent liquidation was unavoidable, he or she took every step with a view to minimising the potential loss to the company's creditors.

Fraudulent trading under the Insolvency Act and Companies Act: Section 213 of the Insolvency Act permits a liquidator[30] to apply for contributions from any person, including a director,[31] who was knowingly party to the carrying on of business with the intent to defraud creditors. Liability under this section requires actual dishonesty involving, according to current notions of fair trading among commercial players, real moral blame.[32]

The facts supporting a claim under Section 213 of the Insolvency Act will also render every person knowingly party to the carrying on of business with the intent

---

25 *Liquidator of West Mercia Safetywear Ltd v Dodd* (1988) 4 BCC 30; *Gwyer v London Wharf (Limehouse) Ltd* [2002] EWHC 2748 (Ch).

26 Or an administrator.

27 See the section below entitled "Investor directors and executive and non-executive directors".

28 Actions under Section 214 of the Insolvency Act are personal to a liquidator. Administrators cannot bring claims for wrongful trading.

29 'Directors' for these purposes includes *de jure*, *de facto* and shadow directors. In short, *de jure* directors are those directors legally appointed as such. A *de facto* director is a person who acts as a director and is generally regarded as being a director, but who has not been legally appointed as a director. A shadow director is a person in accordance with whose direction or instructions the directors of a company are accustomed to act (Section 251 of the Insolvency Act).

30 As with Section 214 of the Insolvency Act, claims under Section 213 are personal to a liquidator and may not be brought by an administrator.

31 Again, this includes *de jure*, *de facto* and shadow directors.

32 See *Re Patrick & Lyon Ltd* [1933] Ch 786.

to defraud creditors liable to criminal penalties under a distinct and separate offence of fraudulent trading under Section 993 of the Companies Act.

Further remedies: If a director of the holding company breaches his or her duties and obligations, then in addition to the remedies noted above, two further categories of remedy will be available against the director concerned:

- Misfeasance – Section 212 of the Insolvency Act applies where, in the course of the winding-up of a company, it appears that a person who is or has been a director of the company[33] has misapplied or retained, or become accountable for, any money or other property of the company, or has been guilty of any misfeasance or breach of any fiduciary or other duty to the company. Under this section, the liquidator is provided with a summary remedy enabling an application to be made to the court for the examination of the conduct of the director concerned and an order compelling him or her to repay, restore or account for the money or property, or to contribute a sum to the company's assets by way of compensation in respect of the misfeasance or breach of fiduciary or other duty. This provision applies only when a company goes into liquidation, although the remedy is available not only to the liquidator of the company, but also to a creditor or contributory.[34]
- Company Directors' Disqualification Act 1986 – pursuant to the Company Directors Disqualification Act 1986, the liquidator of a company subject to an insolvent winding-up may report to the secretary of state for the Department of Business, Innovation and Skills, who may apply for a disqualification order.[35] The report may take into account any misfeasance, breach of fiduciary duty, misapplication of company property and the director's responsibility for entering into any transaction liable to be set aside.[36] Incompetence, as well as commercially or morally culpable behaviour, can be sufficient to enable the court to disqualify a director.

During the period in which a person is subject to disqualification, it is a criminal offence for that person to be a director of a company or take certain other roles relating to company management.

The liquidator's reporting requirement relates only to directors of insolvent companies. Therefore, if the holding company can be given a solvent burial through a members' voluntary liquidation, the reporting requirement does not apply.

Investor directors and executive and non-executive directors: The duties, obligations and liabilities referenced above apply generally to the directors of a holding company which is insolvent or close to insolvency. However, it is also useful

---

33 In fact, the section applies to 'officers', which includes directors (whether *de jure*, *de facto* or shadow directors), as well any other person who is or has been concerned, or has taken part, in the promotion, foundation or management of the company.

34 An administrator cannot seek relief under this section.

35 An administrator may make the same report.

36 See section 3.3(c).

to consider specifically the position of investor directors, given the obvious potential for conflict between their roles for the holding company and the private equity investor, as well as the relative positions of so-called 'executive' and 'non-executive' directors:

- Investor (nominee) directors – investor directors will need to distinguish between their role as a director of the holding company and their employment with the private equity investor. When acting in their capacity as a director of the holding company, they will need to have regard only to the interest of that company and their duties as a director of that company. These may well be at odds and conflict with the interests of the private equity investor – particularly where the company is insolvent or close to insolvency, as the directors must then have regard predominantly to the interests of the company's creditors in determining what is in the best interests of the company. Where the interests of the private equity investor and the company conflict, this is likely to mean that the investor director is precluded from taking part in any decisions of the board relating to the subject matter of the conflict. This could, of course, include any decision to sell the operating business.
- Executive and non-executive directors – many companies have what are colloquially referred to as 'executive directors' and 'non-executive directors' (or, sometimes, 'independent non-executive directors'). The latter are frequently part time and play no part in the day-to-day operation and management of the company, but instead have specific roles such as oversight of remuneration of senior management or audit matters. By contrast, executive directors are usually those engaged in the daily operation and management of the business, and will include the chief executive officer and chief financial officer. The law as it relates to the conduct of directors, which includes each of the matters noted above, does not distinguish between executive and non-executive directors. It applies to all persons who are directors,[37] regardless of any badge that may be given to them to describe their role with respect to the company.

(c) ***Transaction avoidance***

In the event that the holding company becomes subject to an insolvent winding-up, the Insolvency Act provides that the liquidator may apply to court on certain grounds to 'unwind' transactions that the company has entered into within certain specified periods prior to the onset of insolvency (often referred to as 'hardening periods').[38]

The grounds upon which a liquidator may challenge a transaction are as follows:[39]

37 'Directors' for these purposes includes *de jure*, *de facto* and shadow directors.

38 If the holding company enters administration under the Insolvency Act, the administrator of the company may seek to unwind transactions on the same bases.

39 The avoidance provisions of the Insolvency Act are complex and only an overview is provided. Reference should be made to the relevant sections of the Insolvency Act and leading insolvency texts for a detailed analysis.

- Transactions at an undervalue (Section 238 of the Insolvency Act) – a liquidator may apply to set aside a transaction entered into at an undervalue within two years of the onset of insolvency. For this purpose, a transaction is at an 'undervalue' if it constitutes a gift or if the value of the consideration received (in money or money's worth) is significantly less than the consideration provided by the company. It is a defence to a challenge under Section 238 to show that the company was solvent at the time that it entered into the relevant transaction; or even if the transaction was entered into at the relevant time, it may not be challenged unless the company was unable to pay its debts within the meaning of Section 123 of the Insolvency Act[40] at the time of entry into the transaction or became unable to pay its debts in consequence of the transaction. However, where the transaction is entered into with a person connected with the company,[41] there will be a rebuttable presumption of inability to pay debts. It will also not be possible to challenge a transaction under Section 238 where it was entered into in good faith and there were reasonable grounds for thinking that the transaction would benefit the company.
- Preferences (Section 239 of the Insolvency Act) – a liquidator may apply to set aside transactions which occurred within six months of the onset of insolvency (this period is extended to two years for transactions involving connected parties),[42] which had the effect of putting the creditor, surety or guarantor in a better position in the liquidation than would otherwise have been the case, and where the company was influenced by a desire to produce that (preferential) effect. A company must have been influenced in deciding to give the preference by a desire to produce the effect of putting the creditor in a better position. Where the transaction was entered into at the relevant time, it may not be challenged unless the company was unable to pay its debts within the meaning of Section 123 of the Insolvency Act[43] at the time of entry into the transaction or became unable to pay its debts in consequence of the transaction.
- Transactions defrauding creditors (Section 423 of the Insolvency Act) – the court may, on the application of the liquidator of a company (or with the leave of the court, on the application of a 'victim of the transaction', even if the company is not in liquidation), set aside a transaction entered into by the company at an undervalue if the company entered into the transaction for the purpose of putting assets beyond the reach of a person who is making, or may at some time make, a claim against it or of otherwise prejudicing the interests of such a person in relation to the claim which it is making or may make. 'Undervalue' has the same meaning as under Section 238 of the Insolvency Act. It is not a condition of the making of such an order that the company was insolvent at the time of the transaction.

---

40 See generally section 2.3 below.

41 'Connection' is defined in Section 249 of the Insolvency Act and covers a broad range of relationships. Common ownership and control is a typical hallmark of connection.

42 *Ibid.*

43 See generally section 2.3 below.

Remedies: If the liquidator makes out its case under these provisions, the court has wide powers to restore the position to that which prevailed before the sale.[44] This includes the power to order the transfer back to the holding company of the property sold by it (ie, the shares in the operating companies), effectively unwinding or reversing the transaction. The court also has the power to require the investors to return to the holding company or, if the sale was unwound completely, the purchaser any amounts paid to them in respect of the proceeds of the sale. The impact of such provisions will clearly be of concern to any purchaser and, ultimately, to the private equity investor, given the potential for preventing realisation of its investment.

(d) Disclosure of insolvency

In the event of the holding company becoming insolvent and being wound up, its directors and private equity investors may become subject to obligations of disclosure concerning the winding-up which may have ramifications for both.[45]

Directors: For directors, their involvement in the management of a company that has become subject to insolvency proceedings will need to be disclosed in several different scenarios:

- Listing Rules – first, it will need to be disclosed within the context of any directorships that they have or may have in the future of companies whose shares are listed and admitted to trading on the London Stock Exchange. This is mandated by the UK Listing Authority's Listing Rules and requires disclosure through the exchange's Regulatory Information Service, to which major news organisations subscribe. The obligation applies only if the director of the listed company was also a director of an insolvent company either at the time of the company becoming insolvent or within the 12 months prior to this and also, unusually perhaps, only if he or she was an executive director of the insolvent company.[46] This is one of the few areas where a distinction is drawn between the obligations of executive and non-executive directors. A similar obligation, which also extends to non-executive directors, exists for companies wishing to have their shares listed and admitted to trading on AIM.[47]
- EU Prospectus Regulation – disclosure will also be necessary (for both executive and non-executive directors) if they later become involved with a company that wishes to issue new shares or securities for which a prospectus needs to be produced that complies with Section 85 of the Financial Services and Markets Act. A prospectus must include the information in the referenced annexes to the EU Prospectus Regulation,[48] including whether the senior management of the issuing company had been in a similar position of

44 See Section 241 of the Insolvency Act.
45 If the holding company enters administration under the Insolvency Act, the same considerations apply.
46 Listing Rule 9.6.13 requires this information to be disclosed on any new director joining a listed company and Rule 9.6.14 requires the company to update the information should it change.
47 Rule 3 and Schedule 2, AIM Rules for Companies.
48 Commission Regulation (EU) 809/2004.

management for a company that became insolvent within the previous five years. This obligation is particularly widely drafted, with regard to both what positions constitute 'senior management' and the extent of involvement necessary to trigger the disclosure.

- Financial Services Authority – involvement in past insolvencies is a matter relevant to the Financial Services Authority's 'fit and proper' test for determining whether someone should be an 'authorised person' under the Financial Services and Markets Act. It must be disclosed when applying for this status[49] and also forms part of an authorised person's continuing disclosure obligations.[50]

Clearly, for the director concerned, disclosure in all of these situations may be most unwelcome, given the adverse comment and publicity that it could attract. Whether this is in fact the case may in part depend on the circumstances leading to the insolvency. A difference may be perceived between a 'good' insolvency, which has come about due to reasons outside the board's control and despite its best efforts to avoid insolvency (eg, because of the collapse of a particular market due to the imposition of new law or regulation), and a 'bad' insolvency, which has been brought about, for example, by inept management. For an investor director, disclosure may prove problematic in the context of directorships of other portfolio companies, particularly where an exit by way of an initial public offering on the London Stock Exchange or AIM is being considered.

Private equity investor: For the private equity investor, the fact of an investee company becoming insolvent and subject to insolvency proceedings may have an adverse effect on its business. The fact of the failure may need to be disclosed when looking to raise new funds, affecting its ability to do so – particularly given the ever-expanding range of opportunities and competition for potential investors' money.

Insolvency proceedings also tend to make 'good' business news, so even in the absence of any obligation to disclose, press coverage may generate adverse comment and publicity with an equally negative effect.

4. Solvent winding-up after exit

4.1 Avoiding insolvency as a result of exit

In a non-distressed scenario, there will be few, if any, circumstances in which the directors of a holding company should or could enter into a sale which would result in the company's insolvency.[51] However, it may be the case that there is a fine line between achieving an insolvent or a solvent outcome that then permits a solvent burial of the holding company, thereby avoiding the damaging effects of an insolvent winding-up.

The gateway to a solvent winding-up of the holding company may well lie in the

49 FSA Handbook FIT 2.1 to 2.3.
50 FSA Handbook SUP 10.13.16 and 10.13.17.
51 See section 3.2.

structuring of the sale transaction and, specifically, in the limits imposed on the liabilities incurred by it as part of the sales process. This may be a necessity where, following the sale, the holding company will have no assets beyond the proceeds of sale. Chief among such liabilities will be those incurred under the sale and purchase agreement, and in particular under any warranties and indemnities that may be given. Other liabilities under the sale agreement that may be of concern will include further assurance obligations and any transitional service or other arrangements. The sale and the sales process itself may also generate other liabilities on the part of the holding company, such as professional advisers' fees, corporation tax and value added tax, which will need to be factored in. The liabilities incurred are likely to include not only actual liabilities, but also, by reason of any warranties or indemnities provided, prospective and/or contingent liabilities. Liabilities of all types will need to be taken into account when assessing the holding company's solvency.

(a) ***Limiting liability***

While every sale agreement will be different, its content dictated by the facts at hand, there are nonetheless standard approaches to limiting a vendor holding company's liability under a sale agreement.

No warranties or indemnities: Not providing warranties or indemnities is an obvious means of limiting liability. However, both commercially and from the perspective of the purchaser, it is unlikely to be an option. Even if it were, it would be expected to lead to one of two results (or both). The purchaser would seek a reduction in the purchase price to reflect the balance of risk, and the purchase price may then be at a level which is unacceptable for the private equity investor. Alternatively or additionally, the purchaser would wish to retain a part of the purchase price, or place it in escrow, for a period as a reserve against matters that might otherwise have been the subject of a warranty or indemnity, releasing the sums in question to the holding company only at an agreed point in time and provided that no claim has arisen.[52]

Limited scope and duration: The scope and duration of any warranties and indemnities could be limited. The extent of the reduction in scope and duration will be a matter for negotiation. In terms of the scope of warranties, there will be an expectation that these extend to matters connected with, among other things, the conduct and operation of the business and not merely title to the shares being sold. This is in contrast to the position of a vendor private equity investor, where the norm is for only limited warranties as to the ownership of the shares to be given.[53]

---

52 Where a company is financially distressed and either insolvent or close to insolvency, and is undertaking a sale of assets as part of a rescue process (see further section 4.2), it is not unusual for no warranties to be provided and only limited confirmations to be given as to ownership of the shares being sold. This is on the basis that, given the circumstances of the sale, it is essentially akin to a sale by an administrator, liquidator or receiver, and warranties are not given on sales by such office holders in order to minimise the risk of liability resulting from the sale (the proceeds then being readily available for distribution).

53 The usual rationale given for limited warranty coverage is that as the private equity investor is not involved in the day-to-day operation and management of the business, it is incapable of giving representations and warranties that speak to these matters.

Limited recourse: It may be possible to negotiate a limit to the holding company's liability for breach of warranty or under any indemnities, to the extent that any are given. Quite often, only management will give any substantive warranties in these circumstances.

Warranty support: The holding company may be able to lay off the risk under warranties to another party. This could be done through warranty insurance if it is available for the risks in issue, although price will be a key factor in determining whether this is a realistic option. Alternatively, a guarantee (with limited rights of counter-indemnity) might be sought from the private equity investor. In practice, a guarantee is unlikely to be forthcoming as the constitution of the fund entity that holds the investment will typically prohibit the grant of guarantees.

4.2 Distressed situations

Where the holding company is or is likely to become insolvent, it may be questionable whether any purchaser would wish to transact. Likewise, the directors of the holding company may be loath to transact.

In the case of the purchaser, this is primarily due to the risk of a subsequently appointed liquidator[54] reviewing the transaction to ascertain whether it might be challenged, and possibly set aside, on any of the grounds set out in section 3.3(c) above or as result of a breach of the directors' duties to the company.[55] A liquidator's attentions will inevitably result in cost and uncertainty for the purchaser. These factors alone may be something that a purchaser is unwilling to countenance, given that they may hinder or delay integration of its newly acquired business with its own investment in the new business or simply steps to stabilise the newly acquired business. A well-advised purchaser might instead prefer to wait for a liquidator (or administrator) to be appointed to the holding company and deal instead with the company's insolvency office holder. This is because a sale by a liquidator (or administrator) will not be subject to challenge on the grounds set out in section 3.3(c); nor, by definition, could it be challenged on the basis of a breach of a director's duty to the company.[56]

For the directors of the holding company, in such circumstances their decision as to whether to enter into a sale is likely to be framed by two potentially conflicting duties. On the one hand, the directors will want to ensure that they act in the best interests of the company (having regard predominantly to the interests of the creditors) by maximising its value.[57] On the other, they will not want to fall foul of

---

54 Or an administrator.

55 See section 3.3(b).

56 The liquidator or administrator will normally execute the sale agreement as agent of the company. The liquidator or administrator will also usually be party to the sale agreement, but only for the limited purpose of taking the benefit of certain provisions in his or her favour. Those provisions are aimed at excluding any liability on the part of the liquidator or administrator personally, the office of liquidator or administrator being a personal appointment. They would normally include an express exclusion of any representations and warranties, including as to title, and an exclusion of liability extending also to the liquidator's and administrator's partners (those who take appointments as liquidators or administrators are licensed 'insolvency practitioners' and tend to be partners in accountancy firms), employees, agents and advisers.

57 See section 3.3(b).

the 'wrongful trading' provisions of Section 214 of the Insolvency Act, which may be the case if they have reached a point where there is no reasonable prospect of avoiding an insolvent liquidation and, by continuing on, loss will result to the creditors and they will incur personal liability. While the two requirements may not be competing or conflicting in any particular case (eg, a proper analysis of both might lead to the conclusion that insolvency proceedings should be commenced and the sale consummated by the insolvency office holder), it can often be a difficult decision for the directors.

In the context of a private equity-owned group acquired as part of a leveraged buy-out, the position of the secured lenders that have in part financed the acquisition also needs to be considered. In a distressed scenario – whether brought about by poor trading, management problems, adverse market conditions or for some other reason – the group's banking facilities may be in or close to default. In certain cases the situation may be such that the business or parts of it cannot be rescued on a going concern basis, so that upon default, enforcement by the lenders of their security over the group and the sale of the secured assets is unavoidable. That process is likely to amount to a 'fire sale' of the assets, with the amounts realised being applied in satisfaction of the secured debt. Clearly, this outcome will produce no return for the private equity investor or other shareholders, given the fact of insolvency and the scheme of priority of claims under English law, which dictates that shareholders are to receive nothing on a winding-up unless and until all creditors of the relevant company have been paid in full with interest.[58] Worse still, the private equity investor will be left to contend with the inevitable winding-up of the holding company, the possibly damaging commercial effects for itself and the prospect of liability for the holding company's directors, including any investor directors, as noted in section 3.

(a) Clean break

In other cases, where the business or a part of it is fundamentally sound, the lenders concluding that the equity has no value and that the company's creditors are to be regarded as the real owners of the business may wish to restructure the group's

58 The scheme of priority can be discerned from various provisions of the Insolvency Act and case law. The scheme of priority can be summarised as follows in respect of the distribution of proceeds of sale of the secured and unsecured assets of a company:
- secured proceeds –
  - cost and expenses of the liquidator (or administrator) in preserving the assets;
  - holders of fixed (as opposed to floating) security;
  - costs and expenses of the winding-up (or administration);
  - payment of the 'prescribed part' under the Insolvency Act;
  - preferential creditors under the Insolvency Act;
  - holders of security which, as created, is floating charge security;
  - unsecured creditors; and
  - shareholders; and
- unsecured proceeds –
  - cost and expenses of the liquidator (or administrator) in preserving the assets;
  - costs and expenses of the winding-up (or administration);
  - preferential creditors under the Insolvency Act;
  - unsecured creditors; and
  - shareholders.

financial liabilities and take control, recouping their original lending over a period of time or by way of a subsequent sale, or force a sale to a third party in order to pay down so much of their debt as may be possible. While on its face this may appear to be an equally poor outcome for the private equity investor, as it will still lose its investment and make no return, this is perhaps an overly pessimistic view of the situation. It may in fact provide an opportunity for the private equity investor to secure a solvent outcome for the holding company, avoiding the negative consequences of an insolvency and an insolvent winding-up of the holding company.

Working with the lenders and other stakeholders on a consensual basis to deliver the lenders' plan not only may be a correct course of action for the directors in light of their duties, but may also, as part of this process, enable what is sometimes referred to as a 'clean break' to be negotiated between the holding company and the operating group which the lenders wish to own or sell. From the perspective of the private equity investor, the holding company and its directors, the overriding aim of such an arrangement will be to ensure that the holding company can be given a solvent burial.

A comprehensive and detailed analysis of clean-break arrangements cannot be provided, as their content will inevitably be determined by the facts of the particular case. However, such an arrangement might be expected to include provision for the following matters:

- Provision for or assumption of liability – arrangements must be made with a view to either providing for or removing liabilities from the holding company (eg, provision of limited indemnities or novation of any contracts held by the holding company to the operating group or its new holding vehicle).
- Maintenance of holding company – if it is necessary or desirable to keep the holding company in existence for a period after the sale (eg, because of ongoing services that it provides to the operating group or in order to allow time for its tax or other affairs to be settled ahead of a solvent winding-up), then the costs of its ongoing maintenance will need to be covered. Items to be funded might include completion of its annual report and accounts, other statutory filings with Companies House, returns to Her Majesty's Revenue & Customs or other tax authorities, as well as more practical matters such as administrative support.
- Claims against holding company – agreements will need to be reached with respect to any claims (whether or not asserted) that the operating group, the investors (eg, by way of loan note) and/or the lenders (eg, under any guarantees or the balance of any direct borrowings where the acquisition debt has not been 'pushed down' to the operating group) might have against the holding company and/or its directors. In a distressed situation, creditors that are facing a loss may look for avenues of recourse and the holding company and its directors will wish to close off as many as possible. This might amount to a release of such claims or limiting recourse for liability to, in the case of the holding company, any residual assets after its other

liabilities have been met (so as not to jeopardise the prospect of a solvent winding-up). Tax will play an important part in structuring any releases. If the release generates a tax liability, this may render the company insolvent if that liability cannot be met.

- Transitional arrangements – these arrangements might operate both ways. For example, the holding company might need continued access to information, management or the premises of the operating group for a period post-sale in order to facilitate its orderly wind-down and subsequent solvent winding-up. The operating group might also require the continued provision of services by the holding company, such as the maintenance of software or other licences held for the 'old' group pending their transfer to the new group.[59]
- Members' voluntary liquidation costs – provision will need to be made for the costs and expenses of the solvent winding-up of the holding company. In addition to the liquidator's costs and expenses, other professional costs are likely to be incurred, including fees for lawyers and tax accountants.

Experience shows that in negotiating such arrangements, the holding company and its directors need to be realistic and prepared. Lenders that may be facing a loss on their investment will wish to avoid further dilution on their ultimate return and as such will seek to limit any financial support provided by the new group to the holding company under the arrangement, in terms of both its scope and amount. In particular, the lenders are most unlikely to countenance support (eg, by way of indemnity) that is open ended in either duration or amount. Accordingly, ahead of negotiating such an arrangement, the holding company and its directors will need, as far as possible, to have undertaken due diligence to ascertain the liabilities and the amounts that will need to be satisfied, and to have worked out the other costs for its solvent winding-up, including obtaining quotes from advisers. Specific and quantified items are much more likely to be capable of agreement in a timely fashion than unspecified and uncosted items.

In addition to negotiating a clean break, there might be the possibility of negotiating a small equity interest in the new group in consideration for assistance in executing the transaction. In practice, where this is possible, that interest might be expected to be anywhere between 1% and 10% of the equity in the new holding vehicle, although the precise amount will be a matter for negotiation. While this will not provide control and may be of little economic value, particularly when compared with the original investment, it may make all the difference to the private equity investor in terms of reputation and performance record, where the alternative is the complete loss of the original investment and the insolvent winding-up of the holding company. Whether this is possible will depend on the leverage and negotiating position of the holding company and the private equity investor in relation to that of the lenders. This will be dictated by a range of factors, including the terms of the underlying transaction documents for the original buy-out and

59 Transitional arrangements might also be addressed in the sale agreement.

timing (the general perception being that a consensual transaction will be quicker to implement than a non-consensual transaction). In order to gauge negotiating strength, the private equity investor will usually commission a review of the lenders' options for reaching their goal, both consensual and non-consensual, and as part of this, a review of the transaction documentation to ascertain points of weakness or uncertainty that can be leveraged by the holding company or the private equity investor.

It may appear that the benefit of a clean-break arrangement is all one way and there is little advantage for the lenders; however, this is not necessarily the case. A solvent outcome for the holding company through a consensual process and avoiding enforcement, which might itself entail insolvency proceedings in the guise of administration (or overseas insolvency proceedings where there are foreign group companies over which the lenders hold security), will have three key benefits for the lenders:

- Time and cost – generally, a consensual transaction will be quicker and, partly as a function of the reduction in implementation time, cheaper to implement than a non-consensual transaction. In distressed situations, the need to minimise cost is self-evident. However, the group's cost burden typically increases for a range of reasons that might include suppliers reducing or eliminating credit terms and the expectation (and possibly the right) of stakeholders, such as lenders, to have the group bear the costs and expenses of their professional advisers occasioned in connection with the distress.
- No enforcement – it should avoid the possibly damaging effects of a lender-led enforcement process on the operating group's goodwill, long-term and key contractual arrangements (eg, by avoiding the occurrence of defaults pursuant to enforcement) and other commercial arrangements and relationships fundamental to the operation of the business (eg, with credit insurers). This can be particularly important where counterparties may be looking for a reason and grounds to take advantage of the company's distress to further their own agenda (eg, renegotiating contracts on less favourable terms or exiting the contract altogether ahead of term). In certain cases an enforcement process may still be required to implement the transaction even on a consensual basis,[60] but where this is the case, it is much easier in a consensual environment to manage and take steps to mitigate the otherwise damaging effects.
- Holding company stability – if the holding company is given a solvent winding-up, the potentially adverse effects and uncertainty generated by an insolvent winding-up for the purchaser (see section 3) can be avoided, lending to the overall strength and integrity of the transaction.

---

60 This might be the case where a majority of the lenders are in agreement, but a minority are not; however, through an enforcement process commenced by the majority, their preferred outcome can be implemented.

Tax issues

David Harkness
Nick Mace
Anthony Stewart
Kevin Thompson
Clifford Chance LLP

1. Introduction

At each stage of a private equity investment, commercial, regulatory and tax objectives will determine how the transaction should be structured. From a tax perspective, when an investment is first made the focus will be on ensuring that the initial investment itself and any returns made throughout the life of the investment are structured in a tax-efficient way. However, since private equity investors will always make an investment with a view to its ultimate realisation, a key consideration will be ensuring that investors can maximise their proceeds when they come to exit by minimising tax 'leakage'.

This chapter is designed for a reader who does not necessarily have a background in taxation, and the intention is to highlight the principal issues that need to be considered rather than set out a detailed discussion of technical tax issues. Although this chapter considers UK tax issues, it is likely that similar considerations will arise in other jurisdictions (although of course the answers will not necessarily always be the same).

The issues outlined in this chapter are most easily considered by reference to a paradigm structure as set out in Figure 1 overleaf (although there is a wide variety of private equity fund structures and many cases will not exactly fit this paradigm).

At the acquisition stage of an investment, a chain of companies (Topco, Midco, Midco 2 and Bidco in the above example) is often established to acquire the investment (Investee Company). This is normally done for the non-tax reason of ensuring that senior creditors can lend to a company (Bidco) which is lower in the group structure than the companies into which the junior creditors and shareholders lend. This 'structural subordination' ensures that the junior creditors and shareholders rank behind creditors lower down in the group structure.

2. Sales

A sale may take various forms and the tax consequences will vary accordingly. Ideally, the fund would wish to dispose of the whole of its participation in an investment (Investee Company) and would (for the reasons described below) generally wish to do so at the highest possible level in the group structure (ie, by selling the shares in Topco). If a 'full' exit cannot be achieved, the fund may consider a 'partial exit'. This may be a sale of part of an investment (eg, a sale of a 25% stake in Topco or Investee Company, or a sale of part of the underlying business of Investee Company).

Figure 1

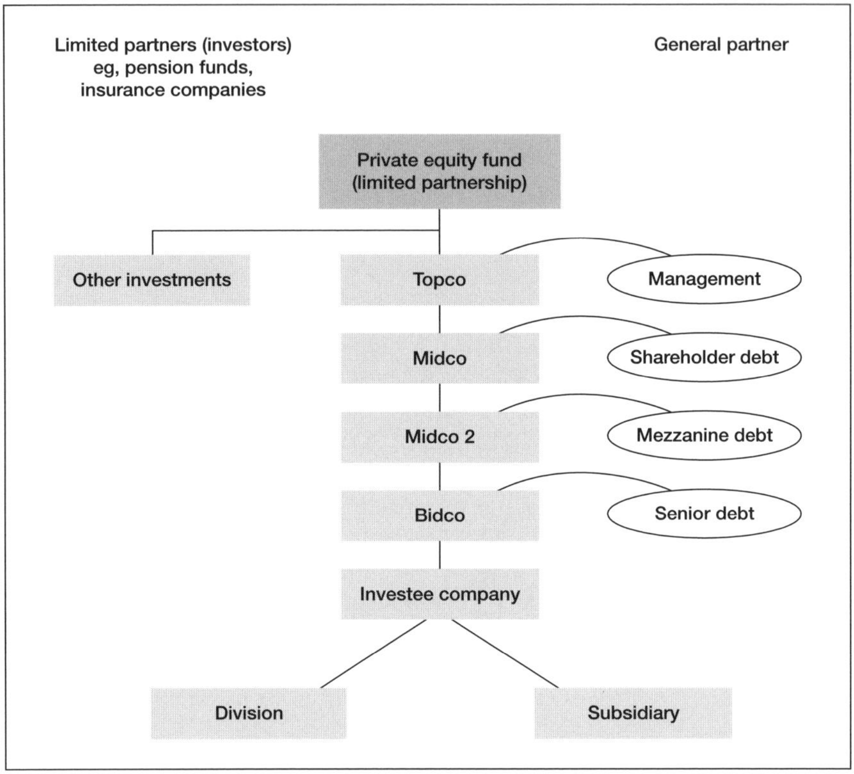

The purchaser may be a third-party trade purchaser or, in the case of secondary buy-outs, the management team supported by a new private equity fund.

3. Sale of whole investment

In any private equity sale where the whole investment is being disposed of, the tax issues affecting both investors and management will be crucial. These are considered in turn in sections 3.1 and 3.3 below. The transaction itself may also give rise to transactional taxes (eg, stamp duty), which are considered in section 3.4 below.

3.1 Tax issues for investors

In the United Kingdom, a private equity fund is often established as a fiscally transparent limited partnership, which is not itself subject to tax. When the partnership disposes of an asset, any gains or losses arising will be apportioned among the various partners.

Most funds have a wide range of investors that will invariably have different tax profiles. Many of the large institutional investors will not be subject to UK tax on capital gains. For example, the investors may be resident outside the United Kingdom and therefore outside the charge to UK tax (because the United Kingdom does not generally tax capital gains made by non-residents). Alternatively, the investors may be non-tax paying entities, such as tax-exempt pension funds. As a result of these different tax profiles, the aim in any exit will generally be to maximise the proceeds which the fund can distribute to investors as a whole, rather than seeking to accommodate the specific tax concerns of particular investors. In other words, the aim is to minimise any taxes arising at the level of the fund itself or lower down in the holding company structure.

A sale of the shares in Topco should result in the least tax leakage since, as described above, the fund will typically be structured so that it will not itself be subject to UK tax on the sale proceeds. However, a purchaser may be unwilling to acquire all of the holding companies within the group and may instead wish to acquire the actual investment (ie, Investee Company). In such cases the issues set out below should be borne in mind (these will also be relevant where, exceptionally, the sale takes place at a level above Investee Company (eg, where Midco 2 sells Bidco)).

(a) Substantial shareholding exemption

If the selling entity (Bidco in the above example) is resident in the United Kingdom or is otherwise subject to UK corporation tax, a key issue will be whether the conditions of the substantial shareholding exemption are met.[1] If the conditions are met, any gain arising on the disposal by Bidco of the shares in Investee Company will be exempt from UK corporation tax on chargeable gains (and any loss on the disposal will not be available to set off against gains). Broadly, the exemption applies where:

- the selling company (Bidco) disposes of shares or an interest in shares in the target company;
- the selling company has held a 'substantial shareholding' (at least 10%) in the target company (Investee Company) for a continuous period of at least 12 months in the preceding two years; and
- the selling company is a trading company or a member of a trading group, and the target company is a trading company or the holding company of a trading group or sub-group.

Determining whether the conditions for exemption are met can be a complex process requiring a detailed analysis of the activities of both the seller and the target companies. For example, a key aspect is that the exemption is aimed at trading companies and groups (rather than investment companies and groups); whether that condition is satisfied is ultimately a question of fact. In many private equity structures, Investee Company and its subsidiaries may well form a trading group. However, potential issues which affect whether a group is treated as a trading group for these purposes include:

- the holding of significant investment assets (eg, real estate) which are not used for the company's trade;
- interests in joint venture companies;

1 Schedule 7AC of the Taxation of Chargeable Gains Act 1992.

- where the target has substantial non-trading activities with other members of the seller's group (eg, intra-group receivables); and
- where the target holds substantial surplus cash balances.

In addition, the legislation provides that the selling company must be a sole trading company or a member of a trading group both before and immediately after the disposal.[2] For these purposes, the group constitutes Topco and its subsidiaries. Any other investments held by the fund will not be grouped with Topco for these purposes, since if the fund is structured as a limited partnership, a group relationship cannot be established through the fund. After the disposal, it is therefore unlikely that Bidco will be a trading company or a member of a trading group. However, there is a subsidiary limb of the substantial shareholding exemption[3] which is potentially available where this condition is not met, but the selling company is liquidated shortly after the disposal (eg, where Topco sells the shares in Midco and Topco is then liquidated). However, the wording of the legislation is problematic and requires careful consideration.

(b) *Extraction of proceeds*

Where an entity other than the fund (eg, Bidco) receives the proceeds of sale, further structuring will be required to ensure that the proceeds are extracted in a tax-efficient manner. Generally, the most straightforward way to achieve this is by distributing the proceeds to higher companies in the chain by way of dividend (which may also require the undertaking of reductions of share capital to create the necessary distributable reserves to ensure that lawful distributions can be declared).

Although dividends received by UK companies are *prima facie* taxable on receipt, there are wide-ranging exemptions,[4] one or more of which are likely to apply in the vast majority of private equity structures (although care must be taken to ensure that one of the exemptions is satisfied and associated anti-avoidance legislation[5] is not applicable). In addition, a company paying a dividend will not be required to make any withholding or deduction on account of UK tax.

The proceeds of sale can also be used to repay debt in the structure.

Once the proceeds of sale (after any repayment of debt) have been distributed to Topco, Topco can then be liquidated in order to distribute the proceeds to the fund for onward distribution to the investors.

3.2 Repayment of shareholder debt

The sale may comprise both a sale of shares in the target company and a repayment of any shareholder debt provided by the fund to Topco or to other members of its group.

If the target group has surplus cash available to it, it may be possible to use some or all of that cash to repay shareholder debt before the sale. Alternatively, it would

---

2 Paragraph 18, Schedule 7AC of the Taxation of Chargeable Gains Act 1992.
3 Paragraph 3, Schedule 7AC of the Taxation of Chargeable Gains Act 1992.
4 Chapter 3, Part 9A of the Corporation Tax Act 2009.
5 Sections 931J to 931Q of the Corporation Tax Act 2009.

be usual for the parties to agree to reduce the debt-free purchase price for the shares by the amount of shareholder debt, with the purchaser then procuring that the target group repay the shareholder debt on completion (the purchaser could provide the necessary funds to the target group as either debt or equity, or a combination, in order to suit its own commercial and tax objectives). Provided that care is taken when drafting this obligation in the share purchase agreement to ensure that the repayment of debt is not treated as additional consideration for the shares for stamp duty purposes, reducing the price of the shares in this manner also has the advantage of reducing the amount of stamp duty payable on the transaction.

Although UK withholding tax (equal to the basic rate of income tax – currently 20%) is generally payable on interest, the shareholder debt will usually have been structured at the investment stage to ensure that it falls within an available exemption (eg, the debt may have been structured so as to qualify for the quoted Eurobond exemption from UK withholding tax).[6]

Additional considerations arise where the shareholder debt is worth less than face value because the target group has fallen in value. In these circumstances care must be taken to ensure that tax liabilities do not arise for the borrowing company as a result of a release of part of the indebtedness.

3.3 Tax issues for management shareholders

The percentage shareholding held by management will generally be a small fraction of that held by the fund, but given the need to incentivise management, care will usually have been taken at an earlier stage to ensure that management participation is structured in a tax-efficient manner. UK tax resident shareholders will generally wish to ensure that proceeds are subject to tax as capital gains, given the difference in rates of capital gains tax and income tax.[7] Moreover, if the proceeds are taxed as employment income (as opposed to other income, such as dividend or interest), national insurance contributions will be due for both the employee and employer (in the latter case, potentially reducing the value of the fund's investment).

(a) Form of management participation

Management will generally participate in Topco alongside the fund through a holding of shares in Topco. The managers may also hold some of the shareholder debt issued by Topco. On basic principles, a disposal of shares in Topco should give rise to proceeds taxable as capital gains. Any profit arising on shareholder debt is likely to be taxed as income, whether it takes the form of interest payments or profit on disposal.

However, two main sets of considerations can affect this basic treatment. First, under the rules relating to the taxation of 'employment-related securities' in Part 7 of the Income Tax (Earnings and Pensions) Act 2003, profits from shares and securities received by reason of employment may, in certain circumstances, be recharacterised as employment income.

---

6 Section 882 of the Income Tax Act 2007.

7 The rate of UK capital gains tax for the tax year 2011/2012 is 28% for higher and additional rate taxpayers. The rate of UK income tax for the tax year 2011/2012 is 40% for higher rate taxpayers and 50% for additional rate taxpayers (those that earn more than £150,000).

Second, Her Majesty's Revenue & Customs (HMRC) has the power to recharacterise consideration as income where HMRC considers that the transaction has given rise to a tax advantage under the 'transactions in securities' rules.[8]

(b) *Employment-related securities*

The employment-related securities rules comprise a number of anti-avoidance provisions which are intended to prevent benefits from being provided to employees through the medium of shares and securities which might otherwise (ie, in the absence of these provisions) be taxed as other forms of income or (more frequently) capital gains. Several different provisions can be relevant in the context of a private equity investment by management, although the most likely to be on point are those that relate to 'restricted securities'.[9]

Essentially, the restricted securities provisions can apply to shares (or securities) whose value is depressed by one or more 'restrictions' attaching to them (eg, in particular, transfer and forfeiture restrictions). Since management shares will generally be subject to so-called 'leaver provisions' (ie, the obligation on the employees, in certain circumstances, to sell their shares back to the company/other shareholders if they cease to be employed), they will almost invariably be restricted securities. If the employee pays less than the value of the shares, ignoring the effect of these restrictions (the 'unrestricted market value') when he or she acquires them, a proportion of the ultimate sale proceeds of the shares will be recharacterised as employment income. The proportion is calculated by reference to the *pro rata* amount of the deemed underpayment – thus, if shares that would otherwise be worth 100 are subject to restrictions such that their value is only 80, and if they are acquired for 80 and sold for 200, then 20% of the ultimate sale consideration (40) will be taxed as employment income.

However, it is possible for the employer and employee jointly to elect out of this treatment so that an immediate tax charge arises in respect of any discount to the unrestricted market value (20 in the above example) when the shares are acquired. The effect of making this election is that any subsequent proceeds are not subject to recharacterisation as employment income.

Although the management team will almost invariably pay the same amount for the shares that it receives as the fund pays for the same equity, there can be circumstances where this may not represent the full value of the shares. For example, if the fund also provides shareholder debt and this debt has a low coupon, the effect will be to shift value into the equity and thus into the hands of management. To provide certainty as to the tax treatment of management shareholders in private equity transactions, HMRC has agreed a memorandum of understanding with the British Venture Capital Association on the treatment of management equity.

This memorandum of understanding effectively provides a 'safe harbour' from the restricted securities rules, provided that certain conditions are satisfied. In brief,

---

8 Chapter 1, Part 13 of the Income Tax Act 2007.

9 Other chapters of Part 7 of the Income Tax (Earnings and Pensions) Act 2003 may also apply (eg, if shares have previously been acquired on deferred payment terms or if the shares are convertible).

the managers must acquire the shares on the same terms and at the same time as the fund, and if the fund is providing shareholder debt, this debt must bear a coupon at a rate no less than that applicable to the most expensive unconnected debt (the idea being to stop value being shifted into equity by providing 'cheap' debt to the company). If there is a ratchet, there is a further condition whereby the managers must pay the full amount for their shares on the basis of their maximum possible entitlement under the ratchet.

(c) *Transactions in securities*

The transactions in securities rules are intended to stop arrangements under which shareholders turn income into capital through dealings in shares or securities. Although a sale of shares to a third-party purchaser should not generally trigger the application of these rules, if management is to retain an interest in the investment and Investee Company has large distributable reserves, HMRC may argue that Investee Company should have distributed the reserves by way of dividend prior to the sale, and that by selling shares the sellers have sold the distributable reserves for a capital return. It is possible to apply for HMRC clearance on this point.

(d) *Capital gains tax – entrepreneurs' relief*

If a sale of management shares is subject to UK capital gains tax, the tax will broadly be due on the difference between the base cost of the shares and the sale proceeds, subject to the availability of any relief[10] or exemption.

One relief which may be available is entrepreneurs' relief.[11] If the conditions for entrepreneurs' relief are met, capital gains tax is chargeable at a rate of 10% on gains that benefit from the relief. There is a lifetime cap[12] on the amount of capital gains which qualify for entrepreneurs' relief. For higher and additional rate taxpayers that would otherwise pay capital gains tax at a rate of 28%, entrepreneurs' relief currently gives a potential maximum tax saving of £1.8 million.[13] Entrepreneurs' relief applies in various circumstances. In the context of private equity transactions, the circumstance which is likely to be the most relevant is a disposal by an individual of shares or securities in that individual's 'personal trading company'.[14] A company is an individual's personal trading company where:

- the company is a trading company (or the holding company of a trading group);
- the individual holds at least 5% of the company's ordinary share capital, allowing the individual to exercise at least 5% of the voting rights; and
- the individual is an officer or employee (full or part-time) of the company or a member of the trading group.

In general, a management shareholder is unlikely to satisfy the requirement of

10 For example, the annual exempt amount (£10,600 for individuals for 2011-12).
11 Chapter 3, Part 5 of the Taxation of Chargeable Gains Act 1992.
12 Currently £10 million in 2011/12.
13 £10 million x 18%.
14 Section 169I of the Taxation of Chargeable Gains Act 1992.

holding 5% of both the ordinary share capital and the voting rights. However, careful structuring of the terms of a manager's investment may enable this requirement to be satisfied.

(e) ***Capital gains tax – reinvestment***

While a sale will usually involve the end of the fund's interest in Investee Company, the same will often not be true of the management shareholders. While they will often want to realise at least part of their investment for cash, a purchaser may want the management team to remain with the business and retain a stake in it. If a purchaser buys Topco, management shareholders can achieve this by selling only part of their shareholding.

However, in many cases a purchaser will want management shareholders to have an interest in the purchaser's acquisition company (Newco) rather than in the target company. In these circumstances management shareholders will, in effect, be forced to dispose of all of their existing shareholding in Topco in return for cash and shares in Newco. While managers could simply sell their existing shares and acquire new shares with the cash proceeds that they receive, this will generally crystallise an immediate tax charge in respect of the whole of their original holding in Topco, even though in real terms they may have made only a part disposal.

Therefore, managers will generally prefer to defer their tax liability on the stake in the business that they retain by seeking to benefit from 'rollover relief', under which they can exchange their shares in Topco for shares or securities[15] in Newco.[16] This will enable the managers to postpone their charge to capital gains tax until the consideration shares or securities are later sold or redeemed. These provisions require an 'exchange' to take place and care needs to be taken that the proposed transaction meets the statutory definition of an 'exchange of securities' in Section 135 of the Taxation of Chargeable Gains Act 1992. In the context of a private equity transaction, it will generally be necessary to ensure that Newco acquires (or already holds) at least 25% of the shares in Topco. However, difficulties can arise where the purchaser wants to issue shares or securities to management shareholders out of a company other than Newco. Rollover relief can be denied to any shareholder that (together with connected persons) holds more than 5% of the target, unless the transaction is carried out for *bona fide* commercial purposes and does not form part of a scheme or arrangement of which the main purpose, or one of the main purposes, is the avoidance of a liability to capital gains tax or corporation tax.[17] It is usual to apply for HMRC clearance on this point and, in fact, a single clearance is usually made to cover both rollover relief and the transactions in securities rules discussed in section 3.3.3 above.

3.4 Transaction taxes

In addition to tax liabilities arising on the institutional investors and the

---

15 Where the consideration consists of securities, careful planning is needed to ensure that the correct type of loan notes are issued. Generally, it is preferable to ensure that the new securities are not 'qualifying corporate bonds'.

16 Sections 127 to 138A of the Taxation of Chargeable Gains Act 1992.

17 Section 137 of the Taxation of Chargeable Gains Act 1992.

management shareholders, the transaction itself may trigger tax charges, and in large transactions such transactional taxes can be material.

(a) ***Stamp duty***

When a purchaser acquires shares and certain types of debt security in a UK company, it will usually be liable to stamp duty or stamp duty reserve tax at a rate of 0.5% of the consideration (rounded up to the nearest £5). Stamp duty and stamp duty reserve tax are usually borne by the purchaser in a transaction. However, depending on the type of transaction, the stamp tax costs may be significant and may therefore affect the overall price that a purchaser is willing to pay. Therefore, sellers are also usually interested in mitigating any stamp taxes.

Often, no stamp tax issues will arise – the purchaser will simply pay the tax on the consideration. However, a number of complications can arise (in particular, care needs to be taken where there is an element of deferred contingent consideration because stamp duty can be charged on the maximum amount payable).

While stamp duty is payable on sales of UK shares, no liability arises on transfers of 'exempt loan capital'. Thus, in many cases the sale of shareholder debt will not attract tax. However, care needs to be taken to ensure that the shareholder debt really is exempt loan capital. Provisions that permit conversion of the debt into equity or give a right to acquire more debt securities will prevent it from being exempt. Similarly, if the interest payable is dependent on the results of the business or is excessive, or if the redemption amount exceeds a reasonable commercial return, the shareholder debt will not be exempt.

In contrast to the sale of shareholder debt, the repayment of such debt would not be subject to UK stamp duty.

(b) ***Value added tax***

A sale of shares will be exempt from value added tax (VAT). However, the costs related to the sale (eg, advisers' fees) are likely to include VAT, which will be a cost to the fund if the fund is based in the United Kingdom, as it will be unable to recover the VAT.

4. Partial exits

In this chapter the term 'partial exit' is used to describe a situation where only part of an investment is to be sold. A partial exit may be achieved by:

- a sale of part of an investment (eg, a sale of a 25% stake in Topco or Investee Company); or
- a sale of part of the underlying business of Investee Company.

Alternatively, investors may realise part of their interest in an investment by way of a refinancing, under which some (or all) of their debt is repaid, allowing cash to be returned to the investors.

4.1 Sale of part of an investment

Where the fund is disposing of a proportion of its participation in Topco or Investee

Company, the tax issues will broadly follow those arising on a sale of the whole investment (see section 3 above).

4.2 Sale of part of the underlying business

Where a purchaser wishes to acquire only part of the underlying business of Investee Company, the part in question may be operated as a subsidiary of Investee Company or through a division of Investee Company (see Figure 1 above). In the United Kingdom, there are significant tax differences between a share sale and an asset sale. These are outlined in the table in Figure 2 below.

Figure 2

	Share sale	**Asset sale**
Substantial shareholdings exemption	Yes, if conditions are satisfied	No
Ability to use tax losses (trading losses)	Yes, subject to anti-avoidance provisions	No
Tax relief on intangible assets	No	Yes*
Capital allowances	No	Yes*
Balancing charges	No	Yes *
Crystallisation of taxable gains on assets	No – however, degrouping charges may apply	Yes
Double taxation	No	Yes**
Historic tax liabilities of target inherited	Yes	No
Stamp taxes	0.5%	Up to 4% if any UK real estate purchased
VAT	No	No***

**Where assets are acquired by a purchasing company within the charge to UK corporation tax, it may be able to obtain relief from corporation tax in respect of the price paid for goodwill and other intangible assets. The relief broadly follows the accounting amortisation. Capital allowances should also be available for qualifying expenditure on plant and*

machinery.[18] *However, a sale of the assets may lead to tax charges for the seller under the same regimes if the sale proceeds exceed the tax written down value of the assets.*
***When a UK company disposes of its assets, a charge to UK corporation tax will arise if those assets have increased in value. This will reduce the funds which are ultimately available to return to investors which may also be subject to tax when the funds are distributed to them.*
****A sale of assets by a company which is registered (or liable to be registered) for UK VAT purposes is generally subject to VAT at the standard rate,*[19] *unless the transfer constitutes a 'transfer of a going concern'. A number of conditions must be satisfied, but in general terms this relief is intended to apply where the assets are to be used by the buyer to carry on the same kind of business as the seller. If the conditions are met, the sale will be outside the scope of VAT and no VAT will be due. Where the assets include real estate, further issues arise.*

In general, due to the availability of the substantial shareholdings exemption on a share sale, a share sale will usually achieve a more favourable tax outcome for a corporate seller. Conversely, due to the potential tax reliefs for acquisition costs on an asset deal, a purchaser will generally favour an asset acquisition. However, in practice, transactions are more commonly structured as share sales for non-tax reasons (eg, due to the legal and practical difficulties of transferring large numbers of assets in a business). Nevertheless, there are circumstances where the structure may be driven by tax considerations. For example, where the seller has capital losses, it may be able to shelter the gain that would otherwise arise on an asset sale. If the purchaser favours an asset deal and is prepared to increase the purchase price as a result of the benefits which it obtains, the transaction may be structured as the sale and purchase of assets.

4.3 Refinancings

A refinancing typically involves the repayment of an existing loan or loans (together with accrued interest) with new debt finance. A detailed analysis of refinancings is beyond the scope of this chapter; however, in broad terms, a repayment of the principal amount of a loan should give rise to no tax liabilities for the investors, although tax will be due on any accrued interest (for further discussion on UK withholding tax on interest payments see section 3.2).

5. Pre-sale reorganisations

For non-tax reasons, it may be preferable to structure a sale as a share sale. However, in some circumstances this may not be possible (eg, where a company owns assets which are not part of the target business or which the seller wishes to retain), and it may be necessary to carry out a pre-sale reorganisation such as a 'hive-down' or a 'hive-out'. In such cases the key tax consideration will be to minimise any taxes arising as a result of the pre-sale reorganisation.

---

18 The main rate of capital allowances is 20% for the tax year 2011/12. From April 2012, the 20% rate will be reduced to 18%.

19 20% for the tax year 2011/12.

5.1 Hive-down

Effectively, a hive-down is a combination of an asset sale and a share sale. The target business/assets are first transferred into a new company and the shares in that company are then sold to the purchaser. This ensures that the purchaser acquires the business assets that it wants in a new (clean) company. Although it is generally possible to transfer the target assets to the new company without adverse consequences (tax reliefs for intra-group transactions are available to treat the new company as 'standing in the shoes' of the transferor), this structure can give rise to a number of tax issues.

(a) Degrouping charges

A problem with hive-down transactions is that a sale of shares in the hive-down company may give rise to 'degrouping charges' if, following the hive-down, the transferee company leaves the seller's tax group within a certain period. Degrouping charges may arise in respect of intra-group transfers that include transfers of land, shares, intangible assets, loan relationships and derivative contracts. Three of these degrouping charges (chargeable gains, intangible assets and stamp duty land tax) are considered in further detail below.

Chargeable gains: Where an asset that is subject to corporation tax on chargeable gains is transferred between companies within the same corporate group, no tax liability generally arises at that time.[20] However, if the transferee company is sold out of the group, while holding the assets that it has acquired from another group company within the previous six years, a degrouping charge can arise.[21] The degrouping charge is calculated on the gain that would have arisen had the company sold (and immediately reacquired) the asset for consideration equal to its market value immediately after the intra-group transfer and (before the Finance Act 2011) the charge arose in the target company leaving the group at the beginning of the accounting period in which the degrouping occurred. However, following the enactment of the Finance Act 2011, the degrouping charge is generally treated as an adjustment to the seller's gains/losses on the disposal of shares, rather than as arising in the company leaving the group.[22] The effect of this is that if the disposal qualifies for the substantial shareholding exemption (see section 5.1.a), any degrouping charge will also be exempt. However, somewhat unfortunately, the Finance Act 2011 amendments do not apply to degrouping charges arising under the intangible assets regime. As many companies hold assets under the intangible assets regime rather than under the chargeable gains rules, this is likely to undermine the utility of the reforms to the latter.

Intangible fixed assets: Broadly, the intangible assets regime applies to the tax treatment of intangible fixed assets (principally goodwill and intellectual property) acquired or created on or after April 1 2002. Under the regime, profits on disposals are

---

20 Section 171 of the Taxation of Chargeable Gains Act 1992.

21 Section 179 of the Taxation of Chargeable Gains Act 1992.

22 However, the new provision applies only where the degrouping charge arises as a result of a company leaving a group because of a disposal of shares or a share-for-share exchange to which the reorganisation provisions in Section 127 of the Taxation of Chargeable Gains Act 1992 apply.

taxed as income and the buyer receives a tax deduction for accounting amortisation of acquisition costs. A degrouping tax charge is triggered if an intra-group transfer (of an asset within the intangibles regime) has taken place and the transferee company leaves the group within six years.[23] The company is deemed to have sold and immediately reacquired the asset at its market value at the time that it originally acquired the asset from the other group member. If the market value at that time exceeds the amortised value, a degrouping charge will arise, giving rise to a taxable profit. The charge is treated as arising immediately before the transferee company leaves the group. As mentioned above, the Finance Act 2011 amendments to the chargeable gains tax rules on degrouping charges do not apply to charges arising under the intangible assets regime, so that a degrouping charge which arises as a result of an intra-group transfer of an asset within this regime still arises in the target company.

Stamp duty land tax: Relief from stamp duty land tax will generally be available if UK real estate is transferred between companies in the same group. However, a degrouping charge arises (and the stamp duty land tax relief is clawed back)[24] if the transferee company subsequently leaves the group. The relevant period is different from that for chargeable gains and intangible assets. Stamp duty land tax may be clawed back where the transferee company ceases to be a member of the same group as the transferor company within three years of an intra-group transfer of the assets, or where the transferee company ceases to be a member of the same group as the transferor company in pursuance of, or in connection with, arrangements made before the end of that period.

(b) ***Substantial shareholding exemption***

In the past, the sale of a hive-down company would not have benefited from the substantial shareholding exemption because, unless the hive-down had been carried out sufficiently far in advance, the seller was unlikely to satisfy the 12-month holding period requirement (see section 3.1(a)). However, the Finance Act 2011 extended the substantial shareholding exemption by:

- extending the ownership period of the hive-down company so that the seller is treated as having held the shares in the hive-down company at any time during the 12-month period when the asset was used for the purposes of a trade carried on by the group; and
- treating the investee company condition as met in those circumstances.

(c) ***Trading losses***

Subject to certain conditions, trading losses can be transferred to a hive-down company. However, a number of anti-avoidance provisions potentially apply where there is a change of ownership of the target company. In particular, trading losses can be carried forward following a change of ownership of the target company only if there is no major change in the nature or conduct of the acquired trade within three years of the change of ownership.

---

23 Section 780 of the Corporation Tax Act 2009.

24 Paragraph 3, Schedule 7 of the Finance Act 2003.

5.2 Hive-out

An alternative structure to a hive-down is a hive-out. Under this structure, the company which owns the target business hives out all of the assets which are not intended to be sold to another company in its group. The transferor company (which now no longer owns the 'unwanted' assets) is then sold to the buyer. Hive-outs are sometimes considered in order to avoid the degrouping risks associated with hive-down structures, since the transferred assets do not leave the seller's group.

One of the principal difficulties with a hive-out is that where the retained business is large and complex, it can be very difficult and costly to transfer it; this, in combination with the changes to the chargeable gains tax degrouping charge in the Finance Act 2011, may result in hive-downs becoming more common structures.

6. Key transaction documents requiring tax input

The main transaction documents requiring tax input on a sale of a private equity backed company are as follows:

- the due diligence report (or a vendor due diligence report when acting for a seller);
- the share purchase agreement, which includes tax warranties and provisions implementing the structure generally; and
- the tax covenant (or tax deed), which will typically be either a separate document or in the form of a schedule to the sale and purchase agreement.

The tax covenant apportions risk for unexpected tax liabilities that arise prior to completion and also deals with other more administrative issues, such as responsibility for preparing and filing tax returns for the pre-completion periods and for the period straddling completion, and mechanisms for dealing with disputes with the tax authorities. In the United Kingdom, on a non-private equity trade sale a seller would usually expect to give a tax covenant for pre-completion tax liabilities, subject to customary exclusions and limitations. However, in UK private equity sales, market practice is that institutional shareholders will usually give no tax covenants or warranties. In such cases tax warranties and covenants may be given by the management team. However, the managers' personal financial liability under such warranties and indemnities is often limited (usually to a proportion of the consideration that they will personally receive under the transaction).

In the case of a 'partial exit' (ie, a sale by Investee Company of one of its subsidiaries), a buyer may argue that tax warranties and a tax covenant should be given by the seller, since the transaction is similar to a non-private equity trade sale (ie, it would expect Investee Company to give usual tax covenants and warranties). On an asset deal, the buyer is not acquiring the tax history and other liabilities of the target. Therefore, the seller will not usually give a tax covenant and only limited tax warranties are usually given. However, where the sale includes a UK business, the asset purchase agreement will often contain detailed provisions dealing with VAT, covering (in particular) whether the sale constitutes a transfer of a going concern.

7. Initial public offerings

As is the case for a sale, an initial public offering (IPO) (and, in particular, any reorganisation steps leading up to it) may be structured in different ways and the tax consequences will vary accordingly.

When considering how the IPO should be structured, the fund would ideally (as with a sale) wish to dispose of its participation in an investment at the highest possible level in the group structure. Therefore, the IPO would ideally take place at the level of Topco.

However, there may be situations where this is not possible or desirable, or where only part of the investment is to be listed and a pre-IPO reorganisation is therefore required (see section 12).

8. New holding company

For commercial reasons, the group may decide to establish a new holding company to act as the vehicle to be listed, and in doing so it must consider the best location for that holding company. This will largely be driven by factors other than tax (eg, requirements for inclusion in indices and local company law regime), but tax issues may also be important. When considering the appropriate location for a group's holding company, tax considerations include:

- the extent to which incoming dividends and capital gains are taxed;
- the level of withholding taxes on dividends and interest;
- the availability of benefits under double tax agreements;
- how the jurisdiction taxes profits made by foreign subsidiaries; and
- whether transfers of shares in the company are subject to stamp duty or other transfer taxes.

This chapter considers the position where a UK holding company is used or interposed as the vehicle to be listed.

Where a new holding company is established, it will be important to ensure that its interposition is carried out in a tax-neutral manner for both the group and its shareholders.

8.1 Capital gains tax – rollover relief

From a UK capital gains tax perspective, where a shareholder exchanges its original shares (eg, shares in Topco) for shares in a new holding company (Holdco shares), provided that certain conditions are met,[25] the shareholder is not treated as having made a disposal of the Topco shareholding for capital gains tax purposes. Instead, the shareholder is treated as having exchanged its shares in Topco for Holdco shares. The Holdco shares take over the history and base cost of the Topco shares, and the charge to capital gains tax is postponed until the Holdco shares are later sold. This is known as 'rollover relief'. If a shareholder (together with connected persons) holds more than 5% of Topco, rollover relief is available only if the transaction is carried out for *bona fide* commercial purposes and does not form part of a scheme or arrangement

---

25 See section 3.3 (e).

of which the main purpose, or one of the main purposes, is avoidance of liability to capital gains tax or corporation tax.[26] It is usual to apply for HMRC clearance on this point.

8.2 Stamp duty

A transfer of shares in a UK company generally gives rise to a liability to stamp duty or stamp duty reserve tax at a rate of 0.5%. However, where a new holding company is interposed, it may be possible to mitigate the stamp duty costs.

Where the new holding company is interposed by way of a 'share-for-share exchange', relief from stamp duty[27] is generally available provided that certain conditions are satisfied. Broadly, these conditions are as follows:

- The transaction is effected for *bona fide* commercial reasons and does not form part of a tax avoidance scheme;
- The consideration for the acquisition consists only of the issue of shares in the new holding company;
- Following the acquisition, each person that immediately before it was made was a shareholder of the target company is a shareholder of the new holding company and the shares in the new holding company are of the same class; and
- Following the acquisition, the proportion of shares of any particular class in the new holding company held by any particular shareholder are the same (or as nearly as may be the same) as the proportion of shares of that class in the target company held by the shareholder immediately before the acquisition.

If these conditions cannot be satisfied, it may be possible to mitigate a stamp duty liability by undertaking a cancellation of the existing Topco's share capital and a reissuance of Topco shares to the new holding company, with the new holding company issuing shares to Topco shareholders. As such a transaction does not involve a transfer of shares in Topco, no UK stamp duty or stamp duty reserve tax should arise. Although this structure will not constitute an 'exchange' of shares for the purposes of rollover relief,[28] rollover relief should still be available under the reconstruction provisions.[29]

9. Tax issues for investors and management shareholders

The IPO may involve both an issue of new shares and a sale of existing shares to new investors. For institutional investors and management shareholders, an IPO may therefore involve a sale of some or all of their existing shares in Topco. The tax issues arising on a disposal of shares as part of an IPO will be the same as those arising when the exit is structured as a sale (for further discussion of the tax issues for institutional investors that sell shares in Topco on exit, see section 3.1, and for further discussion

---

26 Section 137 of the Taxation of Chargeable Gains Act 1992.
27 Section 77 of the Finance Act 1986.
28 Under Section 135 of the Taxation of Chargeable Gains Act 1992 (see section 3.3 (e)).
29 Section 136 of the Taxation of Chargeable Gains Act 1992.

of the tax issues for management shareholders that sell or dispose of shares, see section 3.3).

10. Transaction taxes

Generally, no stamp duty or stamp duty reserve tax is payable when new shares are issued.[30] However, where shares in a UK company are transferred, there is a charge to stamp duty or stamp duty reserve tax at a rate of 0.5%, and so a stamp duty or stamp duty reserve tax liability will arise in respect of sales of existing shares. Stamp duty is generally paid by the purchaser. However, in the context of an IPO the company (or existing shareholders) will often bear the stamp tax costs arising on the sale of existing shares, since the purchaser will not be in a position to know whether it is acquiring newly issued shares or existing shares.

11. Key transaction documents requiring tax input

The main transaction documents requiring tax input on an IPO are a prospectus and an underwriting/placing agreement.

A prospectus is broadly required if a company makes an offer to the public or requests admission to trading of transferable securities in the United Kingdom. The Prospectus Rules and the Financial Services and Markets Act 2000 govern the content of a prospectus. In relation to tax, the Prospectus Rules require specific disclosure to be given only in relation to any withholding taxes and taxes specifically charged to the subscriber or purchaser.[31] However, it is customary for the tax disclosure section to contain a wider and more general summary of the tax issues that are associated with investing and holding shares in the company.

The underwriting agreement may contain tax warranties which are usually given by the company itself. These are usually limited tax warranties relating to the basic tax position of the company, such as compliance issues. The underwriting agreement also contains provisions governing how certain costs and expenses should be borne. In relation to stamp duty, the agreement generally provides that the existing shareholders or the company itself will pay any stamp duty or stamp duty reserve tax arising in connection with a sale of existing shares in the company.

12. Pre-IPO reorganisations

In any exit structure, the fund would ideally wish to dispose of the whole of its participation at the highest possible level in the group structure. However, this may not be possible if potential investors are unwilling to invest in a group with multiple holding companies or where the group has non-core assets or activities.

---

30 However, where chargeable securities (including shares) are issued or transferred to a depositary or clearance system, a liability to stamp duty reserve tax or stamp duty at a rate of 1.5% generally arises. While the securities remain in the depositary or clearance system, there will normally be no further charge to stamp duty reserve tax or stamp duty. Following the European Court of Justice decision in *HSBC Holdings v HMRC* (C-569/07), the government announced that from October 1 2009 and subject to anti-avoidance provisions, the 1.5% stamp duty reserve tax charge would not apply on the issue of shares into a clearance service or a depositary receipt system within the European Union.

31 There are also general content requirements which require additional tax disclosures to be made in certain circumstances.

In such cases the group may have to carry out a reorganisation before the IPO. For example, where the group has non-core assets or activities which will not be included in the IPO, the group may wish to carry out a demerger transaction to split the assets or activities into separate companies. This enables the non-core assets and activities to be kept in a parallel company for the benefit of existing shareholders. While it is generally possible to structure such demerger transactions so that they are tax neutral for both the company and its shareholders, careful planning is required to ensure that the demerger transaction is structured to fall within the various exemptions and reliefs from UK tax. These exemptions and reliefs are complex and beyond the scope of this chapter.

A Luxembourg perspective

Pierre Beissel
Arendt & Medernach

1. Introduction – the place of Luxembourg in the private equity world

In order to understand the relevance of the Luxembourg perspective on private equity exits, it is first important to appreciate Luxembourg's place in the private equity world.

Despite Luxembourg's longstanding tradition in the structuring of national and international private equity acquisitions, it is not easy to collect precise figures on the presence of the private equity industry in Luxembourg. There are various reasons for this. With some exceptions, most of the private equity houses rarely communicate publicly on their Luxembourg operations. A second factor is the absence of a Luxembourg private equity lobby. This gap has now been filled by the creation in 2010 of the Luxembourg Private Equity and Venture Capital Association, which is likely to lead to a better understanding of the Luxembourg private sector in the near future.

Although they may not specifically advertise it, it is common knowledge that most of the major private equity and buy-out firms, including CVC, KKR, Blackstone, Carlyle, Apax, Advent, Warburg Pincus and Cinven, have a more or less substantial presence in Luxembourg and channel a certain amount of international deals through Luxembourg.

In addition to non-regulated vehicles, Luxembourg has certain lightly regulated private equity vehicles such as the *société d'investissement en capital risque* (SICAR), a vehicle created specifically for venture capital and private equity investments, and the specialised investment fund (SIF). The Luxembourg regulated private equity industry is much younger than the unregulated industry and effectively began in 2004 with the creation of the SICAR.

The number of fund structures may yet increase in the near future with the implementation of the EU Alternative Investment Fund Managers Directive. Although not necessarily favourable to the European private equity industry as a whole, the directive will transform Europe into a level playing field for private equity funds and may attract funds with an international investment strategy to Luxembourg due to the regulatory experience that Luxembourg has acquired so far with undertakings for collective investment in transferable securities (ie, regulated open-ended retail funds operating freely throughout the European Union on the basis of a single authorisation from one member state, for which Luxembourg represents a hub).

While the regulated private equity industry has developed significantly in recent years in Luxembourg,[1] the most popular vehicle remains the unregulated holding company (*société de participation financière*), incorporated in the form of a public limited company (*société anonyme*) (SA), a private limited liability company (*société à responsabilité limitée*) (Sarl) or a partnership limited by shares (*société en commandite par actions*) (SCA), which can be used as a fund, joint venture or structuring vehicle. Given the significant number of structures set up through Luxembourg in recent years, exits are made increasingly frequently from a Luxembourg holding company.

Luxembourg private equity structures follow established models created in the United States and the United Kingdom, with some specificities depending on tax constraints due to the country of origin of the private equity investors or the country of the target company.

Unsurprisingly, Luxembourg started to see an increase in the number of private exits in 2010 after a virtual standstill in 2009. Exit activity is expected to rise further in 2011, the major part of which should comprise secondary buy-outs, although some high-profile trade sales and initial public offerings (IPOs) have already been announced during the first quarter of the year.

This chapter does not purport to give a comprehensive view of the mechanisms and techniques used for private equity exits in Luxembourg, which are largely similar or identical to those seen in other countries; rather, it aims to examine a few selected topics and issues more specific to the Luxembourg market.

2. Exit at which level?

A Luxembourg private equity structure may involve one or several layers of Luxembourg companies above the target company, depending on the jurisdictions involved, the requirements of the co-investors or, more rarely, the financing banks, and the most likely exit scenarios.

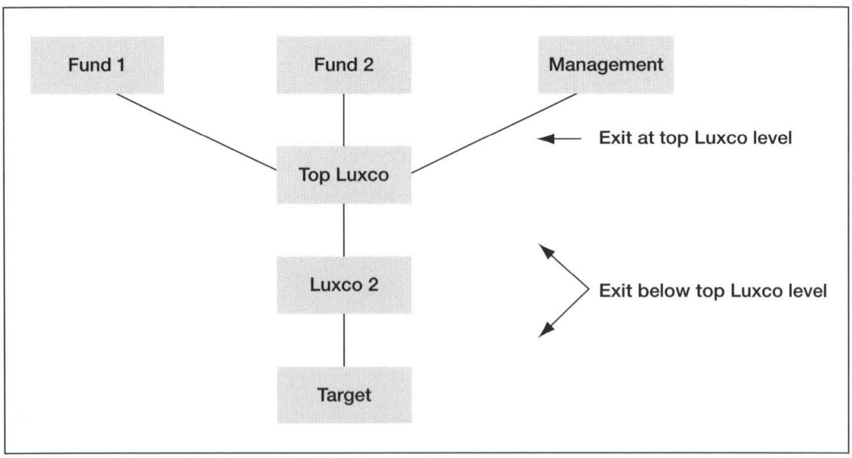

1 As of the end of 2010, there were more than 300 regulated private equity funds in Luxembourg, with more than €40 billion fund assets under management.

Exit scenarios cannot be predicted with absolute certainty, since they depend in part on the acquirer, which by definition is unknown at the time that the structure is being set up. Nevertheless, some scenarios are more likely than others.

The Luxembourg legal and tax treatment will differ depending on whether the exit takes place at the level of the top Luxembourg company or at a level below. An exit at the level of the top Luxembourg holding will trigger various provisions of the shareholders' agreement and, most notably, drag-along rights. An exit at one or more levels below the top Luxembourg company will have as a consequence an upstreaming of the sale proceeds to investors and, except in case of a partial exit, liquidation of the top Luxembourg company.

Generally, the exit strategy will involve a sale at the level below the top Luxembourg holding. An acquirer and, in particular, a buyer in a trade sale will have an interest in the target company, but not necessarily in a holding company which has been tailor made for one or more private equity investors without necessarily suiting the specific needs of the acquirer. Also, often private equity sellers and acquirers prefer to avoid incurring the risk of a forced sale further to a shareholders' agreement in relation to, or the articles of incorporation of, the top Luxembourg holding.

However, in some circumstances an exit at the level of the Luxembourg top holding may be of interest to the acquirer, be it because the tax situation of this company can benefit the acquirer or because the acquirer desires to take over the existing financing organised through this company.

3. Exit by way of securities sale at the level of the Luxembourg top holding

An exit at the level of the Luxembourg top holding may raise certain pre-contractual and contractual issues.

3.1 Parallel negotiations

Without going through a costly organised auction process, private equity sellers may tend to have parallel negotiations with two or more potential buyers with which letters of intent have been signed, without openly disclosing to all parties involved that parallel negotiations are taking place. Under Luxembourg law, a potential seller and acquirer are under an obligation to negotiate in good faith (ie, with a view towards obtaining a result and executing a final agreement between them). The courts have considered that the sudden termination of an undisclosed parallel negotiation may represent a violation of the duty to negotiate in good faith and may lead to the selling party being liable for any damage caused to the potential acquirer whose bid is not retained. The liability risk will increase if it turns out that the terminated negotiation was undertaken for tactical reasons only, with no intent to conclude a final agreement.

The damage will in most cases consist of the advisers' fees paid by the plaintiff during the due diligence process, but could also include the loss of other opportunities during the negotiation process.

3.2 Break fees

Break fees are fees payable by a buyer or seller in case the deal aborts, and are permissible. However, they may be considered contractual penalties if they have a punitive nature, in which case a court may reduce such penalties if it deems them clearly excessive. Therefore, courts may compare the amount of the break fee, which usually lies in the range of 1% to 3% of the transaction value, with the prejudice actually incurred. Break fees should therefore be drafted to cover reasonable costs and fees incurred by the seller or the buyer only.

3.3 Issues related to transfers of shares generally

Depending on the type of company, transfers of shares may raise certain issues under Luxembourg law which must be addressed when drafting the document containing the provisions relating to the transfer of shares, be it a shareholders' agreement or the articles of incorporation of the company.

Shares of an SA[2], as well as the limited shares of an SCA,[3] are freely transferable. Consequently, limitations to the transferability of such shares must be closely monitored. While drag-along, tag-along and pre-emptive clauses are unproblematic, provisions tending to prohibit transfers are valid and enforceable only if they are limited in time. Luxembourg law does not set the duration for which shares can be made non-transferable, but the courts generally hold that the prohibition cannot exceed 10 years and should be economically justified. For example, the shares may be made non-transferable for a maximum of 10 years, except in case of an exit at an earlier date.

An alternative way of structuring a transfer restriction would involve subjecting any transfers of shares to the approval of either the co-investors or the company. While this restriction need not be limited in time, approval cannot be withheld unreasonably.

Transfers of shares of an Sarl[4] to non-shareholders are subject to the approval of shareholders representing 75% of the share capital given in a general meeting. This rule has traditionally been considered as mandatory by the courts, which raises the issue of the validity of drag-along and tag-along clauses in Srls. Prior approval cannot be waived in advance by the shareholders, except in the very limited case of share pledges,[5] where the pledgee can be approved as a potential future shareholder in the pledge agreement.

In drag-along situations, the issue is *de facto* solved when the majority shareholder holds at least 75% of the shares of the company. In all other circumstances it cannot be excluded, in the absence of recent case law, that a court would not give effect to a drag-along or tag-along clause initially agreed upon by the parties if the general meeting of shareholders did not approve the share transfer at a

---

2 The *société anonyme* is the equivalent of a public limited company.

3 The *société en commandite par actions* is a company which is generally subject to the same rules as the SA, except that it has two categories of shareholder: limited shareholders, whose liability is limited to their contributions, and unlimited shareholders, which are liable for all of the company's debts.

4 The *société à responsabilité limitée* is the equivalent of a private limited company.

5 Law of August 5 2005, as amended, on Financial Collateral Arrangements.

75% majority. Any one or more shareholders holding more than 25% of the share capital may potentially be able to block a previously agreed-upon transfer provision.

While there are arguments to consider such an action where a shareholder reneges on an earlier agreement in bad faith and as an abusive exercise of a right, legal uncertainty remains.

If the relevant provision is included in a shareholders' agreement governed by a law other than Luxembourg law, the other parties may be able to obtain damages under the shareholders' agreement, although they would be unlikely to succeed in obtaining specific performance in Luxembourg.

There are early-stage plans to transform this approval right into a default rule, which may be abandoned by the shareholders in the articles of incorporation.

3.4 Enforcement of drag-along clauses

Effective enforcement of drag-along clauses in case of exits from management and club deals is an important issue. Neither private equity nor strategic buyers wish to deal with minority shareholders upon purchase of a target company, be they private equity funds or members of management. In practice, issues typically come up in distressed sales where minority, non-controlling private equity owners that may have lost their controlling interest further to a restructuring involving the taking of control by the lenders may try to hold on to their stake in the target company in order to benefit from a potential upside on their investment. Unresponsive investors or dissatisfied management may also be problematic.

The enforcement of drag-along clauses raises three main questions. First, some shareholders' agreements are governed by the law of a country other than Luxembourg. Will those shareholders' agreements be enforceable in Luxembourg, it being understood that only specific performance of the relevant drag-along clause provides a benefit to the private equity seller and the acquirer? Should the drag-along provision be included in the articles of incorporation or does a shareholders' agreement grant sufficient comfort in terms of specific performance? Finally, how must the clause be drafted to guarantee maximum efficiency?

(a) Which law?

The question of which law a shareholders' agreement relating to a Luxembourg company should be subject to may seem to be a structuring rather than an exit issue. However, it is closely related to the enforceability of crucial provisions, such as the distribution waterfall and the drag-along, tag-along and pre-emption clauses.

EU Regulation 593/2008 on the law applicable to contractual obligations (Rome I) gives the parties freedom to make a contract subject to the law of their choice, subject to certain limitations. The consequence of having a shareholders' agreement governed by the law of a country other than Luxembourg is that enforcement of the shareholders' agreement upon exit must, as a general rule, be sought in a country other than Luxembourg, assuming the logical situation that the jurisdiction clause points to the jurisdiction of the country of the governing law rather than to Luxembourg. This causes no particular issues, to the extent that the relief being sought consists of damages only. However, as the foreign court does not have jurisdiction in Luxembourg, it will be unable to order specific performance in respect of a Luxembourg company which is itself governed by Luxembourg law.

Thus, such court will not be in a position to order the registration of a transfer of shares in a share register, or to suspend or cancel such registration. In conclusion, for maximum efficiency, a shareholders' agreement relating to a Luxembourg company should be governed by Luxembourg law.

(b) Inclusion of drag-along clauses

As illustrated above, drag-along clauses are set out in a general shareholders' agreement between all investors in the Luxembourg company. Traditionally, there has been discussion in Luxembourg as to whether contractual obligations providing for specific performance must in all circumstances be specifically enforced. Courts now tend to be more favourable towards specific performance. Nevertheless, they can still decide to grant damages rather than specific performance based on traditional case law.

In addition, the courts have generally held that only clauses included in the articles of incorporation of a company can justify the exclusion of a shareholder. While this is debatable, it remains highly recommended, to the extent conceivable from a confidentiality standpoint, to duplicate clauses relating to the forced exit of a shareholder, and in particular drag-along clauses, in the articles of incorporation.

(c) Drafting of drag-along clauses

Careful attention must be given to the drafting of drag-along clauses.

Most clauses are worded as obligations for the shareholders being dragged along to execute an additional transfer agreement. The dragging shareholder is then granted a power of attorney to take the relevant steps to render the transfer effective, and in particular to register the transfer in the target company's share register.

Under Luxembourg law, powers of attorney are always revocable, even if they are stated to be irrevocable. Given that the power of attorney is likely to be revoked immediately in case of a conflict, the dragging shareholder may have no choice other than to engage in a court proceeding in order to obtain relief.

In some circumstances judicial relief can be obtained quickly in a summary procedure. However, in most cases club and management deals are organised by way of complex shareholders' agreements, partly included in the articles of incorporation of a Luxembourg company, with potentially ancillary documentation (eg, internal debt instruments). A judge in a summary procedure will grant relief if the request is not subject to serious challenge. If the situation is complex, the judge will prefer to maintain the status quo pending a judgment on the merits.

In conclusion, there is a risk that the enforcement of clauses worded as described above will require a judgment on the merits, and an additional risk that the court resolving on the merits will decide to grant damages rather than specific performance.

In most cases this risk can be reduced by structuring the drag-along clause as an option which may be exercised by the beneficiaries in certain circumstances, hence creating an automatic transfer mechanism which avoids having to request a judge's prior authorisation prior to operating the transfer. The clause must include a price-setting mechanism which is independent of either party in order to be valid – the most likely scenario being a price set by reference to the price offered by a *bona fide* third party.

4. Exit by way of a securities sale at a level below the Luxembourg top holding

4.1 Distributions and waterfall

Although there is no general rule and the specific situations may vary, most private equity deals structured through a Luxembourg holding company are financed to a large extent by shareholder debt and to a lesser extent by pure equity, meaning share capital and share premium. There is no legal distinction between shareholder and third-party creditors, which means that shareholder debt is considered as ordinary debt and treated, in the absence of a subordination agreement, *pari passu* with third-party debt, taking priority over distributions on equity.

Luxembourg law is very flexible as far as the economics of distributions on shares are concerned. As a general rule, unequal distributions between shareholders raise no issues, to the extent that they have been accepted by all shareholders in the articles of incorporation. The only limit on dividend distributions is that no shareholder can be entirely excluded from participating in the profits or losses.

The distribution mechanism is typically included in a waterfall section in the shareholders' agreement. The purpose of the waterfall is to organise the priority of allocations of proceeds between the private equity investors and management. The waterfall provisions will first deal with the shareholder debt. If the company is financed by convertible preferred equity certificates or a similar debt instrument (see section 6.2), the capital gain is usually distributed through those instruments.

If no convertible preferred equity certificates, income-sharing loans or other convertible instruments are outstanding at the time of the exit, the capital gain will be distributed by dividend payments or, more frequently, through liquidation or partial liquidation of the company (see section 6.3).

In the absence of any provision to the contrary, each share entitles its holder to a portion of the profits equal to the part that such share represents in the total share capital. Therefore, it is crucial that the waterfall – including the carried interest, management ratchet and the hurdle – be included in the articles of incorporation and approved by all shareholders at the setting up of the structure, as they will diverge from the rule of proportional profit distribution.

4.2 Management participation

As management represents a key value for a private equity investor, it typically participates in the Luxembourg private equity investment vehicle. There are several potential technical aspects in respect of an exit from a management participation.

(a) Management ratchet

Management is generally entitled to a carried interest amounting to a certain percentage of the total profits made, the payment of which will be subject to the private equity investors first receiving the full return of their capital.

In most circumstances the management carried interest is structured as a share class reserved to the management, which may allow management to fall within a capital gains tax rather than an income tax regime, to avoid any withholding under the EU Savings Directive[6] and to benefit potentially from the participation exemption (see section 6.1), in particular if the management's shareholding is bundled in a management investment vehicle. For the reasons set out under section 3.3, the carried interest provisions should be included in the articles of incorporation.

The ratchet is a motivational tool allowing the management team to increase its participation in the profits in case certain criteria are met upon exit. Those criteria are generally defined by reference to a hurdle, which can be a percentage of the internal rate of return or a multiple of the initial investment.

The management ratchet can take various forms. Most frequently, the ratchet is simply a mechanism included in the waterfall distribution provisions of the articles of incorporation, which increases or decreases the amounts allocated to a certain share class depending on whether the hurdle has been met.

By analogy to the well-known mechanism of 'deferred shares' in the United Kingdom, the ratchet may involve a partial conversion of the share class reserved to the managers into a basically worthless share class in case the hurdle has not been met (negative ratchet). Conversely, the management team may subscribe to a lower amount of shares, the shares of the private equity investors being converted into 'deferred shares', entitling it to a bigger slice of the profits if the hurdle has been met.

However, this mechanism is quite cumbersome under Luxembourg law, as it requires the holding of a general meeting of shareholders prior to exit in order to convert part of the management shares to a different class. Furthermore, it causes problems in principle, since the concept of 'deferred shares' is unknown under Luxembourg law and because of the rule that no shareholder can be entirely excluded from participating in distributions of profits.

(b) *Stock options*

Second-tier managers will often be granted stock options rather than a participation in the carried interest. Vested options will become exercisable upon exit, but the holder of the option will receive cash out of the exit proceeds rather than going through the complicated process of first converting its options to shares. The advantage of options under Luxembourg contractual and corporate law is that the option terms can be made to include automatic payment and lapsing provisions, which will avoid any pitfalls related to the exercise of drag-along rights in case management hold shares (see section 3.3).

5. Partial exits

Partial exits generally follow a partial divestment, a refinancing with a view to

6 EU Directive 2003/48/EC on the taxation of savings income.

distributing some or all of the proceeds from the refinancing to investors or a sale of the business with a reinvestment of some or all of the selling investors.

5.1 Partial divestment

Upon partial divestment by the Luxembourg company, the proceeds available from such divestment will be distributed to the investors by repayment of shareholder debt, dividend payments or partial liquidation of the company, depending on the financing of the company and the tax structure (see sections 4 and 6).

In most cases partial exits are subject to approval under the finance documents governing the existing senior or mezzanine loans.

(a) Repayment of shareholder debt

Generally, shareholder loans or loan securities are repayable either at any time prior to their term or upon an exit event.

Repayments to shareholders will be made in accordance with the terms of the relevant shareholder debt instrument and with the waterfall provisions of the shareholders' agreement. The principal of an income tracking loan will be repaid up to the percentage of the total loan representing the divested part of the business as compared with the total business. From a Luxembourg perspective, the capital gain will be repaid as interest.

The features of such debt instruments are examined in more detail in section 6.2 below.

(b) Dividend payments

In the absence of shareholder debt financing or if the shareholder debt has been repaid by exit, partial exits can be organised as dividend distributions. As a general rule, dividend payments will trigger a 15% withholding tax at the Luxembourg level, unless the shareholder can benefit from the participation exemption (see section 6.1).

However, dividend distributions are subject to the capital protection rules of the second European directive.[7] Luxembourg law provides that the amount to be distributed cannot exceed the amount of profits realised since the end of the latest financial year for which the accounts have been approved, increased by any profits carried forward and by any available reserves, and reduced by any losses carried forward and by any mandatory reserves.[8]

Distributions can be problematic when the company has made substantial losses and when it is fully financed by share capital as opposed to share premium, in which case even a slight loss may prevent distributions.

Share premium is subject to no limitations and can be freely distributed as dividends by the management body of the Luxembourg company. Thus, if the intention is to distribute partial exit proceeds by way of dividends, the share premium should be set at the maximum amount possible from a commercial and tax

---

7 Directive 77/91/EEC dated December 13 1976.

8 Article 72-2 of the Law of August 10 1915 on Commercial Companies, as amended.

perspective. The higher the share premium, the lower the risk that it may be entirely consumed by potential losses made by the company.

Clearly, the risk of potential losses is heightened if the bank debt financing has been incurred directly by the Luxembourg company due to the losses created by the interest charge. In that case the availability of share premium is even more important.

Since interim dividend distributions by SAs and SCAs require the establishment of *pro forma* accounts and a report by an auditor, private equity investors seeking to repatriate funds as quickly as possible may resort to an upstream loan from the company to the investors pending fulfilment of these formalities. As a general rule, this is permissible under Luxembourg law, provided that the loan is made and bears interest at arm's-length terms. The company will be reimbursed by its shareholder(s) if it turns out that the criteria above have not been fulfilled and the distributions were not technically possible.

(c) Partial liquidations

For the reasons set out under section 6.3, partial exit distributions are often structured as partial liquidations. Partial liquidations can be contemplated only if the company's share capital has been divided into share classes, often called 'alphabet shares', beforehand. Upon partial liquidation, one share class which may or may not be linked to a specific asset is repurchased and cancelled by the company and the exit proceeds are distributed to the shareholders as the purchase price for the shares.

The amount paid in addition to the nominal value of the shares will be subject to the availability of the distributable funds test applicable to dividend distributions set out above.

5.2 Refinancing

A refinancing with a view to distributing all or part of the proceeds from the refinancing may be a partial exit route in certain circumstances. Apart from the constraints set out under section 5.1 above, this type of exit route raises two fundamental issues under Luxembourg law.

First, there must be arguments that the distribution is in the company's corporate interest. At first sight, a distribution upon refinancing will be considered as being purely in the interests of the shareholders and contrary to the interests of the company. Usually, it is deemed necessary that a non-negligible part of the proceeds of the refinancing be allocated to the benefit of the company and/or its subsidiaries. Then, the presence of the private equity investors must have directly or indirectly favoured the granting of the loan to the company, either because they have actively arranged the financing or because the loan has been granted in consideration of financial investors having control of the company. The management body of the company may be held liable from a civil law perspective in case the distribution is considered to violate the company's corporate interest.

In addition, the management may incur criminal liability for the misuse of corporate assets.[9] 'Misuse of corporate assets' is defined as a use of corporate assets by

9 Article 171-1 of the Law of August 10 1915 on Commercial Companies, as amended.

the management body in a way which it knew to be contrary to the company's corporate interest or in its own personal interest, or with the aim of favouring a business in which it is directly or indirectly interested. As a general rule, the risk of misuse of corporate assets will be avoided if the distribution does not violate the company's corporate interest.

These issues will arise only if the refinancing takes place at the level of the Luxembourg company.

5.3 Reinvestment by seller

A reinvestment by a private equity seller (or management) in the new acquisition structure can be organised in various ways. The seller will not simply remain a shareholder in the entity which is being sold, since this would not allow it to realise its capital gains fully upon a sale.

Generally, the seller will effectuate the sale and thereafter take a minority stake in a structure tailored to the acquirer's tax and commercial needs. While rollovers are frequent in reinvestments by managers, private equity investors often tend to consider this type of transaction as an exit and reinvestment, with a full realisation of capital gains and a new financing.

6. Repatriation of profits from holding companies – tax considerations

In most cases the tax structuring of an acquisition by a Luxembourg company is effected with a view to organising a tax-efficient repatriation of exit proceeds. While the applicable rules are not reserved to private equity, various instruments, such as preferred equity certificates, have been created specifically in a private equity context.

It is difficult to provide a comprehensive outline of all tax issues related to private equity exits, due to the wide variety of investors, targets, instruments and countries involved (the chapter on tax covers specific UK tax issues in some detail). Therefore, this section is mostly limited to the Luxembourg internal tax rules and the most common internal financing documents.

The precise tax structuring will depend on whether the investment is scheduled to produce regular distributable income or whether there will be a single distribution on the capital gain made upon exit.

6.1 Equity-financed acquisitions

The disappearance of the 0.5% capital duty formerly levied on equity contributions to a Luxembourg company as of January 1 2009 has led to an increase in the potential for fully equity-financed acquisitions.

(a) Corporate income tax and municipal business tax

Taxable profits of a Luxembourg company, including upon exit, are generally subject to corporate income tax and municipal business tax.

The maximum aggregate corporate income tax and municipal business tax rate amounts to 28.8% for the year 2011 (in Luxembourg City).

Dividends received by a Luxembourg company are generally taxable and consequently are included in the taxable base. A tax credit is generally available for

Luxembourg or foreign withholding tax retained by the distributing company. The same is true for liquidation proceeds.

Capital gains are taxable only upon realisation. They are generally regarded as ordinary business income and consequently are included in the taxable base for corporate income tax. No special lower taxation rates apply to capital gains.

(b) *Participation exemption regime*

However, dividends, liquidation proceeds and capital gains may be tax exempt under the participation exemption regime. Dividends which do not qualify for the participation exemption can be exempt for up to 50% in certain cases.[10]

The conditions are that the Luxembourg company is fully taxable and holds an interest in another fully taxable Luxembourg company, a company covered by Article 2 of the EU Parent-Subsidiary Directive[11] or a non-resident company limited by shares liable to a tax corresponding to Luxembourg corporate income tax.[12] Finally, at the time that the income is made available, the parent company must have held or must commit itself to hold the participation in the eligible entity for an uninterrupted period of at least 12 months and, during this whole period, either the level of participation must exceed 10% or the acquisition price must not fall below €1.2 million. Holding a participation through a tax transparent entity is deemed to be a direct participation in the proportion of the net assets held in this entity.

In addition to the domestic participation exemption, almost all of the double tax treaties concluded by Luxembourg grant an international participation exemption.

Capital gains realised on the transfer of participations are exempt under the following conditions:

- The parent and the entity in which the participation is held satisfy the same conditions as those applicable for the exemption of dividends; and
- At the time that the participation is disposed of, the parent has held or commits itself to hold a direct participation in the share capital of the eligible entity for an uninterrupted period of at least 12 months and, during this whole period, either the level of participation exceeds 10% or the acquisition price exceeds €6 million.

(c) *Withholding tax*

Outbound dividend payments by a Luxembourg company are liable to a 15% withholding tax applied on the gross amount, except when the withholding can be

10 The 50% exemption is available for dividends derived from a participation in one of the following entities:
- a Luxembourg resident fully taxable company limited by share capital;
- a company resident in a state with which Luxembourg has concluded a double tax treaty and liable to a tax corresponding to Luxembourg corporate income tax; or
- a company resident in an EU member state and covered by Article 2 of the EU Parent-Subsidiary Directive (90/435/EEC), as amended.

11 EU Directive 90/435/EEC of July 23 1990 on the common system applicable in the case of parent companies and subsidiaries of different member states, as amended.

12 According to the administrative interpretation, this condition is met when the company is mandatorily subject to a tax at an effective rate of a certain percentage, calculated on a taxable base similar to that applicable in Luxembourg.

reduced or eliminated on the basis of a tax treaty or participation exemption rules. Some other transactions can be assimilated to a dividend distribution (eg, a share capital reduction to the extent of previously capitalised reserves or, in the absence of such capitalised reserves, if the reduction is not motivated by sound economic reasons; or redemption of own shares by the company when the latter redeems a proportionally equal number of shares from all shareholders).

A withholding exemption applies under the following conditions:

- The distributing entity is a Luxembourg resident fully taxable company.
- The recipient is in substance a company covered by Article 2 of the amended EU Parent-Subsidiary Directive; a Luxembourg resident fully taxable company or a company which is resident in a country that has a double tax treaty with Luxembourg and subject to a tax corresponding to corporate income tax or a permanent establishment thereof; a company limited by shares (*société de capitaux*) or a cooperative society (*société coopérative*) which is resident in a state party to the Agreement Creating the European Economic Area, other than an EU member state, and which is liable to a tax corresponding to corporate income tax; or a Swiss company limited by share capital (*société de capitaux*), which is effectively subject to corporate income tax in Switzerland without benefiting from an exemption.
- At the time that the income is made available, the recipient has held or commits itself to hold directly for an uninterrupted period of at least 12 months a participation of at least 10% or with an acquisition price of at least €1.2 million in the share capital of the distributing entity.
- The recipient holds a direct participation in the share capital of the distributing entity. Holding a participation through a tax transparent entity is deemed to be a direct participation in the proportion of the net assets held in this entity.

If these conditions are not satisfied, distributions made to treaty country resident shareholders benefit as a rule from reduced rates provided by tax treaties.

Unlike dividend payments, distributions of liquidation proceeds (regardless of whether they derive from pre-existing reserves) are not subject to withholding tax.

6.2 Debt-financed acquisitions

(a) *Financing by way of shareholder debt*

In certain circumstances a financing of the Luxembourg company by way of shareholder debt is preferable from an exit perspective.

According to the general practice adopted by the tax authorities, the debt/equity ratio applicable to a fully taxable Luxembourg company is 15 for equity to 85 for all combined liabilities (shareholder and third-party debt, whether represented by an instrument or not). It is understood that these liabilities shall finance the acquisition of participations and bear a market interest rate.

In case of non-compliance with this ratio, interest in relation to the excess liabilities can be considered as dividends for tax purposes. The consequence is that such excess interest is not deductible and is potentially subject to a withholding tax under the same conditions as distributed dividends.

Debt instruments may bear a fixed yield, a floating yield or no yield. If they are non-interest bearing, they are considered as equity for the purpose of the applicable debt/equity ratio.

One important additional factor for preferring a financing by shareholder debt over a pure equity financing may be the flexibility in terms of reimbursement, with shareholder loans not being subject to the constraints applicable to dividend payments (see section 5.1).

(b) Shareholder debt instruments

Luxembourg and international tax practice has developed specific shareholder debt instruments in the context of the structuring of private equity acquisitions. Although there is no limitation to creativity in this area, the best-known instruments are:

- preferred equity certificates (PECs), which may be convertible into shares;
- asset-linked loans or notes; and
- income-sharing or profit-participating loans.

PECs are hybrid financial instruments which have the advantage of being considered, under certain conditions, as debt for Luxembourg tax purposes and as equity for other jurisdictions' tax purposes. Convertible preferred equity certificates (CPECs) are convertible into shares of the issuer upon exit or partial exit. In practice, in most cases they will not be converted but rather repurchased by the company at their fair market price, which will be equivalent to the fair market price of the shares to which they are convertible.

Accordingly, any interest accrued or paid on PECs or CPECs will generally be considered as a deductible business expense[13] for Luxembourg tax purposes. It will not be subject to withholding tax in Luxembourg or to taxation in Luxembourg in the hands of a non-resident taxpayer.

Asset-linked loans or notes are debt instruments for corporate law and accounting purposes that are generally used for the financing of a specific asset. The characteristic feature of an asset-linked loan or note is that its yield is linked to one or more assets defined in advance in the asset-linked loan agreement or note.

According to administrative practice, in the past it has been accepted under certain conditions that a Luxembourg fully taxable company may finance 100% of an asset by an asset-linked loan without being subject to a debt/equity ratio, where the yield under the asset-linked loan corresponds to all income derived from the asset so financed, minus an arm's-length commercial margin.

In case the asset-linked loan finances an asset whose derived income is exempt for corporate income tax and municipal business tax purposes in Luxembourg, the terms and conditions of the asset-linked loan must include a discount on the

---

13 For example, the yield will not be considered as a deductible business expense if the PECs/CPECs finance the acquisition of a shareholding that benefits from the participation exemption regime, to the extent that the yield does not exceed the amount of exempt dividends received for a given year. Any yield exceeding the exempt dividends remains deductible.

reimbursement or redemption price equal to the arm's-length margin multiplied by the number of years elapsed in order to ensure that the taxable spread is realised not only in the commercial balance sheet, but also in the tax declarations.

Repayment of the principal can be contingent upon the disposal of the underlying asset, with a recourse limited to proceeds deriving from such disposal. This limited recourse feature will allow a segregation of risks on an asset-by-asset basis. A loss incurred on one investment would thus not affect the return on another investment and the capacity of the Luxembourg entity to pay variable interest on the related asset-linked loan.

An asset-linked loan is considered as debt for the purpose of all Luxembourg taxes. Interest payments made under the asset-linked loan are considered as deductible expenses (unless they are connected with tax-exempt income or gains) and generally are not subject to Luxembourg withholding tax.[14]

Income-sharing or profit-participating loans are loans bearing low fixed interest (eg, 0.5% or 1%), as well as variable interest. The variable interest on income-sharing loans is determined by reference to the total profit realised by the borrower and is not connected with the income realised on a specific asset.

A back-to-back income-sharing loan financing arrangement can be organised within a two-tier structure in order to finance any underlying investments by the lower-tier entity (eg, participations, loans and bonds). As the income-sharing loan is arranged on a back-to-back basis at the level of the upper-tier entity, the latter is required to realise only an arm's-length commercial margin or spread on this back-to-back activity. The spread is subject to corporate income tax and municipal business tax at ordinary rates (ie, maximum 28.8%). Interest payable under the income-sharing loan will not be subject to withholding tax in Luxembourg[15] or to taxation in Luxembourg in the hands of a non-resident taxpayer.

The lower-tier entity will repatriate all of its net profit to its Luxembourg parent company as variable interest under the income-sharing loan. To the extent that this entity holds and acquires participations, in theory it is required to comply with a debt/equity ratio and a limitation on interest. However, any possible recharacterisation of excess interest as a hidden dividend should lead to no actual tax burden, due to the application of participation exemption rules between the two entities. If the lower-tier entity receives taxable income, the tax authorities generally accept that no spread is retained by this entity, as a spread is already realised at the upper-tier level.

Finally, in a move to clarify its transfer pricing policy, on January 28 2011 and April 8 2011 the Luxembourg tax administration issued two circular letters[16] which provide guidance on the tax treatment of companies conducting intra-group financing activities, and which will thus impact on some debt-financed structures by,

---

14 Subject to the provisions of the Law of June 21 2005 implementing EU Directive 2003/48/EC on the taxation on savings income and certain agreements concluded with other states, and the Law of December 2005 introducing a withholding tax on certain interest payments made to Luxembourg resident individual taxpayers.

15 A withholding tax may be applicable in some cases pursuant to the legislation implementing the EU Savings Directive. However, such a withholding tax is not applicable in the case at hand.

16 Circular Letters 164/2 and 164/2*bis*.

among other things, requesting a transfer pricing analysis for the determination of profit made on their financing activity.

6.3 Liquidations

Distributions made to shareholders upon liquidation are exempt from the 15% withholding tax generally applied on distributions, which explains the success of liquidations as a tool for the repatriation of exit proceeds.

The Luxembourg liquidation process consists of an initial general meeting, to be held before a notary public, which dissolves the company and opens the liquidation procedure. This general meeting also appoints the liquidator, who will be in charge of the liquidation process. The notary public generally verifies whether the company has duly filed its annual accounts prior to passing the deed dissolving the company.

Once the liquidator has liquidated any remaining assets and paid off all third-party creditors, he or she will convene a second general meeting to approve the liquidation report and the distribution of the liquidation proceeds, and appoint an auditor to the liquidation. A third general meeting will then resolve upon the auditor's report and close the liquidation procedure.

Although Luxembourg company law does not set a mandatory timeframe for the liquidation, liquidation proceedings tend to take more time than expected. However, the liquidator is authorised to make advance payments on liquidation proceeds upon the opening of the liquidation procedure, provided that he or she feels comfortable that making such a distribution will not prevent the servicing of the company's debt. Often, the liquidator will retain a certain amount for that purpose.

7. Exits from other types of company

Exits from other types of holding or fund vehicle may be structured slightly differently, due to the different tax regimes applicable to such vehicles.

7.1 SICAR

Created in 2004, the SICAR is a corporate structure which allows for investment in risk and venture capital by direct or indirect investment in entities to be launched, developed or listed with the aim of offsetting the high levels of risk taken by investors against a higher than average return. This vehicle is regulated and limited to well-informed investors (see section 7.2), but is subject to less stringent regulation than investment fund structures. This vehicle specifically targets private equity and venture capital funds.

The SICAR in the form of an SCA, Sarl, SA or *société cooperative* set up as a public limited company is generally fully liable to corporate income tax and municipal business tax. However, income derived from portfolio items consisting of securities and capital gains deriving from such securities, and from temporary investment in liquid assets held for a maximum of 12 months before investment in 'risk capital', are excluded from the tax base.

As a result, the SICAR is subject to corporate income tax and municipal business tax only on any other income (eg, interest income deriving from standard loans, management fees and subscription fees).

Non-resident shareholders of a SICAR that have neither a permanent establishment nor a permanent representative in Luxembourg to which the investments in the SICAR are attributable are subject to no capital gains, income or withholding tax in Luxembourg, subject to the provisions of the EU Savings Directive.

From a Luxembourg perspective, a SICAR set up in the above-mentioned corporate forms may benefit from the application of Luxembourg double tax treaties, as well as the EU Parent-Subsidiary Directive.

The SICAR can be, and in most cases is, created with a variable share capital, exempting it from the capital protection constraints set out under section 5.2. With the exception that the minimum share capital of €1 million cannot be paid out, distributions and share redemptions by a SICAR are subject to no restrictions other than as provided in the articles of incorporation, allowing for the quick repayment of investors upon exit or partial exit. This, added to the SICAR tax regime, avoids the need for a more complex structuring of the equity financing by way of debt instruments.

7.2 Specialised investment fund

The specialised investment fund (SIF) is a vehicle created in 2007 which is reserved to well-informed investors, meaning institutional investors, professional investors or any other investor that meets the following conditions:

- He or she has confirmed in writing that he or she adheres to the status of a well-informed investor, and
- He or she:
  - invests a minimum of €125,000 in the specialised investment fund; or
  - has been the subject of an assessment made by a credit institution within the meaning of EU Directive 2006/48/EC, by an investment firm within the meaning of EU Directive 2004/39/EC or by a management company within the meaning of EU Directive 2001/107/EC certifying his or her expertise, experience and knowledge in adequately appraising an investment in the specialised investment fund.

In practice, this means that sophisticated retail or private investors may invest in an SIF. Similar to the SICAR, the SIF can be structured as an umbrella fund, with two or more compartments which can be separately liquidated in case of an exit or partial exit without the SIF itself being liquidated.

The SIF is subject to a risk spreading rule of 30%, which applies to each individual compartment.

The SIF is tax exempt, except for a 0.01% subscription tax on its net asset value.

Any distributions made by an SIF are not subject to withholding tax, thus allowing for a tax-neutral exit as far as Luxembourg taxation is concerned.

From a corporate perspective, distributions by a SIF are subject to the same rules as those of a SICAR. The minimum share capital of an SIF has been set at €1.25 million.

8. IPO

Until recently, the listing of a Luxembourg vehicle as an exit route for private equity investors was rarely high on the priorities list, mainly for commercial reasons and because of the lack of a Luxembourg track record for equity listings.

This may be about to change, given a number of high-profile listings of Luxembourg companies in 2010 (eg, L'Occitane, which was listed on the Hong Kong stock market, and two special purpose acquisition companies listed on the Frankfurt stock exchange).

There are several advantages of using Luxembourg as the country of choice for an exit by way of an IPO.

Luxembourg has an interesting company law in the sense that the Luxembourg SA and, even though more rarely used, the SCA, although typical civil law entities, can be easily adapted to the requirements of the relevant stock exchange and investors. The main limitation is that the board of directors of an SA may at any time be revoked without cause, thus preventing the creation of effective staggered boards.

The authorised share capital is essentially a delegation by the general meeting of shareholders in favour of the board, which allows the board to increase the share capital of a company up to a certain amount specified in the articles without reserving the existing shareholders a preferred subscription right. It allows for the creation of effective poison pills, to the extent permissible under applicable market regulations.

In the context of European IPOs, the consequence of using a Luxembourg company is that the offer documents must be filed and discussed with the generally more accessible Luxembourg regulator, the *Commission de Surveillance du Secteur Financier.*

Most, if not all, of the IPOs of Luxembourg companies in a private equity context take place on foreign stock exchanges (US, Frankfurt and, more recently, Warsaw), given the relative lack of liquidity of equity instruments listed on the Luxembourg stock exchange.

9. Distressed exits

How to deal with distressed companies has been a hot topic in Luxembourg since 2009.

As a preliminary matter, in order to consider Luxembourg for a distressed debt restructuring, the Luxembourg company must itself be in an insolvency situation (ie, the company must be unable to pay its debts as they fall due and unable to obtain any further credit). In spite of the fact that the entire investment may be in an insolvency situation, if the acquisition financing has been fully structured through a direct or indirect subsidiary of the Luxembourg company, it is unlikely that the Luxembourg company will itself be technically insolvent, unless it acts as guarantor under the finance documents.

The options to restructure a Luxembourg distressed company in preparation for an exit are limited. The traditional insolvency procedure, which dates back to the 19th century, is rarely an option, as it has been conceived as a liquidation procedure, which means that a sale of the company as a going concern is not the primary purpose. Second, and most important, it leads to a complete loss of control by the investors, since the management is replaced by an insolvency receiver, assisted by a judge, and the shareholders are no longer consulted.

However, a second procedure aiming at reorganising a business does exist – it is known as 'controlled management'. The procedure starts with a request by the company, leading to a first court judgment if the court deems that conditions for controlled management have been fulfilled. These conditions are that the company must have difficulties meeting its commitments and be unable to obtain further financing, without being insolvent. There must be realistic prospects for reorganisation (or orderly liquidation). The first judgment automatically stays the enforcement of all proceedings against the company. The major advantage of controlled management is that management remains in charge, although under the supervision of one or more receivers. The success of the procedure will depend on the approval of the reorganisation plan, involving in most cases a sale of the company, by 50% of the creditors representing more than 50% of the debts of the company, thus granting important powers to the company's creditors.

The main obstacle to controlled management as an exit from a distressed investment is the Luxembourg Law of August 5 2005 on Financial Collateral. Although the automatic stay on the first court judgment stops all enforcement proceedings against the company, it does not stop enforcement of Luxembourg security granted over the company's assets or enforcement of security granted over the company's shares.

Consequently, controlled management is of little use when the Luxembourg company has granted substantial security over its assets.

About the authors

Pierre Beissel
Partner, Arendt & Medernach
pierre.beissel@arendt.com

Pierre Beissel is a partner in the investment funds practice of Arendt & Medernach, where he specialises in corporate law, mergers and acquisitions and transactional business law. He advises private equity firms, hedge funds and real funds on fund structuring and formation, as well as on the structuring and financing of international buy-out transactions, joint ventures, corporate reorganisations and corporate governance matters. He serves as co-head of the firm's private equity group.

Mr Beissel is an active member of the Luxembourg Private Equity and Venture Capital Association and the Mergers & Acquisitions Subcommittee of the American Bar Association. He is also a member of the Luxembourg and New York Bars.

He holds a law degree (DJCE – DESS) from the University of Montpellier and is a graduate of Cornell Law School (LLM).

Rachel Bond
Partner, Macfarlanes LLP
rachel.bond@macfarlanes.com

Rachel Bond joined Macfarlanes in 1997 and became a partner in 2006. She advises on all aspects of public and private M&A transactions, as well as private equity and venture capital transactions. She also advises a number of public and private companies on general corporate issues.

Ms Bond was seconded for one year to a major law firm in New York and much of her work is cross-border or has an international dimension. She has developed particular expertise in relation to transactions in the financial services sector, for both corporates and private equity sponsors.

Stuart Boyd
Partner, Linklaters LLP
stuart.boyd@linklaters.com

Stuart Boyd is a managing associate in the corporate department of Linklaters in London. He holds a degree in law and specialises in M&A and equity issues, with a particular focus on private equity.

In particular, he has led Linklaters teams on a number of leading private equity transactions in a variety of sectors. He also has extensive experience of public and private M&A transactions and joint ventures.

Stuart Brinkworth
Partner, Hogan Lovells International LLP
stuart.brinkworth@hoganlovells.com

Stuart Brinkworth is a partner in the banking group at Hogan Lovells in London. He joined the firm in 2010 from SJ Berwin LLP, where he was also a banking partner. He specialises in acting for UK and international lenders, sponsors and bidding consortia on a variety of private equity-backed finance transactions, including leveraged buy-outs, management buy-outs/buy-ins, public bids and recapitalisations, and has experience of senior, second-lien, mezzanine and payment-in-kind debt, as well as acquisition bridge financings. Mr Brinkworth also has experience in advising both lenders and sponsors in the restructuring of leveraged assets.

Mr Brinkworth is widely recognised for his specialist expertise in leveraged finance and is ranked in the leading guides to the legal profession, including *Chambers Global*, *Chambers UK* and *Legal 500*. Mr Brinkworth was also included in the finance section of *The Lawyer's Hot 100 2011*.

Emma Danks
Partner, Taylor Wessing LLP
e.danks@taylorwessing.com

Emma Danks is a partner in the corporate department of Taylor Wessing in London and specialises in private equity.

Ms Danks trained with Clifford Chance and spent nine years in its private equity practice before joining Taylor Wessing. She has advised many of the leading European and international private equity houses and their investee companies on a wide range of leveraged buy-outs and related transactions.

Ms Danks is co-author of the *PLC Cross-Border Private Equity Handbook 2010*. She has also been involved with the Private Equity Foundation since its establishment in 2006.

Ms Danks is a graduate of Newnham College, Cambridge.

Stephen Drewitt
Partner, Macfarlanes LLP
stephen.drewitt@macfarlanes.com

Stephen Drewitt joined the firm in 1993 and became a partner in 2002. He specialises in private equity and acts predominantly for private equity sponsors. His clients include 3i, The Royal Bank of Scotland plc, Phoenix Equity Partners, Darwin Private Equity and Silverfleet Capital.

Tom Evans
Senior associate, Clifford Chance LLP
tom.evans@cliffordchance.com

Tom Evans joined the London private equity team at Clifford Chance in 2006 and spent 18 months in Hong Kong from late 2009. He specialises in advising on cross-border mergers and acquisitions, equity finance and arrangements between private equity investors and management teams. Prior to working with Clifford Chance, Mr Evans qualified as a barrister and solicitor in Australia, where he worked with an Australasian firm advising on mergers and acquisitions in the Asia-Pacific region and as a senior legal adviser for the Australian Capital Territory government.

David Harkness
Partner, Clifford Chance LLP
david.harkness@cliffordchance.com

David Harkness has been a partner at Clifford Chance since 1996 and the global head of its tax, pensions and employment practice since 2006. He specialises in corporate and international tax planning. He has undertaken a wide range of work, including many significant public and private mergers and acquisitions, restructurings, joint ventures, financing transactions and securitisations.

His clients include leading banks and insurance companies, and industrial and commercial enterprises. Mr Harkness has particular experience in advising large corporates, banks and financial institutions on public takeover issues, tax structuring and disputes. Geographically, he has experience in advising on tax issues throughout Europe and North America.

Mr Harkness is listed as a leading tax adviser in *Chambers*, *Legal 500* and the *Guide to the World's Leading Tax Advisers* (2010), and has written and lectured on a number of tax issues. He recently co-authored a chapter on European tax issues for the *Inward Investment and International Taxation Review*.

Philip Hertz
Partner, Clifford Chance LLP
philip.hertz@cliffordchance.com

Philip Hertz is a partner in Clifford Chance's restructuring and insolvency group. His practice involves general insolvency and restructuring work. He is a member of the Association of Business Recovery Professionals, INSOL and the Insolvency Lawyers' Association. Mr Hertz is also a member of the Insolvency Lawyers' Association Council and serves on its technical committee. He is the co-author of the chapters entitled "Schemes of Arrangement" in *Tolley's Insolvency Law* and "Compromising Shareholder Claims both generally and in listed companies" in *The Law and Practice of Restructuring in the UK and US*, as well as numerous articles on insolvency-related topics.

Mr Hertz's recent experience includes advising senior creditors' committees, companies and private equity houses in relation to the restructuring of a number of distressed international groups.

David Holdsworth
Partner, Linklaters LLP
david.holdsworth@linklaters.com

David Holdsworth is a partner in the corporate department of Linklaters in London. He holds a degree in law and specialises in M&A and equity issues, with a particular focus on private equity.

Kem Ihenacho
Partner, Clifford Chance LLP
kem.ihenacho@cliffordchance.com

Kem Ihenacho is a partner at Clifford Chance in London and joined the firm in 1999. He specialises in private equity investment, cross-border mergers and acquisitions and corporate finance, and is also a lead partner in the firm's Africa group. Mr Ihenacho is a member of the Legal and Regulatory Council of the Emerging Markets Private Equity Association, sits on the advisory board of the Clifford Chance Foundation and regularly advises charities and not-for-profit organisations on a pro bono basis.

John Lane
Partner, Linklaters LLP
john.lane@linklaters.com

John Lane is a partner in the corporate department of Linklaters in London. He specialises in equity capital markets transactions and has done so for over 15 years while based in London. He has extensive experience of equity capital raisings and international public M&A transactions.

Recently, he has advised both issuers and underwriting banks on primary and secondary equity capital raisings on the London Stock Exchange, including various proposed private equity exits by way of IPO with a focus on shareholder structures, pre-IPO reorganisations and management incentive packages.

John MacLennan
Partner, Clifford Chance LLP
john.maclennan@cliffordchance.com

John MacLennan is a partner in Clifford Chance's restructuring and insolvency group in London. He specialises in international and domestic restructuring and insolvency, advising lenders, companies, directors, private equity sponsors, insolvency officeholders, government institutions and other stakeholders. Mr MacLennan has also spent a period working as a restructuring banker on secondment to the restructuring team of a leading UK clearing bank. As well as being published in restructuring and insolvency and finance and banking journals, he is a member of the Association of Business Recovery Professionals (R3), the Insolvency Lawyers' Association and INSOL.

Chris McLaughlin
Partner, Hogan Lovells International LLP
chris.mclaughlin@hoganlovells.com

Chris McLaughlin is a partner in the banking group at Hogan Lovells, London. He specialises in the origination and restructuring of domestic and cross-border leveraged acquisitions, and acts for a wide variety of banks, private equity sponsors and borrowers. He also has significant experience in real estate finance and provision of working capital facilities alongside high-yield bond financing.

Nick Mace
Partner, Clifford Chance LLP
nicholas.mace@cliffordchance.com

Nick Mace is a partner in the tax group at Clifford Chance, having been with the firm since 1998. Mr Mace specialises in advising on corporate tax issues and has advised his clients on a wide range of transactions, focusing principally on public and private mergers and acquisitions, joint ventures, corporate reorganisations, financing transactions and initial public offerings. He has extensive experience of advising on private equity investments and exits, and also advises on international tax issues arising on cross-border transactions.

Amy Mahon
Partner, Clifford Chance LLP
amy.mahon@cliffordchance.com

Amy Mahon is a partner in the corporate practice of Clifford Chance who specialises in private equity transactions. She has advised on a range of transactions, including domestic and international leveraged buy-outs, divestments, consortium transactions and minority investments, and has acted for financial sponsors, including private equity houses, infrastructure funds and investment banks. She has advised on a number of spin-outs of private equity businesses.

Fraser Robson
Associate director, The Carlyle Group
fraser.robson@carlyle.com

Fraser Robson is an associate director focused on European buy-out opportunities in the industrial, consumer and services sectors. He is based in London.

Since joining Carlyle in 2005, he has been actively involved with Carlyle's investments in Britax and Talaris, where he serves as a member of the board of directors. He was also a member of the transaction team that executed Carlyle's investment in RAC.

Prior to joining Carlyle, he worked at Lazard in London. He received a BA with honours in economics and politics from the University of Durham.

Gabrielle Ruiz
Senior associate, Clifford Chance LLP
gabrielle.ruiz@cliffordchance.com

Gabrielle Ruiz is a senior lawyer at Clifford Chance LLP. She has over 13 years' experience, specialising in all aspects of corporate restructuring and insolvency law. Ms Ruiz is the co-author of "Compromising Shareholder Claims both generally and in listed companies" in *The Law and Practice of Restructuring in the UK and US*, as well as numerous articles on insolvency-related topics in restructuring and insolvency and finance and banking journals. She is a member of the Association of Business Recovery Professionals (R3), as well as the Insolvency Lawyers' Association, where she serves on its technical committee.

Philip Sanderson
Partner, Travers Smith LLP
philip.sanderson@traverssmith.com

Philip Sanderson is head of the private equity practice at Travers Smith. He specialises in UK and international buy-outs and M&A deals. As a member of the firm's private equity group since its inception, he has spent over 17 years advising private companies, institutional investors and management teams.

Chambers and Partners lists Mr Sanderson as one of the United Kingdom's leading lawyers in private equity.

Anthony Stewart
Partner, Clifford Chance LLP
anthony.stewart@cliffordchance.com

Anthony Stewart has been a partner in the tax group at Clifford Chance since 2005. Mr Stewart advises on all aspects of investment fund taxation, with a particular focus on private equity-related matters, including fund formation, cross-border structuring and incentive arrangements. He has written a number of articles on investment fund taxation and is a regular speaker at private equity tax conferences.

Kevin Thompson
Partner, Clifford Chance LLP
kevin.thompson@cliffordchance.com

Kevin Thompson is a partner in the employee benefits group at Clifford Chance in London. Mr Thompson has specialised in employee benefits and employee tax matters for over 20 years. He advises on all aspects of employee benefit arrangements – in particular, employee stock plans (including institutional guidelines, tax and corporate aspects and accounting implications), tax-efficient remuneration for managers and employees (including international aspects) and termination arrangements. He also advises on the employee benefits aspects of a wide range of corporate transactions, including takeovers, initial public offerings, disposals, demergers/returns of capital and private equity-related transactions.
Mr Thompson is a member of the steering committee of the Employee Share Ownership Centre and a member of the company law and accounts committee of the Share Plan Lawyers' Organisation.

David Walker
Partner, Clifford Chance LLP
david.walker@cliffordchance.com

David Walker is a partner at Clifford Chance and global head of private equity. For more than 18 years he has focused on private equity clients and their portfolio companies, assisting them with all types of corporate transactions. He is rated as a leader in his field in numerous legal directories.

Tim Wright
Partner, SJ Berwin LLP
tim.wright@sjberwin.com

Tim Wright is a partner at European law firm SJ Berwin LLP. He qualified in 1993 and since 1997 has specialised in UK and cross-border private equity transactions. This includes primary and secondary buy-outs, bolt-on acquisitions and associated equity fundraising, as well as ultimately the exits. Mr Wright acts for a number of private equity houses and management teams. Over his last 10 years as partner he has acted on more than 60 private equity acquisitions and disposals with a total value in excess of £6 billion. Notable completed private equity exits include the sale of Xafinity, acting for key managers on the listing and takeover of Gartmore and the disposal of Inchape Shipping Services. He is recognised by *Chambers* as a leading individual in private equity.